What They Say about Us

"One organization with a long record of success
in helping people find jobs is The Five O'Clock Club."
FORTUNE

"Many managers left to fend for themselves are turning to the camaraderie offered by [The Five O'Clock Club]. Members share tips and advice, and hear experts."
The Wall Street Journal

"If you have been out of work for some time . . . consider The Five O'Clock Club."
The New York Times

"Wendleton has reinvented the historic gentlemen's fraternal oasis and built it into a chain of strategy clubs for job seekers."
The Philadelphia Inquirer

"Organizations such as The Five O'Clock Club are building . . . an extended professional family."
Jessica Lipnack, author, *Professional Teams*

"[The Five O'Clock Club] will ask not what you do, but 'What do you want to do?' . . . [And] don't expect to get any great happy hour drink specials at this joint. The seminars are all business."
The Washington Times

"The Five O'Clock Club's proven philosophy is that job hunting is a learned skill like any other. The Five O'Clock Club becomes the engine that drives [your] search."
Black Enterprise

"Job hunting is a science at The Five O'Clock Club. [Members] find the discipline, direction and much-needed support that keeps a job search on track."
Modern Maturity

"Wendleton tells you how to beat the odds—even in an economy where pink slips are more common than perks. Her savvy and practical guide[s] are chockablock with sample résumés, cover letters, worksheets, negotiating tips, networking suggestions and inspirational quotes from such far-flung achievers as Abraham Lincoln, Malcolm Forbes, and Lily Tomlin."
Working Woman

What Job Hunters Say

"During the time I was looking for a job, I kept Kate's books by my bed. I read a little every night, a little every morning. Her common-sense advice, methodical approach, and hints for keeping the spirits up were extremely useful."
Harold Levine, coordinator, Yale Alumni Career Resource Network

"I've just been going over the books with my daughter, who is 23 and finally starting to think she ought to have a career. She won't listen to anything I say, but you she believes."
Newspaper columnist

"Thank you, Kate, for all your help. I ended up with four offers and at least 15 compliments in two months. Thanks!"
President and CEO, large banking organization

"I have doubled my salary during the past five years by using The Five O'Clock Club techniques. Now I earn what I deserve. I think everyone needs The Five O'Clock Club."
M. S., attorney, entertainment industry

"I dragged myself to my first meeting, totally demoralized. Ten weeks later, I chose from among job offers and started a new life. Bless You!
Senior editor, not-for-profit

"I'm an artistic person, and I don't think about business. Kate provided the disciplined business approach so I could practice my art. After adopting her system, I landed a role on Broadway in Hamlet.*"*
Bruce Faulk, actor

"I've referred at least a dozen people to The Five O'Clock Club since I was there. The Club was a major factor in getting my dream job, which I am now in."
B. R., research head

"My Five O'Clock Club coach was a God-Send!!! She is truly one of the most dynamic and qualified people I've ever met. Without her understanding and guidance, I wouldn't have made the steps I've made toward my goals."
Operating room nurse

"The Five O'Clock Club has been a fantastic experience for my job search. I couldn't have done it without you. Keep up the good work."
Former restaurant owner, who found his dream job with
an organization that advises small businesses

What Human Resources Executives Say about
The Five O'Clock Club Outplacement

"**This thing works.** *I saw a structured, yet nurturing, environment where individuals searching for jobs positioned themselves for success. I saw 'accountability' in a nonintimidating environment. I was struck by the support and willingness to encourage those who had just started the process by the group members who had been there for a while.*"
Employee relations officer, financial services organization

"**Wow! I was immediately struck by the electric atmosphere** *and people's commitment to following the program. Job hunters reported on where they were in their searches and what they had accomplished the previous week. The overall environment fosters sharing and mutual learning.*"
Head of human resources, major law firm

"*The Five O'Clock Club program is **far more effective** than conventional outplacement. Excellent materials, effective coaching and nanosecond responsiveness combine to get people focused on the central tasks of the job search. Selecting The Five O'Clock Club Outplacement Program was one of my best decisions this year.*"
Sr. vice president, human resources, manufacturing company

"**You have made me look like a real genius** *in recommending The Five O'Clock Club [to our divisions around the country]!*"
Sr. vice president, human resources, major publishing firm

Go to our website
www.fiveoclockclub.com
Join our mailing list and receive FREE periodic
emailings on job search or career development.

The Five O'Clock Club®

Find your personal path in job search and career success

Packaging Yourself:
The Targeted
Résumé

KATE WENDLETON

CENGAGE
Learning·

Professional • Technical • Reference

Australia • Canada • Mexico • Singapore • Spain • United Kingdom • United States

CENGAGE Learning®

Professional • Technical • Reference

Packaging Yourself: The Targeted Resume
Kate Wendleton

Vice President, Career Education SBU: Dawn Gerrain
Director of Editorial: Sherry Gomoll
Publisher and General Manager,
Cengage Learning PTR: Stacy L. Hiquet
Associate Director of Marketing: Sarah Panella
Manager of Editorial Services: Heather Talbot
Senior Marketing Manager: Mark Hughes
Acquisitions Editors: Martine Edwards and Mitzi Koontz
Developmental Editor: Kristen Shenfield
Editorial Assistant: Jennifer Anderson
Director of Production: Wendy A. Troeger
Production Manager: J.P. Henkel
Production Editor: Rebecca Goldthwaite
Technology Project Manager: Sandy Charette
Director of Marketing: Wendy E. Mapstone
Channel Manager: Gerard McAvey
Marketing Coordinator: Erica Conley
Cover Design: TDB Publishing Services
Text Design: Bookwrights

Learning, Inc., within the United States and certain other jurisdictions. All other trademarks are the property of their respective owners. All images © Cengage Learning unless otherwise noted. Cartoons courtesy © Jerry King of Cartoons, Inc.

For product information and technology assistance, contact us at
Cengage Learning Customer & Sales Support, 1-800-354-9706
For permission to use material from this text or product,
submit all requests online at cengage.com/permissions
Further permissions questions can be emailed to
permissionrequest@cengage.com

Cengage Learning PTR
20 Channel Center Street
Boston, MA 02210
USA

Cengage Learning is a leading provider of customized learning solutions with office locations around the globe, including Singapore, the United Kingdom, Australia, Mexico, Brazil, and Japan. Locate your local office at:
international.cengage.com/region
Cengage Learning products are represented in Canada by Nelson Education, Ltd.
For your lifelong learning solutions, visit **cengageptr.com**
Visit our corporate website at **cengage.com**

For information, please contact: The Five O'Clock Club®
300 East 40th Street
New York, New York 10016 www.fiveoclockclub.com
Library of Congress Cataloging-in-Publication Data
Packaging Yourself: The Targeted Resume / Kate Wendleton.
p. cm.
"The Five O'Clock Club."
Includes index.
ISBN 978-1-285-75358-4
2013935348

Preface

Dear Reader:

Do you ever feel your résumé isn't representing you in the best way possible? You're probably right. A résumé is not just a recap of what you have done and where. It's a marketing piece that should dynamically present you just the way you want a prospective employer to see you.

Studies show that the average résumé is looked at for only 10 seconds! You want a résumé that positions you properly so the reader quickly gets your message. And you not only want a résumé that people look at, you want them to find it so compelling that they look forward to meeting you.

Packaging Yourself: The Targeted Résumé will take you through the entire process of developing a résumé that's right for you. We'll make sure you're "positioned" properly for your target market. If your positioning is wrong, your résumé is wrong, and it becomes a handicap rather than a help. In addition, we'll cover the use of LinkedIn and other social media where the positioning should match what you have on your résumé.

This book starts with an overview of The Five O'Clock Club approach to job search. Then we'll work on your accomplishment statements—the backbone of your résumé. We'll teach you the Seven Stories Exercise, which will help you express your accomplishments in an interesting way. You'll also learn how to effectively describe any consulting, freelance, temporary, or volunteer work you have done. That's just the beginning of how we'll make your résumé more exciting to read.

Then we'll work on your summary—the most important part of your résumé and the most difficult. Your summary increases your chances of getting exactly the kind of job you want.

Next we'll put it all together by stepping you through lots of sample résumés. The case studies will teach you the nuances of how to *think* about résumé preparation. You'll take your important accomplishments and incorporate them into the body of your résumé, making sure it supports the statement you created for your summary.

Finally, we'll make sure your résumé is appropriate for your level. We don't want you positioned higher or lower than where you want to be.

Be sure to look in the index under "Industries and professions." You will then be able to find the résumés in this book that refer to your field.

Be careful not to simply copy segments of the résumés in this book. ("This one sounds just like me.") It's better to use the most important things unique to *your* background that you want the hiring manager to know.

This is the only résumé book on the market with case studies, and all the case studies are of actual people. The beginning of this book also contains a brief overview of The Five O'Clock Club job-search process. If you really want to land that next job or if you want to think more about your long-term career, be sure to read the other books in our series. Together, these books provide the most detailed explanation of the search process:

• *Targeting a Great Career* tells you where to look for a job. It is a relatively painless way to think about the career-planning process. It also contains an extensive overview of the entire Five O'Clock Club approach to job search.

• *Shortcut Your Job Search: Get Meetings That Get You the Job* tells you how to get job leads— part-time or full-time, freelance or consulting. It also contains worksheets, which you may copy for your own use. In addition, it contains the most comprehensive job-search bibliography around.

• *Mastering the Job Interview and Winning the Money Game* tells you The Five O'Clock Club way to interview, get the offer, and negotiate.

• *Packaging Yourself: The Targeted Résumé* (this book) is quite simply the best résumé book on the market. It uses the résumés of real people and tells you their stories. It refers to more than 100 industries and professions.

All of this information is based on the highly successful methods used at The Five O'Clock Club, where the average, regularly attending member finds a job within 10 weeks. Take a look at our website: www.FiveOClockClub.com. You'll find over 200 articles from past issues of *The Five O'Clock News,* the basics of The Five O'Clock Club approach to job search, and information on our coaches, among other things.

We are guided by the original Five O'Clock Club, where the leaders of Old Philadelphia met regularly to exchange ideas and have a good time. Today's members are the same. They exchange ideas, operate at a high level, brainstorm to help each other, and truly enjoy one another's company.

I hope the résumés in this book will give you a feel for some of the wonderful and intriguing people I have met. That's what you want your résumé to do: entice the reader and make him or her want to meet the author.

I thank the members of The Five O'Clock Club, people who care about their careers. Their hard work is reflected in this book. Thanks to all of our coaches. They're committed to bringing the highest quality career counseling—along with some fun—to those who care.

Finally, thanks to you for buying this book. Your appreciation of these materials makes it possible for us to continue this effort. Our goal is, and always has been, to provide the best possible and the most affordable career advice. With your help, we will continue to stand by you to help with your career.

Cheers and good luck!

Kate Wendleton
New York City, 2013
www.fiveoclockclub.com

Contents

The Five O'Clock Club®

PART ONE

The Five O'Clock Club Method of Job Search

Getting Up to Speed

You've got to think about "big things" while you're doing small things, so that all the small things go in the right direction.

ALVIN TOFFLER, *Newsweek*

When most people think of job hunting, they think *résumé*. And certainly a résumé is an important ingredient. After all, I devoted this whole book to résumés! But a résumé is only part of the process that you will see here. What's more, a good résumé is usually the result of a thorough evaluation (or assessment) in which you have identified specific job targets (industries and fields) and learned to position yourself to look desirable to hiring managers in those target areas.

On the other hand, you usually need a résumé just to get started in the job-search process—even before you may clearly know the industries or fields you want to target.

It's fine to take a crack at a résumé without going through the assessment—just understand that you have skipped an important step that you should return to later and that there are several other steps that follow the writing of a résumé.

As your targets become clearer, you may want to revise your résumé to create a better match between you and your targets.

The importance of a long-term perspective cannot be overstated. It can make the difference between a career of major contributions and one characterized by early burnout. Savvy managers typically seem to have a longer view than other managers.

JOEL M. DELUCA, PH.D., *Political Savvy*

The Job-Search Process

The charts in this chapter outline each part of the process. It's best to do every part, however quickly you may do it. Experienced job hunters pay attention to the details and do not skip a step.

The first part of the process is **assessment** (or evaluation). You evaluate yourself by doing the exercises in our book *Targeting a Great Career*, and you evaluate your prospects by doing some preliminary research in the library or by talking to people.

Assessment consists of the following exercises:
- The Seven Stories Exercise
- Interests
- Values
- Satisfiers and Dissatisfiers
- Your Fifteen- or Forty-Year Vision

If you are working privately with a career coach, he or she may ask you to do a few additional exercises, such as a personality test.

Assessment results in:
- a listing of all the targets you think are worth exploring
- a résumé that makes you look appropriate to your first target (and may work with other targets as well)

Even if you don't do the entire assessment, the Seven Stories Exercise is especially important because it will help you develop an interesting résumé. Therefore, we have included that exercise in the next chapter.

Research will help you figure out which of your targets

- are good fits for you
- offer some hope in terms of being a good market

You can't have too many targets—as long as you rank them. Then, for each one, conduct a campaign to get interviews in that target area.

First say to yourself what you would be;
and then do what you have to do.

Epictetus

Step I: Campaign Preparation

Conduct research to develop a list of all the companies in your first target. Find out the names of the people you should contact in the appropriate departments in each of those companies.

Develop your cover letter. (Paragraph 1 is the opening, Paragraph 2 is a summary about yourself appropriate for this target, Paragraph 3 contains your bulleted accomplishments ("You may be interested in some of the things I've done"), and Paragraph 4 is the close. (Many sample letters are in the other two books.)

Develop your plan for getting **many interviews in this target**. You have four basic choices:

- Networking
- Direct contact
- Search firms
- Ads

You can read about each of these methods for getting interviews in our book *Shortcut Your Job Search*.

Step II: Interviewing

Most people think interviews result in job offers. But there are usually a few intervening steps before a final offer is made. Interviews should result in getting and giving information.

Did you learn the issues important to each person with whom you met? What did they think were your strongest positives? Where are they in

the hiring process? How many other people are they considering? How do you compare with those people? Why might they be reluctant to bring you on board, compared with the other candidates? How can you overcome the decision makers' objections?

Interviewing is one of the most important and yet most overlooked parts of the job-search process. It is covered in extensive detail in the other two books.

Step III: Follow-Up

Now that you have analyzed the interview, you can figure out how to follow up with each person with whom you interviewed. Aim to be following up with 6 to 10 companies. Five job possibilities will fall away through no fault of your own.

What's more, with 6 to 10 things going, you increase your chances of having 3 good offers to choose from. You would be surprised: Even in a tight market, job hunters are able to develop multiple offers.

When you are in the Interview Step of Target 1, it's time to start Step I of Target 2.

This will give you more momentum and ensure that you do not let things dry up. Keep both targets going, and then start Target 3.

Develop Your Unique Résumé

Read all of the case studies in this book. You will learn a powerful new way of thinking about how to position yourself for the kinds of jobs you want. Each of the résumés in this book is for a unique person aiming at a specific target. You and your exact situation are not in here. But seeing how other people position themselves will help you think about what you want a prospective employer to know about you.

After you look at the charts, we'll start gathering important information about you—through the Seven Stories Exercise.

Steps of the Job Search and the Results of Each Step

ASSESSMENT

Consists of:

- The Seven Stories Exercise
- Interests
- Values
- Satisfiers and Dissatisfiers
- Your Fifteen- or Forty-Year Vision

Results in:

- As many targets as you can think of
- A ranking of your targets
- A résumé that makes you look appropriate to your first target
- A plan for conducting your search

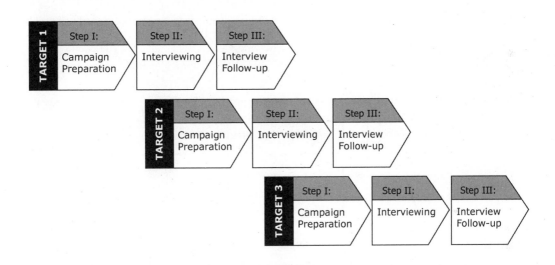

TARGET 1

Step I: Campaign Preparation | Step II: Interviewing | Step III: Interview Follow-up

TARGET 2

Step I: Campaign Preparation | Step II: Interviewing | Step III: Interview Follow-up

TARGET 3

Step I: Campaign Preparation | Step II: Interviewing | Step III: Interview Follow-up

RESULTS

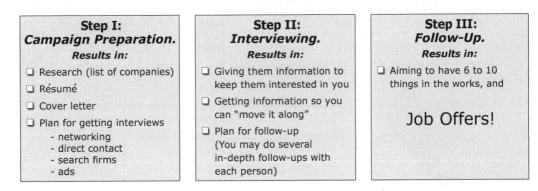

Step I:
Campaign Preparation.
Results in:

- ❑ Research (list of companies)
- ❑ Résumé
- ❑ Cover letter
- ❑ Plan for getting interviews
  - networking
  - direct contact
  - search firms
  - ads

Step II:
Interviewing.
Results in:

- ❑ Giving them information to keep them interested in you
- ❑ Getting information so you can "move it along"
- ❑ Plan for follow-up (You may do several in-depth follow-ups with each person)

Step III:
Follow-Up.
Results in:

- ❑ Aiming to have 6 to 10 things in the works, and

Job Offers!

Getting Interviews and Building Relationships

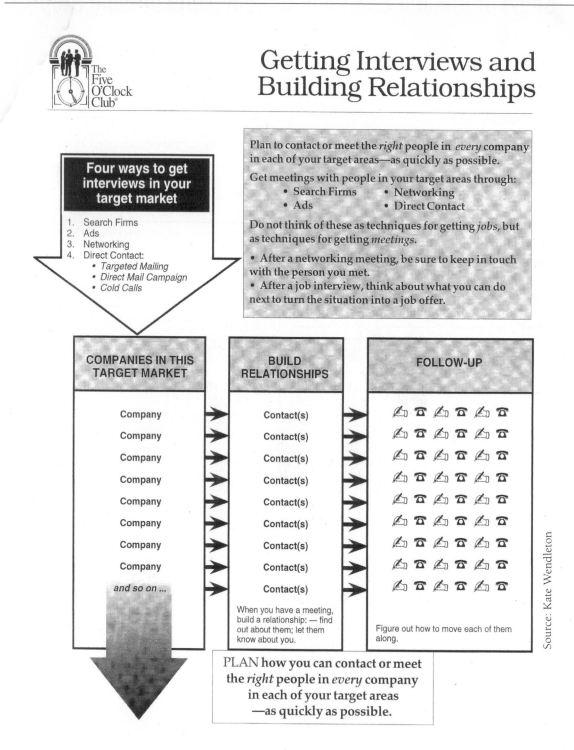

The Five O'Clock Club®

Four ways to get interviews in your target market

1. Search Firms
2. Ads
3. Networking
4. Direct Contact:
   - Targeted Mailing
   - Direct Mail Campaign
   - Cold Calls

Plan to contact or meet the *right* people in *every* company in each of your target areas—as quickly as possible.

Get meetings with people in your target areas through:
- Search Firms
- Networking
- Ads
- Direct Contact

Do not think of these as techniques for getting *jobs*, but as techniques for getting *meetings*.

- After a networking meeting, be sure to keep in touch with the person you met.
- After a job interview, think about what you can do next to turn the situation into a job offer.

COMPANIES IN THIS TARGET MARKET	BUILD RELATIONSHIPS	FOLLOW-UP
Company	Contact(s)	
Company	Contact(s)	
Company	Contact(s)	
Company	Contact(s)	
Company	Contact(s)	
Company	Contact(s)	
Company	Contact(s)	
Company	Contact(s)	
and so on ...	Contact(s)	

When you have a meeting, build a relationship: — find out about them; let them know about you.

Figure out how to move each of them along.

PLAN **how you can contact or meet the** *right* **people in** *every* **company in each of your target areas —as quickly as possible.**

Source: Kate Wendleton

The Five O'Clock Club®

PART TWO

Accomplishments: The Backbone of Your Story

The Five O'Clock Club

Elizabeth: What a Difference a Story Makes

Concentrate your strength against your competitor's relative weakness.

BRUCE HENDERSON,
Henderson on Corporate Strategy

Every résumé has a pitch—although it may not be what the job hunter wants it to be. In scanning Elizabeth's "before" résumé, we can easily see that she has had communications and advertising positions in a number of computer companies. That's the total extent of her pitch. When she went on interviews, managers commented: "You sure have worked for a lot of computer companies." Her résumé read like a job description: She wrote press releases, product brochures, employee newsletters, and so on.

Thousands of people can write press releases, so citing those skills will not separate Elizabeth from her competition. But we can get to know her better if she tells us about specific accomplishments.

Elizabeth agreed to do the Seven Stories Exercise. She didn't feel like writing down "the things she enjoyed doing and also did well" because she felt as though she kept doing the same things again and again in every company for which she worked, and she enjoyed them all. Still, I urged her to be specific—details can make a résumé more interesting. And working on the Seven Stories Exercise is a sure way to develop a strong overall message.

She started with an experience on a job early in her career. She had thought of a terrific idea: Her company's product could be sold through the same computer systems that were used to sell airline tickets and car and hotel reservations. She convinced the company to let her go ahead with the idea, and she promoted it to travel agents across the country and also to the salespeople in her own company. It was so successful; it became the standard way to sell foreign currencies when people were going on a trip.

Most job hunters tend to ignore accomplishments that took place when they were young. But if you had accomplishments early in your career, they may be worth relating because they let the reader know that you have always been a winner.

I said, "That sounds great. Where is it on your résumé?" Elizabeth said, "Well, it's not said exactly that way...." Many times job hunters are constricted when they write their résumés, but the Seven Stories Exercise can free them up to express things differently. So we restated that accomplishment.

Elizabeth then worked on another story. She had participated in a conference that had "generated 450 letters of intent."

I said, "It's nice the conference generated 450 letters of intent. But from what you said, I can't tell that you had anything to do with those results, and I don't know if 450 is good or not. Tell me more about it."

Elizabeth said, "There were only 1,500 participants in the conference, and 450 letters of intent is a lot because our product is very expensive. I had a lot to do with those results because I developed an aura of excitement about the product by putting teasers under everyone's hotel door every morning.

"And before the conference, I had sent five weekly teasers to everyone who planned to attend. For example, one week, I sent each person a bottle of champagne. This direct-mail campaign had everyone talking about us before the convention started. People were asking one another whether or not they had gotten our mailers. When they got to the convention and found teasers under their doors, they were eager to come to our booth.

"I also trained the teams of employees who were demonstrating the product at the convention. I made sure that each demonstrator delivered the same message."

Now I understood how Elizabeth had played a major part in generating those letters of intent.

Next we needed to think of the message behind this accomplishment. Was her message that she could stick mailers under doors? Or send out bottles of champagne? No, her message was that she knew how to launch a product, and that's what we put on her résumé as the main point for that accomplishment.

In her "before" résumé, Elizabeth said that she wrote press releases and did direct-mail campaigns. Her "after" résumé provides some examples of what she accomplished with those efforts and gives us a feel for her ingenuity and hard work.

The successful person has the habit of doing things failures don't like to do. They don't like doing them either necessarily. But their disliking is subordinated to the strength of their purpose.

E. M. Gray, *The Common Denominator of Success*

The Summary

After we reviewed all of her accomplishments, we tackled the summary. What was the most important point Elizabeth wanted to get across? It wasn't just that she could write press releases and speeches or do direct-mail campaigns.

She had to think hard about this. The most important thing was that Elizabeth was a key member of the management team. She sat in on meetings when the company was discussing bringing out a new product or planning how to handle a possible crisis. Elizabeth would not be happy—or effective—in a job where she simply wrote press releases. She needed to be part of the strategy sessions.

What you put on your résumé can both include you and exclude you. A company that does not want the communications person included in those meetings would not be interested in Elizabeth—but then, she wouldn't be interested in them either.

In her summary, instead of highlighting the companies she had worked for, Elizabeth highlighted the industries represented by those companies. She listed Information Services and High-Tech first, because they represented areas of greater growth than Financial Services did.

Elizabeth was—and wanted to be again—a corporate strategist, a crisis manager, and a spokesperson for the corporation. That's how we positioned her.

In every summary in this book, the reader can tell something about the writer's personality. It is not enough that someone knows what you have done; they also need to know your style in doing it. For example, a person who had run a department and doubled productivity could have done it in a nasty, threatening way or could have motivated people to do more, instituted training programs, and encouraged workers to come up with suggestions for improving productivity. Your style matters.

Look at this case study, and then do the Seven Stories Exercise. Come up with accomplishments that will interest your reader. Let him or her know what to expect from you if you are hired.

In Elizabeth's case, we hope the hiring manager will look at her résumé and say: "That's exactly what I need: a corporate strategist who knows how to handle crises and can also serve as a spokesperson for us."

This is the response you want the reader to have: "That's exactly the person I need!" Look at your résumé. What words pop out? Is this how you want to be seen? If not, let's get going.

Great minds have purposes, others have wishes.
Little minds are tamed and subdued by
misfortune; but great minds rise above it.

WASHINGTON IRVING, *Elbert Hubbard's Scrap Book*

ELIZABETH GHAFFARI

207 Dobbs Ferry
Phoenix, AZ 44444

Home: (602) 555-6666
liz.ghaffari321@hotmail.com

EXPERIENCE

CITRUS COMPUTER SYSTEMS   2009-Present

Director Corporate Communications

Plan and supervise all corporate communications staff and activities for diversified financial information Services Company on a global basis.

- Develop, direct, and implement global media, public relations, and internal-communications programs in support of corporate and sales objectives, working closely with executive management team.
- Direct all media-relations activities related to new product introductions and product enhancements; initiate media contacts; respond to press inquiries; coordinate and conduct interviews; and develop all press materials.
- Develop and direct advertising and promotional literature activities, overseeing all corporate publications, including corporate and product brochures, sales materials, and customer and employee newsletters.

ELECTRONIC DATABASE SYSTEMS   2007-2009

Manager, Advertising and Promotion

Developed and implemented marketing and promotion strategies for the company and its North American subsidiaries.

- Worked with market and product managers to identify opportunities for product and sales promotions and new product development for multiple market segments. Conducted market research, developed marketing strategies, and implemented tactical plans (e.g., direct response marketing and sales incentive programs).
- Responsible for planning biannual securities analyst meetings and communication product information to investors and industry analysts.
- Orchestrated six product introductions during three-month period, including public-relations activities, promotional literature and training materials.
- Responsible for forecasting and maintaining $4 million budget.
- Managed corporate and product advertising programs, hiring and working with various agencies.

ELIZABETH GHAFFARI

CREDIT LYONNAIS 2005-2007

Corporate Investment Officer and Product Manager

Planned and directed the sales and promotion efforts for the bank's corporate and correspondent sales staff for a variety of products including foreign exchange and precious metals.

- Developed active and profitable business relationships with correspondent banks for sale of precious metals and foreign exchange products.
- Established and developed new account relationships. Brought in eleven new corporate accounts which produced significant business in precious metals and foreign exchange trading areas.
- Managed market study to identify size, segments, and opportunities of various markets. Prepared analysis and recommendations for new product development and trading vehicles.

WASSERELLA & BECKTON 2000-2005

Director of Marketing

Managed all activities of the Marketing Department, including product development, sales promotion, advertising, and public relations activities for diversified financial services company.

- Conceptualized and developed national marketing strategy for foreign exchange services offered to travel industry professionals via automated airline reservation systems.
- Developed and implemented business plans for a variety of products, including responsibility for product positioning, pricing, contracts, advertising, and promotional materials.
- Promoted from Foreign Exchange Trader to Marketing Representative to Director of Marketing in three years.

EDUCATION

B.A., Psychology, University of Phoenix 2000

ELIZABETH GHAFFARI

207 Dobbs Ferry
Phoenix, AZ 44444

liz.ghaffari321@hotmail.com

Residence: (602) 555-6666
Work: (602) 345-7777

CORPORATE COMMUNICATIONS EXECUTIVE
with 14 years' experience in

- High-Tech   • Information Services   • Financial Services

Experience includes:

- Global Media and Investor Relations
- Social Media/Employee Newsletters
- Advertising/Promotional Literature

- Employee Roundtables/Awards Programs
- Customer Videos and Newsletters
- Speech Writing/Papers/Public Speaking

- **A corporate strategist and key member of the management team** with extensive knowledge of financial markets.

- **A crisis manager**: bringing common sense, organizational skills, and a logical decision-making process to solving sensitive, time-critical problems.

- **A spokesperson for the corporation**: developing and communicating key corporate messages accurately and convincingly, under deadline pressure, to multiple audiences including employees, the media, customers, and investors.

Proven team leader and troubleshooter with highly developed analytical, organizational, and strategic planning skills.

CITRUS COMPUTER SYSTEMS   2009-Present
Director, Corporate Communications

- Gained extensive positive media coverage in conjunction with launch of company's first product for new market segment.
  - Planned and conducted **media events in 8 countries**.
  - Resulted in **positive stories in 30 major publications** and trade press: *The Wall Street Journal, The New York Times, Barron's, The Financial Times, Forbes,* and various foreign publications.
  - A first for the company, **positive TV coverage in the United States**: CNN, CNBC, **and Europe**: Sky Financial Television, Business Daily, The City Programme.
  - Integrated **new media** into conventional public relations campaigns. Gained extensive social media coverage with 14 high-profile **bloggers**, tripled **website traffic** and instituted a successful corporate **Facebook** page and a dozen **webinars** for customers.
- Successfully **avoided communications crisis**, gained positive press coverage and customer support when company sold a major division. Within a 60-day period:
  - Planned and managed all aspects of a **13-city, interactive teleconference**.
  - Developed all written and web-based materials including various employee and customer communications, background materials, and press releases.
  - Wrote speeches for six executives including both company presidents (present and acquiring companies).
  - Wrote and produced an extensive question-and-answer document covering **union, compensation, and benefits issues and business rationale**.
  - Selected and trained staff representatives for each of 13 cities.

ELIZABETH GHAFFARI - Page 2

CITRUS COMPUTER SYSTEMS, contd.

Director, Corporate Communications, contd.

- Developed and implemented **company's first employee awards program** for service excellence.
  - Honored employees who participated in planning sessions.
  - **Led to changes in key areas** including improvements in software manufacturing efficiencies, shortening of the product development cycle, and improved employee morale.
- **Introduced desktop publishing** program for in-house production of all promotional materials and various customer and employee newsletters. Newsletters were then primarily sent via email.
  - **Reduced outside services expense by 75%.**
  - Created new **corporate standards manual** and reorganized promotional literature system to replace inconsistent product literature.
- Conducted group and individual **employee meetings** to gain and disseminate critical information in identifying and resolving employee-relations problems.
- Prepared quarterly management reports and written/oral presentations to top management and employees to describe corporate accomplishments compared to goals.
- Managed all customer/media/employee communications for sale of three business units.

ELECTRONIC DATABASE SYSTEMS   2007-2009

Manager, Advertising and Promotion

- Prepared written and oral **presentations to boards of directors** and senior managers on various services, concepts and results.
- Planned **product launch** and company participation in global foreign exchange conference. Successful product launch resulted in **generating 450 letters of intent from 1,500 participants**. Assured successful product introduction:
  - Developed 5-week **direct-mail campaign** to stimulate interest and create an aura of excitement around product prior to conference. Campaign continued at conference with daily newsletter and door stuffer.
  - Maximized impact of **product demonstrations** through use of compelling visual presentation and environment.
  - **Trained teams** of product demonstrators to assure that information regarding benefits and features would be delivered in a consistent way.
- Strengthened company relationships with **industry analysts and investors** by arranging product demonstrations in conjunction with biannual industry analyst meetings. Demonstrations stimulated interest and **gained support for strategic direction from investor community** by communicating important strategic and product information.
  - Selected products to be demonstrated, developed promotional materials, organized display area, selected and trained product demonstrators to assure delivery of consistent corporate message.

CREDIT LYONNAIS   2005-2007

<u>Product Manager</u>

- Established and developed new account relationships.
  - **<u>Brought in 11 new corporate accounts during 10-month period</u>**, producing significant business in precious metals and foreign exchange trading areas.

WASSERELLA & BECKTON   2000-2005

<u>Director of Marketing</u>

- **<u>Developed breakthrough idea to sell</u>** foreign exchange services (currency and travelers' checks) through travel agents the same way hotel space and airline tickets are sold

  <u>via automated airline reservation systems.</u>

- Sold concept to senior management and **<u>negotiated contracts with three major airlines</u>**.

- Developed sales and operational procedures. **<u>Hired and trained 10-person sales and operations staff.</u>**

- **<u>Promoted concept to travel agents</u>** across the country through industry trade shows and sales program.

EDUCATION

B.A., Psychology, University of Phoenix, 2000

The Seven Stories Exercise® Worksheet

This exercise is an opportunity to examine the most satisfying experiences of your life and to discover those skills you will want to use as you go forward. You will be looking at the times when you feel you did something particularly well that you also enjoyed doing. Compete this sentence: "There was a time when I…" List enjoyable accomplishments from all parts of your life: from your youth, your school years, your early career up to the present. Don't forget volunteer work, your hobbies and your personal life. Other people may have gotten credit or under-appreciated what you did. Or the result may not have been a roaring success. None of that matters. **What matters is that you enjoyed doing it and did it well.**

This exercise usually takes a few days to complete. Many people review different life phases in order to capture the full scope of these experiences. Most carry around a piece of paper to jot down ideas as they think of them.

List anything that occurs to you, however insignificant. When I did my own Seven Stories Exercise, I remembered the time when I was 10 years old and led a group of kids in the neighborhood, enjoyed it, and did it well.

When you have 25, select the seven that are most important to you by however you define important. Then rank them: List the most important first, and so on. Starting with your first story, write a paragraph about each accomplishment. Then find out what your accomplishments have in common. If you are having trouble doing the exercises, ask a friend to help you talk them through. Friends tend to be more objective and will probably point out strengths you never realized.

Section I

Briefly outline below *all* the work/personal/life experiences that meet the above definition. Come up with at least 20. We ask for 20 stories so you won't be too selective. Just write down anything that occurs to you, no matter how insignificant it may seem. **Try to think of concrete examples, situations, and tasks, not generalized skills or abilities**. It may be helpful if you say to yourself, **"There was the time when I . . ."** You may start with, for example, "Threw a fiftieth birthday party for my father," "Wrote a press release that resulted in extensive media coverage," and "Came in third in the Nassau bike race."

Don't just write that you enjoy "cooking." That's an activity, not an accomplishment. An accomplishment occurs at a specific time. You may wind up with many cooking accomplishments, for example. But if you simply write "cooking," "writing" or "managing," you will have a hard time thinking of 20 enjoyable accomplishments.

RIGHT

- Got extensive media coverage for new product launch.
- Delivered speech to get German business.
- Coordinated blood drive for division.
- Came in third in Nassau Bike Race.
- Made basket in second grade.

WRONG

- Writing press releases.
- Delivering speeches.
- Coordinating.
- Cycling.
- Working on projects alone.

1. _____
2. _____
3. _____
4. _____
5. _____
6. _____
7. _____
8. _____
9. _____
10. _____
11. _____
12. _____
13. _____
14. _____
15. _____
16. _____
17. _____
18. _____
19. _____
20. _____
21. _____
22. _____
23. _____
24. _____
25. _____

Section II

<u>Choose the seven experiences from the above</u> that you enjoyed the most and felt the most sense of accomplishment about. (Be sure to include non-job-related experiences also.) Then rank them. Then, for each accomplishment, describe what you did. Be specific, listing each step in detail. Notice the role you played and your relationship with others, the subject matter, the skills you used, and so on. Use a separate sheet of paper for each.

If your highest-ranking accomplishments also happen to be work related, you may want them to appear prominently on your résumé. After all, those were things that you enjoyed and did well. And those are probably experiences you will want to repeat again in your new job.

Here's how you might begin:

Experience #1: Planned product launch that resulted in 450 letters of intent from 1,500 participants.

a. Worked with president and product managers to discuss product potential and details.
b. Developed promotional plan.
c. Conducted five-week direct-mail campaign prior to conference to create aura of excitement about product.
d. Trained all product demonstrators to make sure they each presented product in same way.
e. Had great product booth built; rented best suite to entertain prospects; conducted campaign at conference by having teasers put under everyone's door every day of conference. Most people wanted to come to our booth.

—and so on—

*Action may not always bring happiness,
but there is no happiness without action.*

BENJAMIN DISRAELI

In the next section, we'll get started on your résumé. First, you'll read some general guidelines and see a couple of examples of how job hunters have implemented them. Then you'll work on your accomplishments, including any relevant experience that you had while you were a consultant, freelancer, temporary worker, or volunteer.

After that, we'll *position* you to look appropriate for that next move by developing your summary statement, which goes at the top of your résumé. It's the most important thing your reader will see, and it's also the most difficult part to do well. That's okay. You will have lots of summary statements to look at, so you will be able to develop one that is right for you.

Finally, we'll put it all together by looking at the résumé case studies for people at your level. They will help you understand the thinking and the strategy that go into a really great résumé.

People cannot let others limit their imagination of what it is they want to do or can do. Otherwise, we would never have discoveries or advance.

MAE C. JEMISON, PHYSICIAN, CHEMICAL ENGINEER, AND AMERICA'S FIRST BLACK WOMAN ASTRONAUT

The Five O'Clock Club®

PART THREE

Developing
Your Résumé

The Five O'Clock Club®

General Résumé Trends and Guidelines

...For while history does not teach that honesty, in this world, is the best policy, it surely teaches that dishonesty ultimately is the worst policy.

JOHN LUKACS, *A History of the Cold War*

Your résumé is the equivalent of a sales brochure. It is not supposed to tell every detail, but to entice the reader—grab his or her attention.

Your résumé softens the reader. It predisposes him or her to think of you in a certain way, so that when you meet, he or she will already have a preconceived notion about you. Tailor your résumé to make the impression you want. Most people never consider using their résumé to create a certain impression of themselves; they simply write down their work experience. Job hunters who think of their résumé as a tool for communication tend to be more effective than those who play it safe and use a bland approach. Your credentials and experience are only half of what you are selling. Your style and personality are the other half.

Your résumé can serve as a guide to the interview. If you highlight certain areas in your résumé, the interviewer cannot help but ask about them. If you play down or even leave out certain things, you reduce the chances of having the interview center on those areas.

This chapter will present some new thoughts on résumé writing. Some ideas may suit your style; others may not. Use what you want. But do not reject these ideas too hastily: If you have not been as successful as you would like, you may find it useful to try a different style.

Make yourself necessary to someone.

RALPH WALDO EMERSON

What Happens to Your Résumé

Your résumé crosses the desk of someone. This person is not looking to hire, but something about your résumé or cover letter strikes a responsive chord. If one of your achievements addresses the reader's problems at the moment, you may be called in.

The reader says to his or her administrative assistant, "Ask this person to come in for a chat, but be sure to say that we have no openings." You are called in for an exploratory meeting.

In most cases, there truly is no specific job opening. If the chemistry is right, and if things progress smoothly, however, a position may be developed for you. This happens more often than the average job hunter may realize—and is the ideal scenario. A position created for you has the best chance of being a successful and satisfying one.

The Purpose of Your Résumé

Your résumé serves a number of purposes:

1. **It is your marketing piece.**

It's important to realize that your résumé—your brochure about yourself—*will be looked at for only 10 seconds.* You must make that 10 seconds worthwhile. The reader will usually look at the top of the first page and perhaps glance at the rest. You want him or her to see your opening paragraph—your summary—and other parts that you intend to stand out. If something sparks the reader's interest, he or she may spend a little more time on your résumé.

We don't care whether they do more than glance at your résumé. *What we care about is whether they call you in for a meeting.* At this point, you are not looking for a job—you are looking for a meeting to have the opportunity to explore what is going on in their company and tell them more about you. You want to build a relationship and see if perhaps there is a place for you *in the long run.*

2. **It is your sales tool in your absence.**
   After you leave the meeting, the manager may want to discuss you with someone else. Your résumé can speak for you in your absence and convince that second person that you have a lot to offer.

3. **It can guide your interview.**
   The interviewer is likely to ask about those sections you've highlighted. We each have things we'd like to talk about and things we'd rather not.

Emphasize:

- things you have done well and also enjoyed doing and would like to do again
- areas that make you more marketable by differentiating you from your likely competitors
- areas that support your *pitch*—the main argument you are advancing about yourself
- things you think will sell you and will be of interest to the readers in your marketplace.

If any man wishes to write in a clear style, let him be first clear in his thoughts; and if any would write in a noble style, let him first possess a noble soul.

GOETHE

The Typical Résumé: Historical

Most résumés are historical documents. They list the positions a person has had and what was done in each position. It's as if the résumé writer were saying: "I've put it all down. Now you figure out where I fit in or what I should be doing next."

But if the reader doesn't *get* it—doesn't figure out in just 10 seconds what you could do for him or her—you will be passed over.

A good résumé allows readers to imagine you working in their company. Something in the résumé grabs them, and they can see some as-yet-undefined possibility for you.

Your Résumé: Strategic

Your résumé should not be a historical document but a future-oriented, strategic one. It should select from your background and highlight those areas you want to offer and state them in ways that relate to the needs of the market.

What kinds of things would you like to do next?

What do you have to offer that the market may also want?

And what do you have to offer that may give you credibility or negotiating leverage (as in "I'll do this for you, providing you allow me to do this other

Your Résumé Is Completely under Your Control

An unlearned carpenter of my acquaintance once said in my hearing: "There is very little difference between one man and another, but what little there is, is very important." This distinction seems to me to go to the root of the matter.

WILLIAM JAMES, *"The Importance of Individuals"*

You have complete control. Determine exactly what will hit the reader's eye on each page and the impression you want him or her to have of you. For example, you may want to appear to be a person with a certain background. Be sure to mention that area in your summary and highlight it in the body of your résumé. You may want to stress your long-term managerial experience or your technical expertise. Your résumé can show that you are the kind of person who constantly comes up with new ideas and implements them or one who solves problems for the company.

Tell the reader outright the kind of person you are. Most résumés focus on credentials, but with so many qualified people vying for the same position, a résumé with personality is more readable and stands out. Résumés that are detached and cold are not as effective as those that seem more human. Résumés and cover letters should be alive and enthusiastic.

What you write predisposes the reader to see you in a certain way. If, for example, you describe yourself as dynamic, the interviewer will tend to see that part of your personality. You will not have to work as hard to come across as dynamic. Even if you feel you're not acting very dynamic that day, do not be surprised if the interviewer happens to mention how dynamic you are.

This is your story. It is one you want to be proud of. Don't be boring about it.

Always bear in mind that your own resolution to succeed is more important than any one thing.

Abraham Lincoln

General Guidelines for Writing Résumés

1. Before you start, do yourself a favor. Go back and do the Seven Stories Exercise. The effort you put into this will dramatically affect the quality of your résumé. It will give you the substance you need to work with and add depth and detail to your résumé in those areas you want to highlight. It will also loosen you up and increase your chances of telling a good story about yourself.

Whether I'm working with someone making $20,000 a year or $400,000, they each go through this exercise. Then I have a better idea of what they may want to emphasize on their résumés and what they'd rather not highlight. If your past accomplishments are important to you, they should take up some room on your résumé.

2. Most people need only one résumé. However, you can modify your résumé to make it suitable for other targets. And if your targets are completely different (such as being a customer service manager or a chef), you will probably need two completely different résumés.

If your résumé positions you the way you want to be positioned, it's a good résumé. If it doesn't, it's not good.

---

3. Aim to have a reverse chronological résumé (starting with your most recent job). Functional résumés are organized by type of work done rather than by dates. They are usually written to hide something, and they are looked upon with suspicion. Chances are, there is a way for you to say what you want to say without resorting to a totally functional résumé. For example, try a chronological résumé that has a particular job broken down functionally—that is, by the different types of work done.

4. **<u>You will probably want to have a summary statement on your résumé.</u>** It's an opportunity to dramatically influence the way the reader sees you and the rest of the information you have included. Take advantage of this powerful tool. But remember, it's not easy. (The cover letter is your other opportunity for positioning, to influence what the reader notices in your résumé.)

They are able because they think they are able.

Virgil

Job Target

In developing your résumé, your job target must be clearly in your mind. Major changes in your target may require different résumés. Minor changes will not.

With your target in mind, go through the accomplishment statements you developed. Select those that support your job target, and leave out those that do not support it.

If the accomplishments that best support your goal occurred a long time ago, select excerpts from them and put the excerpts in your summary. This will make it easier for the reader to see that you have had that experience.

Though you have your target clearly in mind—*do not* put it on your résumé. Your résumé could then exclude you from the hiring process.

People sometimes use a "job objective" statement to describe the kind of job they want to have next. However, if you do this, it may seem as if you only want a specific position. It can limit your search. Even if you are open to other positions, it may seem that you are not.

On the other hand, if you know exactly what you want, and if there are plenty of jobs with the title you are going after, then it is all right to put a job objective on your résumé.

An objective statement is also appropriate when the job hunter wants to reassure the hiring manager that he truly is interested in the area he is looking at.

. . . My experience says that it is possible to study and imagine where we may be headed. By imagining where we are going, we reduce this complexity, this unpredictability which... encroaches upon our lives.

Peter Schwartz, *The Art of the Long View*

Your Summary Statement

In differentiation, not in uniformity, lies the path of progress.

Louis Brandeis

The summary statement sets the tone and highlights the theme—the threads that bind your accomplishments. Your summary statement describes what makes you qualified and yet different from others who may be aiming for the same position.

The summary statement goes at the top of your résumé, after your name, address, E-mail address, and phone number. It brings all your accomplishments together. If in your summary statement you want to say that you are a financial wizard, your accomplishment statements must support this.

Consider **underlining and boldfacing** what you want the reader to see in the summary. Remember, the reader scans the highlighted parts and then reads the rest of the summary. Highlighting makes some people uncomfortable. They fear it makes them look too aggressive. But in fact you're doing the reader a favor, by helping him or her figure out where to look next.

First, Decide the Story You Want to Tell

Form follows function. Decide the story you want to tell a specific target market, and tell it as briefly as is sensible. Then decide what format to use.

The dynamic principle of fantasy is play, which belongs also to the child, and... appears to be inconsistent with the principle of serious work. But without this playing with fantasy, no creative work has ever yet come to birth.

Carl Jung

The Format

I don't like work—no man does—but I like what is in work—the chance to find yourself.

Joseph Conrad

Your résumé should be attention getting in an understated way, and readable. Lines of type that go clear across the page from one margin to the other are difficult to read. Use bulleted accomplishments to break up the text.

Think about what will show up on the first page. Your summary is most important. If the jobs you want the reader to see are also on the first page, that's lucky. But if the jobs you want the reader to see are on the second page, be aware that you will wind up with a longer summary because you should include information in the summary about those jobs that don't appear until later.

This can happen when the situation you are in right now does not lend itself to where you want to go next. In that case, format your résumé so the reader's eye will see your summary, skip over your most recent job, and go directly to one before that. Simply boldface or underline phrases in your summary and in the body of the résumé to highlight the job you want to call attention to.

The top of page 2 is also important. When the reader turns the page, that's the first thing he or she will see. So make sure you have something important at the top.

Scan your résumé to see where your eye naturally goes. That's the message your reader will get too.

The Length

Your résumé should be as long as it has to be, and no longer. Cut and cut until you cannot cut any more. You do not care if anyone ever reads your entire résumé; the fact is that he or she probably won't read it all, whether it is two pages long or five. You simply want the reader to stop at your résumé and spend more than 10 seconds on it, so perhaps you will be called in.

My own résumé happens to be three to four pages long—I feel it has to be to say what I want to in the way I want to say it. I could cram it into two pages—but instead I make it attractive and readable and *use as many pages as necessary.*

I get *lots* of interviews, even though interviewers almost invariably tell me that my résumé is too long: One thing *everyone* claims to know about job hunting is that a résumé should be no longer than

two pages. That's not necessarily so. Many people mistakenly think a shorter résumé is more likely to be read, so they force a lot of information into one completely unreadable page. It is better to have a longer résumé that is scannable and readable.

The Trends in Résumé Length

In the *old days*, just a few years ago, résumés were one page long. It made sense then. Most people had worked at the same company—and often the same job—for most of their careers. They were expected to stay put. Their entire history could usually fit on one page.

Those who changed jobs were often limited to doing again what they had done before. Things have changed dramatically in the past few years. Today, the average American has been in his or her job only 4 years, and the average person getting out of college today can expect to have 12 to 15 jobs in a lifetime. Simply listing all the jobs one has had could easily take an entire page—without even mentioning what one has done in those jobs.

Furthermore, the job-hunting market has become more sophisticated and competitive. Hiring managers are seeing more and more résumés. Yours has to stand out. It takes a certain amount of space to tell your story in a way that shows how you are different from the competition. If this makes your résumé more than one page long, that's fine.

Say all you have to say in the fewest possible words, or your reader will be sure to skip them; and in the plainest possible words or he will certainly misunderstand them.

JOHN RUSKIN

The Trend in Dates: Put Them on the Right

Job hunters used to put the dates of employment down the left side of the résumé. But now, with people having so many jobs, there might be a string of dates down the left-hand side. Since the reader's eye naturally goes to the left column, the dates become the main message. That's why the trend these days is to put dates on the right.

Do What is Appropriate for Your Level

In the examples on the following pages, a very senior executive may have a one-, two-, three-, or four-page résumé. It depends on how complicated the person's message is.

However, a junior person should never have a three- or four-page résumé. It is inappropriate and makes the person look silly. One page—or two at most—is appropriate.

Middle managers almost always require two pages, and sometimes three, to tell their stories in a way that is clear.

I applied to banks. I have never seen men on Wall Street in such complete agreement on any issue as they were on my application. A few actually laughed at my résumé.

MICHAEL LEWIS, *Liars Poker*

Test Your Résumé

You need to test what you have written. First, show your résumé to a friend. Ask him to describe in 10 seconds how the information comes across. If your friend describes you the way you wanted to come across, then your résumé is presenting you properly. If you come across as having expertise in a field that you did not want to highlight, then your résumé needs to position you better.

The most valuable comments are strategic in nature. If your friend wants you to change the third word on the second page, it will not help you get a job. But if he tells you that you come across as a junior accountant, when you actually headed up a division of a company, that is valuable feedback. Or if you come across as a salesperson,

when you hate sales, that is valuable. It is also important for you to know if you come across as being at a higher or lower level than you really are.

Your Phone Number

List a daytime phone number. If you have a cell phone, answering machine or voice mail, you can list the number as "213-555-1212 (message)"; interviewers will then expect to leave a message but not necessarily talk to you. Do the same if you use the number of a relative who is taking messages for you. (If you get a call on your cell phone, it may be better to let it go to voicemail so you can find out who it is and go to a quiet place where you can be prepared and have good reception. That way, you'll have a better conversation.)

Job Titles

You must be accurate in stating your job title, and sometimes that means *not* using the title your company gave you. Use a title that truly reflects the job you held—one commonly understood outside your company. For example, if your company calls you a programmer C, is that a high-level programmer or a low-level one? It would be better to call yourself a junior programmer or a senior programmer—titles that make more sense to the outside world.

I had a client whose job title was Marketing Representative, yet what she did was market analysis. Since she was applying for positions in market analysis, the title was holding her back—and it was also misleading. Until she agreed to change her title and make it more honest, readers thought she was in sales.

One job hunter had trouble in her search because her most recent job title was Marketing Manager, when what she had actually done was sales. She had to convince the prospective employer that in reality she had had 10 years of sales experience—not marketing. Her title misrepresented her and was a handicap.

Think seriously about your company-dictated

job titles and make sure they truly represent what you did. If they do not represent what you did and the way you want the market to see you, you must change them to make your résumé depict you more honestly. Just be certain that your accomplishments support whatever title you use.

Reporting Relationships, Company Descriptions

Sometimes your reporting relationship gives a good indication of your level of responsibility. If it helps, put it in; for example, "Report directly to the president."

It may help to put in parentheses what your company does. For example: "Complex, Inc. (a computer software company)."

Highlighting or Understating Job Titles

Look at the first job listed on your résumé. Which would be more important to the *reader*: your job title or the name of your employer? Decide which you want the reader to notice for each position. You do not have to be consistent: In one case, it may be your title, and in another, say, if you're looking within the same industry, it may be the name of your employer. Or you may want to highlight both or play down both.

Emphasize or de-emphasize by using caps, spacing, underlining, boldface, and positioning on a page. I list one job that was a bore for me at the bottom of page 2 of my résumé. Both my title and the name of the company are simply written in upper- and lower-case. Nothing stands out. The result is that most interviewers don't ask me about that job.

Here are some examples of highlighting:

Assistant Researcher, ACME CORPORATION
Assistant Researcher, **ACME CORPORATION**
ASSISTANT RESEARCHER, Acme Corporation
ASSISTANT RESEARCHER, Acme Corporation

This practice is effective and not offensive. It helps in the readability and the dynamism of your résumé. When it's done correctly, the interviewer will tend to talk about what you want to talk about.

The Date Your Most Recent Job Ended

If you have recently left a job, or know that your job is ending, should you highlight that fact by putting an end date on your résumé, or should you say "to present"? For example:

Assistant Researcher	2003 to present
Acme Corporation	

or

Assistant Researcher	2003 to 2007
Acme Corporation	

Do whatever feels right. You do not want to be "rejected on paper." You need to make sure that your résumé supports you, not hurts you.

You don't have to have a résumé that is completely up-to-date. If you are now unemployed, you may want to pretend that you wrote your résumé while you were in your last job. If the interviewer asks if you are still there, you can answer truthfully that you are not—but at least you have gotten in for the interview.

Most people do not have completely up-to-the-minute résumés. Let me give you an example. At one point in my career, I was called in for an interview and was asked to bring along my résumé. Because I had been at my current company for over three years, my résumé was out of date. I was so busy, I had no time to write a new one. At the meeting, I explained what I had been doing at my present job for the past three years.

These days, being out of work has little stigma attached to it—so do whatever makes you comfortable. However, if you have been out of work for a while, you are facing a different issue: What have you been doing lately? This issue is addressed in our book *Mastering the Job Interview and Winning the Money Game* in the chapter *How to Handle Those Difficult Interview Questions*.

Rank Your Accomplishments

Within each job, list first the accomplishment most important to the *reader*. If your most important one is listed last, the reader may never get to it.

Where to Spend Your Energy

On the first page—especially the summary.

How to Decide If You Should Put Something on Your Résumé

Always use this philosophy: If it helps your case, put it in. If it does not help your case, leave it out.

The Question of Telling Your Age

If you are older (say, over 55 or 60), the accepted practice is that you would not give a clue in the résumé about your age. But the reader will invariably try to guess how old you are anyway. If, for example, you leave out your years of graduation, it will make your age look like an issue, and the reader may guess that you are older than you are. When I was applying for management positions years ago, my résumé made me sound younger than I actually was—I had worked for a few years before completing my undergraduate work. It helped my case to put my date of birth in my résumé, because I wanted employers to know how old I really was. Admittedly, this is not the usual situation. Look at your own situation to see if putting in dates would help your case or not.

Use the Language of Your Target Market

Restate your background in terms your target market will understand. If you're looking outside your company, don't lapse into company jargon; if you're looking outside your industry, don't lapse into industry jargon. For example, if you want to switch from education to a training position in the corporate world, remember that the corporate world does not have *teachers*; it has *trainers* or even *instructors*. Consider using these words instead. Do not expect the reader to translate the terminology. Show that you understand his or her industry.

Is This Résumé Good or Bad?

Now take a look at the sample résumés. You'll see that it is difficult to judge whether a résumé is good or bad unless you know the circumstances and the pitch the person is trying to make.

People show me résumés all the time and ask me to tell them quickly if they are good or bad. Usually, the ones lacking summary statements are not very good. And those written with large, dense paragraphs are difficult to read, causing the messages to get lost. But other than that, I frankly cannot tell if a résumé is good or bad. I need to know more about the person and his or her goals.

If your résumé positions you the way you want to be positioned, it's a good résumé. If it doesn't, it's not good. I hope the case studies in this book will show you the power of a correctly positioned résumé—one that places you at the proper level and highlights the right areas from your background.

Some people have never seen a positioning statement at the top of the résumé and they're reluctant to use one. "Gee, are you sure that's okay? I've never seen that before. It seems too much to me."

We recommend the positioning statement because it's based on hard research. We have tracked what works for job hunters for 25 years.

Thousands of Five O'Clock Club members have landed better jobs faster because their résumés *positioned them accurately and powerfully.*

Unlike other résumé books, this one is geared to showing you the reasoning behind the résumé. My clients have been delighted to learn the difference a good résumé can make in their searches. And I am delighted to pass on some of this wisdom to you.

Perseverance is a great element of success. If you only knock long enough and loud enough at the gate, you are sure to wake up somebody.

LONGFELLOW

Many of life's failures are people who did not realize how close they were to success when they gave up.

THOMAS EDISON

If you have a job without aggravations, you don't have a job.

MALCOLM FORBES

Maria: Not a Kid Anymore

By Maritza Diaz, Certified Five O'Clock Club Coach

Maria's approach in writing her résumé *used* to be okay for someone just getting out of school: She stated a career objective, which was followed by her education and then a historical listing of her work experience. If someone spends only ten seconds looking at her résumé, she appears to be a recent graduate. Today, we live in an age of sound bites and résumé overload. It would have taken the reader too long to figure out what level Maria was at, the important things she had done and where she might fit in.

Maria's "after" résumé has a summary, which makes it easy for the reader to figure out exactly what she does and her level. In addition, the reader gets a feel for **Maria's personality**: "Passionate, committed and highly skilled professional with technical and customer service skills. Driven to produce results. Known for going the extra mile." Maria's old résumé told us nothing about **her work style**.

Maria had additional problems. One was that **she wanted to transition from accounting into Information Technology** and has an engineering degree. She is foreign born and English is her second language, and she has been taking classes to get a U.S. degree in Information technology. Maria has had IT internships, and has been exposed to aspects of IT in the some of her work assignments.

But her résumé was weak and scattered—and it didn't include any of her IT experience, which could be helpful for getting her foot in the door. **She needed to re-position her résumé and show what she had done in IT** and not just focus on her education and coursework in IT. What's more, the résumé was structured poorly, was hard to read, and had misspellings! A potential employer

could easily get lost or just lose interest. She had not made it easy to see how her past experience could apply to IT positions.

In revising the résumé, we refocused on the type of job she wanted to find. We put that front-and-center in the summary section at the top of the résumé. We listed her work history in reverse chronological order and put the education and skills section at the end. I asked Maria to think hard about her 'job description duties' so that we could add specific accomplishments, achievements and results.

When we listed her past employment, we focused as well on stating all the IT-related duties that she had in her non-IT positions. One example of this was her Graphic Designer job; we highlighted the fact that it was actually more IT-related than design. We also added volunteer work she had done that involved IT duties. **We brought in everything in her past work history, whether paid or unpaid, that demonstrated her IT skills.**

Maria had one more problem: the large number of jobs she had held. A number of those job changes were easily explained, but Maria didn't get the chance to explain them because prospective employers jumped to conclusions. Maria was "rejected on paper." That is, her résumé contained something a prospective employer might object to. Do not allow your résumé to defeat you. Handle those objections on paper.

In this case, **Maria inserted—in small type— the reasons she left a number of those jobs**: In her case, she had been caught in a number of downsizings. In your case, it might be that the company moved, closed, or other explanations that do not reflect on you at all. The explanation is not included for every job—just enough to let the reader know that Maria would and could have stayed longer if the circumstances had been right.

With so many companies in trouble these days, a job hunter may change jobs several times through no fault of his or her own. It may be best to let the reader know those reasons—on paper. But don't overdo it and feel compelled to put in a reason for every job you've left.

Finally, the "after" résumé is scannable. With this new formatting, especially the underlining and bolding, the reader is more likely to notice the things Maria thinks are important.

Maria is working to compete the IT coursework and is being well received for a number of IT positions.

The price one pays for pursuing any profession or calling is an intimate knowledge of its ugly side.

James Baldwin

Maria Lopez

2632 Hoym Street – Apt. 4C
Fort Lee, NJ 08555
Tel: (201) 555-4321
Email: m.lopez.gonzalez@yahoo.com

OBJECTIVE: A position as a Help Desk Technician / Desktop Support

EDUCATION

Long Beach City College, Seeking Associate in Arts Degree on Network Administration   GPA: 4
School of Visual Arts, Photography Course 2002
The new School of New York, Typography Course 2001
Habana University, Cuba, BA Mechanical Engineering 1994-2000

CERTIFICATIONS:

CompTIA A+, Apparel Information Management System Certification

TECHNICAL SKILLS:

- Languages: Java, PHP, HTML, Apache, MySQL
- Operating Systems: UNIX, Windows 98/ME /NT /2000/2003 Server/XP/Vista /7, Mac OS X, Red Hat Linux
- Software: MS Office 2003/2007, Photoshop, Dreamweaver, Macromedia Flash, Microsoft SQL Server, VMware, Microsoft Windows Server, Microsoft Visio 2007, Apparel Information Management System (AIMS), Direct EDI

ADITIONAL SKILLS:

- Excellent interpersonal and communication skills
- Proactive worker with outstanding leadership skills
- Ability to learn quickly and maintain attention to detail in high stress situations
- Fluent in English and Spanish

EXPERIENCE:

Help desk technician (Six Months Internship)

- Installed and configured applications on workstations.
- Troubleshoot and resolve problems as needed.
- Configured and deployed workstations.
- Implemented projects as assigned.
- Answered technical questions regarding software products and their requirements within related industries.
- Documented all support & maintenance activity.
- Maintained a current and accurate inventory of workstations, printers, copiers, fax machines and other LAN devices as assigned.

Maria Lopez - Page 2

- Helped install local area network cabling systems and equipment such as network interface cards, hubs and switches.
- Diligently and consistently followed departmental & organizational policies and procedures.

Operations Coordinator / Database Administrator Assistant
- Update and chase delegated tasks to ensure progress to deadlines: Keep projects on schedule.
- Maintain and develop process and procedures manual to ensure consistent performance of routines.
- Coordinate work flow across multiple projects.
- Provide accurate and timely project updates through both the company's planning tools and written/verbal status reporting.
- Enhanced end users' understanding of database AIMS system by conducting pre-implementation workshops, delivering group and individual training sessions and creating user-friendly training materials.

Graphic Designer /Art Producer
- Designed prototypes, visual layouts, and user interfaces for web sites and web-based applications using HTML, JavaScript, and Photoshop.
- Used a wide range of typography to appeal to specific design.
- Performed color corrections and image manipulation, photo retouching and special effects to digital artwork.
- Created and delivered dynamic website designs and user interfaces.
- Designed various types of printed publications such as brochures, programs, banners, diagrams, graphs, slides and web site graphics.
- Designed thumbnails, roughs, and final comps for web sites.

RELEVANT WORK HISTORY

2010-Present	*Operations Coordinator / Database Administrator Assistant,* Alchem Textile, Inc, Los Angeles, CA
2009-2010	*Help Desk Technician,* Bank of Mexico, New York, NY
2005-2008	*Royalty Manager/Member Relations,* Sociedad General de Autores y Editores, New York, NY
2001-2004	*Graphic Designer /Art Producer,* Sesame Workshop, New York, NY
2000-2001	*Accounts Payable,* Downtown Home Furnishings, New York, NY
1998-2000	*Mathematics Tutor,* Havana University, Cuba

VOLUNTEER EXPERIENCE

Libreria Mexico *(Spanish Bookstore)*
2003 - Present
Responsibilities: Web site design and maintenance, company technical support.

Written references are available upon requests.

MARIA LOPEZ

2632 Hoym Street – Apt. 4C   201-555-4321
Fort Lee, NJ 08555   m.lopez.gonzalez@yahoo.com

HELP DESK TECHNICIAN / DESKTOP SUPPORT SPECIALIST
With over 12 years experience in

Media   Textile Manufacturing   Financial Services

- As a Help Desk Technician, <u>**decreased the turnaround time for installations by two days**</u>.
- **Developed an in-house database training program.**
- Installed and configured workstations and applications for <u>**over 200 customers**</u>.
- <u>**Designed printed publications**</u> (brochures, programs, banners, diagrams, graphs, slides and website graphics as well as <u>**dynamic websites with special effects**</u>.

Passionate, committed and highly skilled technology support professional with technical and customer service skills. Driven to produce results. Known for going the extra mile. Fluent in Spanish.

ALCHEM TEXTILE INC. - Los Angeles, CA   2010–Present
<u>**Operations Coordinator / Database Administrator**</u>

- Developed an in-house training program on AIMS database system including all training materials. Resulted in an enhanced understanding for end users of AIMS and a <u>**decrease in processing time for the Operations group**</u>.
- Played a key role in project scheduling, investigating problems and recommending solutions. <u>**Resulted in a decrease of 10% in turnaround time for order completion**</u>.
- Developed the company's process and procedures manual on data administration. Resulted in a decrease in the number of errors made when processing orders. Overall impact was an <u>**increase in positive customer satisfaction level by approximately 20%**</u>.
- Effective team member with the ability to successfully coordinate work flows across multiple projects.
- Effective communicator responsible for providing accurate and timely project updates throughout the company using multiple in house reporting tools.

BANK OF MEXICO - NEW YORK, NY   2009–2010
<u>**Help Desk Technician**</u>
Internship

- Installed and configured workstations and applications for over 200 customers. <u>**Decreased the turnaround time for installations by two days**</u>.
- Responsible for troubleshooting and resolving problems for internal customers.
- Installed local area network cabling systems and equipment such as network interface cards, hubs and switches.
- <u>**Quickly**</u> address problem situations and <u>**accurately**</u> answered technical questions regarding software products and their requirements.
- Maintained all required documentation on all support and maintenance activity in a timely manner which <u>**contributed to the resolution of an open internal audit item**</u> for the IT group.
- Maintained a current and accurate inventory of workstations, printers, copiers, fax machines and other LAN devices assigned. This <u>**contributed to a no findings report**</u> on inventory by the Federal Banking regulators.

Reason for leaving: Entire department was outsourced.

MARIA LOPEZ – page 2

SESAME WORKSHOP - NEW YORK, NY   2001-2004
<u>**Graphic Designer / Art Production**</u>
- <u>**Designed prototypes**</u>, visual layouts, and user interfaces for websites and web-based applications <u>**using HTML, JavaScript, and Photoshop**</u>.
- Created and delivered dynamic website designs and user interfaces.
- Designed a variety of printed publications including brochures, programs, banners, diagrams, graphs, slides and website graphics.
- Performed **special effects on digital artwork** such as color corrections and image manipulation and photo retouching.
- Designed thumbnails, roughs, and final comps for websites.
- Reason for leaving: Company has a major reduction in force.

Other Positions included:
- Royalty Manager / Member Relations at Sociedad General de Autores y Editores (New York, NY) - 2005 to 2008.
- Accounts Payable Specialist at Downtown Home Furnishings (New York, NY) – 2000 to 2001.
- Mathematics Tutor at Havana University (Cuba) – 1998 to 2000.

Volunteer Work:
- **Website Designer** at Libreria Mexico (Spanish Bookstore) - 2003 to present
  Perform website design and maintenance of website providing extensive technical support
  www.libreriamexicoqueens.com

EDUCATION
- Long Beach City College – Associates in Arts Degree in Network Administration. Expected completion Summer 2014
- School of Visual Arts - Photography Course – 2002
- The New School of New York – Typography Course – 2001
- Havana University, Cuba – BA Mechanical Engineering – 1994 – 2000

CERTIFICATION AND SKILLS
- Certified Comp TIA A+, Apparel Information Management System
- Languages: Java, PHP, HTML, Apache, MySQL
- Operating Systems: IUNIX, Windows 98/ME/NT/2000/2003 Server, XP/Vista/7, Mac OS X, Red Hat Linux
- Software: MS Office 2003/2007, Photoshop, Dreamweaver, Macromedia Flash, Microsoft SQL Server, VMware, Microsoft Windows Server, Microsoft Visio 2007, Apparel Information Management System (AIMS), Direct EDI
- Fluent in Spanish

Andy: His Seven Stories Made the Difference

Andy worked on the West Coast for one of the largest power plants in the country. He had an engineering background, but he saw himself as different from the stereotype of an engineer in that he was very much a people person. In fact, he thought he would like to go into sales in his next job in the energy industry. That was Andy's target.

First, we analyzed Andy's #1 accomplishment from his Seven Stories Exercise. Though he ranked it #1, it wasn't even on his old résumé: "Led the project to redesign the CRDM fan supports during the 2012 refueling outage. My boss said it could not be done. I convinced him to let me go ahead. We completed the project early and solved not only a structural problem but a union/management issue. Saved $3 million and avoided significant potential plant downtime."

Andy told me more and here's how we restated it for his new résumé:

- Conceived of **technological innovation** and **led 50-person project** that **solved heated union/management safety issue**.
  - Problem had been **unsolved for 10 years**.
  - **Saved $3 million** and avoided significant potential plant downtime.

If Andy had not done the Seven Stories, he would have skipped this accomplishment completely. We got rid of unnecessary jargon (CRDM fan supports) to make this accomplishment appealing to a broader range of power plants. We added drama to the accomplishment by stating that the problem had gone unsolved for 10 years. Often **you can add drama to your accomplish-ments by letting the reader know something about the difficulty of the situation you faced.**

Here's another one of Andy's Seven Stories: "During the 2012 refueling outage, a serious problem arose with seismic restraints on the steam generators. It would have kept the plant shut down, costing $1 million a day. I analyzed the situation, organized information-gathering sessions with relevant people, and made field visits to verify measurements and conditions. I came up with a simple solution and saved the day!"

Here's how we wrote it up for his new résumé:

- During the 2012 refueling outage, **selected to solve problem that would have prevented plant from starting up,** costing almost **$1 million/day and major regulatory fines.**
  - Under extremely high-pressure situation, developed simple solution to problem.
  - Achieved regulatory approval.
  - Led team to quickly solve problem.

This accomplishment was impossible to find on Andy's "before" résumé. It was buried as the sixth item in a list of seven bullets. You can see it in the "Second Draft" on the next page.

Here is how he had stated it: "Solved operational difficulties which averted significant plant downtime and $1 million in losses per day."

That wasn't too bad, but we don't see the drama of the high-pressure situation or his ability to get others to cooperate. In addition, he was selected to solve this problem. The Seven Stories helped Andy come up with words that were more alive and better expressed what he did.

Let's take a look at the progression of Andy's description of this particular job. In his first draft, before he was aware of the techniques used at The Five O'Clock Club, the write-up sounded like a job description.

First Draft of Sample Accomplishment

<u>Project Manager</u>, Nuclear Power Department

- Responsible for the engineering and design of plant modifications and the development of plant drawings for installation.
- Conceived, created, and provided implementation support for numerous plant improvements and modifications.
- Assisted construction and maintenance personnel in solving problems related to the installation of plant modifications.
- Interfaced with other departments (Maintenance, NS&L, Operations, QA, Tech. Svcs.) on sensitive issues concerning regulatory inquiries.
- Coordinated department schedule and prioritized engineering projects.
- Performed operability analysis on critical plant components.

In his second draft, completed after he was aware of The Five O'Clock Club techniques but before I started coaching him, Andy tried to take an accomplishment-oriented approach, which worked much better.

Second Draft of Sample Accomplishment

Project Manager, Nuclear Power

- Managed the engineering, design, and installation of critical plant modifications costing from $50,000 to $6 million.
- Directed contractor and company workforces in high-pressure, schedule-sensitive $60 million refueling/maintenance outage.
- Revitalized engineering department and rearranged the way we did business for increased productivity.
- Coordinated the efforts of various departments for the accomplishment of project objectives.
- Conceived, created, and organized the implementation of numerous plant advances and improvements.
- Solved operational difficulties that averted significant plant downtime and $1 million in losses per day.
- Played major role in achieving world record-breaking performance at Stockton Light Station. The plant is now one of the lowest cost nuclear generating stations in the world.

After focusing on his Seven Stories, Andy wrote his final draft, which looked like the following. Notice that we took what was his very last bullet in his second draft and highlighted it. It is a strong statement and an overview of what he did in that job. It will certainly grab the reader's attention.

Final version of sample accomplishment

<u>Project Manager,</u> Nuclear Power

Played major role in making Stockton Light <u>one of the best performing, lowest cost nuclear plants in the world. Plant broke the world record for continuous operation.</u>

- Conceived of **<u>technological innovation</u>** and **<u>led 50-person project</u>** that **<u>solved heated union/ management safety issue.</u>**
  - Problem had been **<u>unsolved for 10 years.</u>**
  - **<u>Saved $3 million</u>** and avoided significant potential plant downtime.
- During the 2012 refueling outage, **<u>selected to solve problem that would have prevented plant from starting up,</u>** costing almost **<u>$1 million/day and major regulatory fines.</u>**
  - Under extremely high-pressure situation, developed simple solution to problem.
  - Achieved regulatory approval.
  - Led team to quickly solve problem.
- Managed the engineering, design, and installation of critical plant modifications ranging from **<u>$50,000 to $6 million.</u>**
- Revitalized the engineering department and rearranged it for increased productivity.

The write-up of that job is now looking pretty good. This restatement better emphasizes Andy's interpersonal skills as well as his knowledge of plant operations, positioning him well for a sales position in the energy field. What's more, by completing this part, Andy has already rewritten a major segment of his résumé.

Andy worked on the other accomplishments from his Seven Stories Exercise and then restated each job they were part of.

Next, he needed to write the summary statement. Below is the first draft of his summary, which he had written before he knew The Five O'Clock Club approach.

First Draft of summary

Skills	Interpersonal Communication, Negotiating, Problem Solving, Planning, Project Coordination, Supervisory, Team Leadership, Writing, Public Speaking
Education	**MBA**, Rensselaer Polytechnic Institute, Troy, New York **MS**, Nuclear Engineering, Rensselaer Polytechnic Institute, Troy, New York **BS**, Physics, SUNY at Stony Brook, Stony Brook, New York **AAS**, SUNY at Farmingdale, Farmingdale, New York

---

Andy made a good effort to jazz up his summary. This is what he wrote before we met:

Second Draft of summary

Summary of Qualifications

- Power industry professional with **extensive experience** in the production of electricity and its associated distribution.
- An **accomplished manager** with **excellent interpersonal skills.**

- **Skilled at financial and operational analysis** for optimal decision making.
- A visionary with keen insight into the emerging competitive electricity marketplace.
- **MBA**

Andy wanted to get into sales, so he stressed skills related to that. He also wanted the reader to know that he is knowledgeable about new developments in the power industry. But after rewriting his accomplishments based on his Seven Stories, he found that he wanted a stronger summary.

I probed further: "What would you like people in the power industry to know about you? How do you see yourself as special and different from the average person in your area?"

Here's Andy's new summary:

Final version of summary

Power Industry Manager with experience in literally every area of power generation

- In-depth understanding of plant operations, engineering, maintenance, and staffing.
  - **Ran a 1000 megawatt power plant.**
- **Negotiate with independent energy producers.** First-year savings of $63 million.
- Managed the engineering, design, and installation of **plant projects of up to $6 million.**
- An innovative problem solver, **skilled at financial and operational analysis.**
- Managed staff of 30. Assembled and **led teams of up to 50** in high-pressure projects.
- **BS, Physics; MS, Nuclear Engineering; MBA**

A visionary with keen insight into the emerging competitive electricity marketplace.
An aggressive, congenial manager who develops strong union/management relations.

The first line positions Andy as a "manager" rather than as a "professional." He wants to stay in the power industry, so that is also in the first line. The second line differentiates him from other power industry managers. In addition, not too many people can say that they actually "ran a 1000 megawatt power plant." That accomplish-ment implies a lot. His education is also unique, so we summarized it here. The italicized section at the bottom of the summary is like the tagline in an ad: It describes the way he works and tells something about his personality. It predisposes the hiring manager to see Andy as a certain kind of person, and it complements the headline.

The final summary is more scannable than the second draft. In the second draft, we see weaker words such as "extensive experience," and "accomplished manager."

In the final, we see punchier and more specific phrases like "Power Industry Manager" and "ran a 1000 megawatt power plant." As Andy remarked, "That pretty much says it all. The rest of my résumé supports those points."

Now let's look at the final product.

Andrew Marks

21 Ocean Avenue
Manteca, CA 54999

andy463@att.net

Home: (222) 555-1234
Business: (222) 556-6734

Power Industry Manager
with experience in literally every area of power generation

- In-depth understanding of plant operations, engineering, maintenance, and staffing.
  - **Ran a 1000 megawatt power plant**.
- **Negotiate with independent energy producers**. First-year savings of $63 million.
- Managed the engineering, design, and installation of **plant projects of up to $6 million**.
- An innovative problem solver, **skilled at financial and operational analysis**.
- Managed staff of 30. Assembled and **led teams of up to 50** in high-pressure projects.
- **BS, Physics; MS, Nuclear Engineering; MBA**

A visionary with keen insight into the emerging competitive electricity marketplace.
An aggressive, congenial manager who develops strong union/management relations.

California Power Company, Inc.   2005-present

Project Engineer, Planning and Inter-Utility Affairs   2012-present

Develop strategy to position company to compete in future electric industry.

- Negotiate with independent power producers. Resulted in $63 million in savings.
- Analyze system requirements and financial advantages of plant repower/retirement.
- Assess electric generating stations future costs, risks and competitive potential.
- Assist operating departments in scheduling the economic dispatch of electricity.
- Evaluate potential purchases and sales of electric capacity.
- Negotiate and prepare contracts for the exchange, purchase and sale of electricity.

Project Manager, Nuclear Power   2010-2012

Played major role in making Stockton Light
one of the best performing, lowest cost nuclear plants in the world.
Plant broke the world record for continuous operation.

- Conceived of **technological innovation** and **led 50-person project** that **solved heated union/ management safety issue.**
  - Problem had been **unsolved for 10 years.**
  - **Saved $3 million** and avoided significant potential plant downtime.
- During the 2012 refueling outage, **selected to solve problem that would have prevented plant from starting up,** costing almost **$1 million/day and major regulatory fines.**
  - Under extremely high-pressure situation, developed simple solution to problem.
  - Achieved regulatory approval.
  - Led team to quickly solve problem.
- Managed the engineering, design and installation of critical plant modifications ranging from **$50,000 to $6 million.**
- Revitalized the engineering department and rearranged it for increased productivity.

Department Supervisor, Performance Engineering   2008-2010

- **Selected to reorganize Performance Engineering Department.**
  - Dept. had dissension, infighting, and extremely low productivity.
  - **Doubled productivity** in less than 1 year.
  - Initiated cutting-edge programs that **saved millions.**
  - Department became one of the **most respected groups** in the plant.
  - Created and implemented Dept. training program. **Program became the model.**
  - Boosted group morale by **creating a team and empowering individuals.**

Fast-Track Training Program   2005-2008

A rigorous 3-year program of rotation supervisory assignments. Positions were critical to the reliable operation of the electric system. Presented to a panel of executives every 3 months. **Achieved top rating in this elite management group.**

Chief Engineering Inspector, Kingsburg Generating Station

- Directed contractor workforces and installed two plant computer control systems.
- Managed the rebuilding of 300-foot-high power plant smoke stack.

Supervisor, Taft Avenue Generating Station

- Managed contractor and company workforces in the overhaul of power plant turbine and control systems. Unit ran better than it had in 20 years.

Operations Supervisor, Kingsburg Generating Station

- Ran a 1000 megawatt power plant.
  - Initiated substantial productivity improvements in worker practices.
  - Persuaded workers to see their efforts as part of the big picture.

Supervisor, Modesto Networks

- Directed crews in the maintenance of underground cable systems and transformers.

Supervisor, Stockton Light Nuclear Generating Station

- Responsible for the testing of critical emergency safe shutdown components.

Engineer, Mechanical Engineering

- Conceived, designed, and developed power plant diagnostic Expert System.

Education

MBA, with fellowship honors, Rensselaer Polytechnic Institute, Troy, NY 2005
MS, Nuclear Engineering, Rensselaer Polytechnic Institute, Troy, NY 2005
BS, Physics, SUNY Stony Brook, Stony Brook, NY, 2003
AAS, SUNY Farmingdale, Farmingdale, NY 1997

Memberships

American Association of Individual Investors
American Society of Mechanical Engineers
American Nuclear Society

Downplaying His Most Recent Position

As you can see from the final version of the first page of Andy's two-page résumé, he played up the second job on the page and played down his most recent job. He felt that the project manager job was one of the most important he had held in his life. His current job was interesting but not as important for making his next move.

You too can highlight what you want to in your résumé and downplay other areas.

Mediocrity obtains more with application than superiority without it.

Baltasar Gracian, *Oraculo Manual*

Font Size, Spacing, Underlining

Your résumé is completely under your control. You can guide the reader's eye. If hiring managers are looking at your résumé for only 10 seconds, what do they see? Make sure every line is great, because if they like what they see in those first 10 seconds, they will be inclined to read more.

Some résumés in this book use underlining and boldface; others do not. With most computers, underlining alone is not sufficient: The presentation looks weak, and it actually may be better to have no underlining at all. **If you are going to underline something, it should also be bolded. If you are going to bold something, it should also be underlined.**

Remember that italicized words are more difficult to read than nonitalicized. Therefore, use italics sparingly and be sure that the font size is not too small.

Use spacing between lines to break up your résumé and make it easier for the reader to make sense of it. In general, leave more space in between each job than there is within each job. Otherwise, your résumé will look like lines and lines of type with no apparent logic.

Andy's final résumé was done in 12-point type, Palatino typeface. The point sizes are differ-

ent depending on the typeface. That is, 12-point New York typeface is smaller than 12-point Palatino typeface.

When Andy makes a line space with his computer by hitting the enter key, that space is 12 points because that is the font size he is using. He can make his résumé look more logical if he leaves two full 12-point spaces between his jobs rather than just one space.

Spacing fine-tuned the look of his résumé in other places. For example, after the line "Project Engineer," Andy has a small space rather than the full 12-point space he would have had if he simply hit the enter key. The line that says "Develop strategy to position company to compete in future electric industry" is followed by another small space. This makes that portion of the résumé tighter. Logical areas are drawn together more.

Andy follows the next job title, "Project Manager," with a small space. The three-line summary for that job is centered and bolded and followed by another small space. These small spaces in Andy's résumé happen to be 4 points each.

This kind of spacing tightens up the résumé and makes the jobs hang together better. Then the reader can more easily see the logic of your résumé.

The same is true in Andy's summary. The line "with experience in literally every area of power generation" is followed by an 8-point space. And the space before the tagline "A visionary..." is also an 8-point space.

If you cannot easily make these kinds of minor adjustments, do not worry about them. They are tiny refinements that ultimately make little difference except to those of us who are perfectionists about the way a résumé looks.

Making a space other than standard size (that is, 10, 12, 14 points) is easy on the Macintosh. You simply highlight the blank line you are trying to change and, depending on the software, use command-D or command-T to enter in a different font size. Four points is usually the smallest font size you can enter.

On a PC, the job can be much more difficult, depending on the software. Highlight the blank line you want to change, and on some programs (such as Microsoft Word), change the font size that shows in the bar at the top of the screen (for example, change "12" to "8") and hit the return key. If this task is too much trouble, simply skip it.

Now that you have an overview of how a résumé gets put together, let's get serious about yours.

How to State *Your* Accomplishments

The fastest way to succeed is to look as if you're playing by other people's rules, while quietly playing by your own.

Michael Korda

The results of your Seven Stories exercise and Forty-Year Vision help you set your long-term direction. In order to go somewhere, you must know where you are right now. In this chapter, you will look down and see where your feet are. You will become more pragmatic. What have you done so far in your life? What do you have to offer the world?

What Do You Have to Offer?

In deciding what you *want* to offer, first list all you *have* to offer—a menu to choose from. When you go after a certain kind of position, emphasize those parts that support your case. If you decide, for example, to continue your career in the same direction, you will probably focus on your most recent position and others that support that direction.

If most of your adult satisfactions have occurred outside your job, you may want to change something about your work life. Someday you may decide to change careers—most of us will have to. If you decide to change careers, activities outside your regular job may help you make that change.

Take my case: When I was interested in changing from computers to advertising, I offered as proof of my ability the three years I had spent at night promoting nonprofit organizations. My portfolio of press coverage for those organizations

was my proof. Later, when I wanted to work as a career coach, my proof was my many years' experience in running The Five O'Clock Club at night, the seminars I had given on job hunting and career development, and so on. When I wanted to continue working in business management, I simply offered my on-the-job experience in making companies profitable.

If you have available the entire list of what you have to offer, you can be more flexible about the direction you want to go in.

Process- versus Project-Oriented Accomplishments

Present what you have to offer in terms of accomplishments. Tell your *story* in a way that will provoke interest in you and let the reader know what you are really like. Accomplishment statements are short, measurable, and results oriented. We each handle the situations in our work lives in different ways. What problems have you faced at work? How did you handle them? What was the effect on the organization?

Some of us are project oriented and others are process oriented. If you are project oriented, you will tend to take whatever is assigned to you, break it into *projects* in your mind, and then get those projects done. You like to solve problems, and you get bored when there are none. Your accomplishments will state the problems you faced, how you solved them, and the impact you had on the organization.

On the other hand, if you are process oriented. you like to run the day-to-day shop. You can be trusted to keep an existing situation running smoothly, and your accomplishments will reflect that. You like stable situations and systems that work. You will state that you ran a department of so many people for so many years.

A project-oriented accomplishment could look like this:

- Designed and directed a comprehensive and cost-effective advertising and sales promotion program that established the company as a major competitor in the market.

A process-oriented accomplishment could look like this:

- Conducted ongoing reviews of market performance of investor-owned utility securities, using multiple equity valuation techniques. Recommended redirection of portfolio mix to more profitable and higher-quality securities.

Developing *Your* List of Accomplishments

There are two ways to develop your complete list of accomplishments: You can start with your most recent job and work backward, or you can start with the results of your Seven Stories Exercise. Do whichever is more comfortable for you.

Do not worry right now if you do not like your job title or do not even like your job. Later on, we will change your title to make it reflect what you were actually doing, and we can emphasize or de-emphasize jobs and responsibilities as you see fit. Right now, get down on paper all of your accomplishments. Then we will have something to work with.

Do not wish to go back to your youth. What was challenging then would probably not satisfy you today. Look for the elements of those early jobs that satisfied you. These elements can help to determine your lifelong interests.

You will feel better after you have developed your list of accomplishments. You will see on paper all that you have to offer. And your accomplishments will be stated in a way that will make you proud. Discipline yourself to do this exercise now, and you will not have to do it again.

Starting with Your Most Recent Position

Write down your current or most recent position. State your title and your company name, and list your accomplishments in that position. Rather than ranking them chronologically, rank them in the order of interest to the reader.

After refining the accomplishment statements for your present or most recent position, examine the job before that one. State your title and your company name, and list your accomplishments.

Work on as many accomplishments as make sense to you. Some people cover in depth the past 10 years. If you can, cover your entire career, because you never know what may occur to you, and you never know what may help you later. In doing this exercise, you may remember jobs you had completely forgotten about—and pleasant and satisfying accomplishments. Ask yourself what it was about that job that was so satisfying. Perhaps it is another clue about what you might do in the future.

After you have listed your work experiences, list accomplishments outside work. These, too, should be short, measurable, and results oriented. These outside experiences can help you move into a new field. In fact, that's how I and many others have made career transitions. By volunteering to do advertising and public relations work at night, I developed a list of accomplishments that helped me move from computers to advertising. In those days, my outside experience included:

- Walnut Street Theatre Gallery
  Planned, organized, and promoted month-long holography exhibition. Attendance increased from fewer than 100 visitors per month to over 3,000 visitors during the month of this exhibition.
- YMCA
  Handled all publicity for fund-raising

campaign. Consulted with fund-raising committee on best techniques for them to use. Received plaque in recognition.
- United Way
  Received four United Way awards for editorial work in 1979; two awards the prior year. Spoke at the United Way's Editors' Conference.

Starting with Your Seven Stories

When people start with their Seven Stories Exercise, they often find that their accomplishments are stated in a more vital way. Their résumé becomes more interesting to read—it is full of "stories." If your résumé sounds dull—and perhaps like everyone else's—try this approach. It will loosen you up.

The next chapter will get you started on this new adventure.

An adventure is the deliberate, volitional movement out of the comfort zone.

James W. Newman, *Release Your Brakes*

The
Five
O'Clock
Club®

Start with Your Seven Stories

Start where you are with what you have, knowing that what you have is plenty enough.

BOOKER T. WASHINGTON

Start with your most important story from the Seven Stories Exercise—if it was work related. Do *not* look at what you wrote on your résumé. This is your opportunity to develop very different words from those you used on your résumé—words that very likely were stilted. Instead, brag about your accomplishments and write down what you did as if you were talking to a spouse or a friend. Chances are, this unstilted description will better capture what you really did.

Then polish up that accomplishment and a few more. If you want your reader to know about these accomplishments, work hard to state them correctly. When you have finished refining three or four major accomplishments, you'll be surprised by how much of your résumé is already done.

You will feel more hopeful about your job search after you have completed this exercise. Your accomplishments will be stated in a way that will make you proud.

Here are a few accomplishment statements. They are written in the context of a complete job so you can see how to bullet and sub-bullet. This technique lets you avoid long, bulky paragraphs that are difficult to read. Bulleting and sub-bulleting can be used on anyone's résumé.

After you have created bullets, look them over. You may find you have too many bullets in a row; for example, a string of nine would be too long. Now see which ones go together. Certain bullets can be made into sub-bullets of others. Sub-bullets will make your résumé even more logical and readable.

This example is written the way it would appear on a résumé. Note that certain parts are underlined so the reader cannot miss them. It makes the résumé more scannable.

VICE PRESIDENT OF MARKETING SERVICES   2004-2006

- Contributed to 3 consecutive years of record 9.7% growth.
- Developed marketing and sales **training programs for 5,000 employees.**
- Program changed "hard sell"/reactive selling to consultative and entrepreneurial approach.
- Program shifted selling culture and positioned company for growth in the 90's.
- **Repositioned subsidiary** by redesigning logo, signage, brochures, direct-mail solicitations, social media efforts and collateral materials.
- Introduced customer-satisfaction measurement program that provided feedback to 1,100 branch operations and produced changes in operational procedures.

Depending on the positions he is going after, these accomplishments may be included or not. They may, for example, be unimportant for 10 years, and later on become important again, depending on his job target.

International Rescue Committee, Sakaeo, Thailand   2007-2008
Educational Programs Coordinator

Directed all educational programs in Thailand's second-largest Cambodian refugee camp, with a population of 35,000.

- Managed a budget of $300,000 and an international staff of 550.

- Conceived of and introduced programs that resulted in both a 250% expansion of participants and national recognition.

- Negotiated regularly with the Thai government and the United Nations.

Always seek the hard, definite, personal word.

T. E. HULME

Her job was basically a process-oriented job: getting things to run smoothly and reducing the reporting cycle. Process-oriented jobs can still be presented in terms of accomplishments.

Vice President, Chief Budget Officer   2011-2013
Major Not-for-Profit

Reported to chief financial officer. Staff of 50 in two cities. Joined management team of new CEO and CFO to implement a more results-oriented culture in a nonprofit environment.
- Coordinated annual corporate budget of $500 million expenses.
  - Introduced top-down approach, PC modeling, and budget programs.
- Developed cost-allocation computer system to transfer over $200 million in indirect back-office expenses.
- Projected program costs, including
  - Correcting cost allocations to collect over $2 million in additional annual revenues.
  - Saving program $3 million in potential cost overruns.
  - Developing product costs for future programs, as a member of product-development teams.
- Improved financial systems and information flow:
  - Streamlined financial reporting **reduced cycle by 5 days**.
  - Presented strategic plan to upgrade financial systems.

Let your own discretion be your tutor: Suit the action to the word, The word to the action.

WILLIAM SHAKESPEARE

Curator, Penobscott Museum   2012-2015
Organized all major exhibitions (5 to 6 per year) and their accompanying catalogues.

- Developed educational programs supplementing these exhibitions.
- Reorganized museum's collection of paintings, sculptures, and graphics.
- Organized special films, concerts, and lectures at museum.
- Maintained an extensive speaking schedule; promoted public relations.
- Supervised the activities of curatorial, library, and installation assistants.

Senior Paralegal   2007-2014
Burstein, Kleinder and Feld, PC

- Trained, directed, and **supervised four support employees.**
- Administered, coordinated, and ran secured-loan transactions.

Served as liaison to clients and attorneys; wrote detailed progress reports.

Office Manager/Chiropractic Assistant   2007-2010
Dr. James Taylor
One-person office force for this busy chiropractic office.

- Transcribed own correspondence.
- Set up Leading Edge Word Processor.
- Assisted doctor with exam preparation.
- Billed patients, maintained patient files, answered phones, ordered medical and office supplies, handled appointments.

Her volunteer work shows that she has the experience necessary to do that next job.

Brevard Elementary School, Parent Volunteer   2005-2013

- Assisted teachers with proofreading/grading students' creative writing assignments.
- Coordinated/edited newspapers for two class groups.

Summer jobs can count, too.

Federated Department Stores, Atlanta, GA
Sales Assistant, Summer 2010

- Sold merchandise in various departments and resolved complaints.
- Balanced daily accounts and prepared displays.

Although he held this job a long time ago, the details are important to what this career-changer wants to do next.

Editor/Public Relations Manager, Outboard Marine   2003-2004

- Edited company magazine and handled company P.R. duties.
- Obtained publicity through most national trade magazines.
- Coordinated freelance artists and writers around the country in producing special on-the-spot application stories about the company's products.
- Distributed innovative ideas and encouragement/promotional letters to dealers.
- Attended meetings and conventions.
- Assisted in advertising campaigns, such as photography of products.

Polish Up Your Accomplishment Statements

Rework the wording of your accomplishments. Think how they will sound to the reader. Do not "tell all." Make the reader want to meet you to find out more.

In addition, rephrase your accomplishments to make them as independent as possible of the particular environment you were working in. Make your accomplishments seem useful in other companies or even other industries.

Here is an accomplishment statement as originally written:

Compared the changes in various categories of revenue to the changes in various categories of labor. Plotted results on a scatter diagram to show the relationships.

Avoid the crowd. Do your own thinking independently. Be the chess player, not the chess piece.

Ralph Charell

That is so boring. What were you really doing and why? Look at what you did as if you were an observer rather than the grunt working on something day in and day out. What were the results of your efforts?

Here is that same accomplishment statement reworked:

Defined the factors that influence profitability in professional service firms. Resulted in launch of major reorganization of company's largest division.

Sounds better, doesn't it? The first example sounds like a person who is technical and adds up numbers all day—which is what this project was. The rewrite sounds like a person who knew what he or she was doing, had some say in how it was done, and was aware of the impact on the organization—perhaps even pushed for the changes that took place in the company. The new wording makes the reader want to meet this person to learn new insights.

It has long been an axiom of mine that the little things are infinitely the most important.

A. Conan Doyle, *A Case of Identity*

Here is another "before-and-after" example. The first one was not bad:

Investor Business Manager,   2007-2008
Middle East, Africa Division

- **Reinvigorated risk-taking; improved credit practices** during rebuilding of business in Gulf region. Managed relationships with selected investors.

- Helped **modernize and strengthen risk management** in various functions of the European division. Led a group critique of risk-management issues.

In the rewrite, the job hunter thought more about what he really did in the job. That became the main focus, with the details subordinate to that.

Manager, Middle East Investor Business,   2007-2008
Middle East, Africa Division
Redefined the opportunities in and helped rebuild Gulf Region business after years during which the company perceived high risks and low profitability. Had operating centers in 5 countries, 400+ staff.

- **Redirected marketing** to focus on clients' needs as investors.

- **Reinvigorated risk-taking** and improved credit practices.

- **Improved profitability.**

- Designated a **senior credit officer** and division risk manager.

We all have ability. The difference is how we use it.

STEVIE WONDER, IN HASKINS,
Growing Up in a World of Darkness

What do you want the reader to see? If you want the reader to know that you have developed training programs, does it hit the reader's eye? If you are proud of having repositioned a subsidiary and think it may be important to your next employer, can he or she find it on your résumé? You will not have to think about highlighting your résumé until it is completely put together. For now, just know that it will be an option later. This book contains many examples of accomplishment statements for people of all levels.

When writing your accomplishments:

- *Focus on results*, as opposed to the process you went through. Focus on the effect your actions had.

- *Use quantitative measures* when possible. If the quantity doesn't sound important, don't use it.

- *Show the part you played* in whatever happened to your company. If the company grew from $50 million to $200 million, were you an observer or did you have something to do with it? What was your key accomplishment?

- Don't just say what you did. *State the magnitude and the effect* it had. For example, if you say you "started up a new computer system," that statement could apply to anyone at any level. What effect did that computer system have on the company? Rework your accomplishment to say:

    Developed spreadsheet program to highlight salary inconsistencies within range. Resulted in a more equitable personnel system and savings of $100,000 a year.

or:

    Solely responsible for the development of a computerized system that resulted in a new way to analyze accounts. Resulted in $2 million profit improvement and the renegotiation of key accounts.

Now go back and rework *your* accomplishment statements.

Other Areas to List

Skills and equipment. If you are in a technical job, you may want to list the equipment you are familiar with, such as computers or computer languages or software, and perhaps foreign languages you know.

Books or articles written; speeches delivered. One important example implies you have done more. If you have addressed the United Nations, do not mention the speech you gave at a neighborhood meeting.

Organizations. List organizations related to the work you are seeking. If you list too many, the reader may wonder how you will have time for work.

How You Will Use Your Accomplishments List

Your list of key accomplishments will help you interview, write cover letters, and prepare your résumé. It is the raw material for the rest of your job hunt.

These are the key selling points about you— the things that will make you different from your competition. They will also whet the appetite of the reader, so he or she will want to meet you. The purpose of a résumé or cover letter is not to tell what you did but to get interviews. During the interview, you can elaborate on what you did.

Figuring out what you really did is much more difficult than simply reciting your job description. That's the importance of doing the Seven Stories Exercise. It helps you step back from a résumé frame of mind so you can concentrate

on the most important accomplishments of your life (in terms of what you really enjoyed doing and know you also did well). Then the exercise helps you to think about each accomplishment in terms of what led up to it, what your role was, what gave you satisfaction, what your motivation was, and so on.

When you write your accomplishments, think about your future and those parts of your accomplishments you may want to emphasize. And think about what you really did.

If You Think You Haven't Done a Thing with Your Life

Many people are intimidated when they see other people's accomplishments. They think they have none of their own. Chances are, you aren't thinking hard enough about what you have done. Even obviously accomplished people struggle to express what they have done.

If you think you haven't done much, think again. Even the most junior employees have accomplishments they are proud of. At all levels in an organization, people can be presented with problems and figure out how to handle them.

Don't compare yourself with others, and don't worry about what your boss or peers thought of what you did. Maybe they did not appreciate your talents. Brag about what you have done anyway—even though your boss may have taken credit for the work you did, and even though you may have done it with others. Think of problems you have faced in your company. What did you do to handle them? What was the result for your company? Think of an accomplishment. Write it down. Then pare it down until you can show the reader what you handled and the impact it made.

Finally, don't say anything negative about yourself. Don't lie, but don't hurt yourself either. For example, never lie about where you got a degree or whether you got a degree. If you are found out, you will be fired. If you have been unemployed for a very long time, see my specific hints on how to discuss this awkward timeframe in "How to Handle Difficult Interview Questions" in our book *Mastering the Job Interview.*

For additional reading on this topic, see the section in this book *Résumés for People with "Nothing to Offer."*

Some of us seem to accept the fatalistic position, the fatalistic attitude, that the Creator accorded to us a certain position and condition, and therefore there is no need trying to be otherwise.

Marcus Garvey

Never allow your sense of self to become associated with your sense of job. If your job vanishes, your self doesn't.

Gordon Van Sauter, Former President, CBS News, *Working Woman*

The ingrained mind-set that resists change causes self-inflicted wounds, and those are the most crippling wounds of all, because they are the hardest to cure. The bottom line is: Change is irresistible; run with it.

Hedrick Smith, *Rethinking America*

Industry is a better horse to ride than genius.

Walter Lippmann

How to Handle Consulting, Freelance, Temporary, or Unpaid Work

Work is work. Experience is experience. It does not matter whether or not you were paid, or how you were paid—on payroll, as a consultant, or through an intermediary firm.

If you are performing work for a certain company but are being paid through an intermediary company, such as a temporary services firm, do not put the name of the intermediary firm on your résumé unless it is in your best interests to do so.

Companies make arrangements with intermediary firms for their own reasons, and those negotiations should not affect the way you position yourself on your résumé.

For example, Sharon is working full-time as a project manager at IBM. The project is expected to last for four years. She reports to people at IBM, works with people there, and even manages IBMers. But she was hired by and is paid by a temporary services firm (and receives no benefits, by the way). Which firm should she put on her résumé: the temporary services firm or IBM? IBM is where she works. The temporary services firm is merely a middleman, and the work she does has nothing to do with them. Therefore, she should indicate that she served as a project manager for IBM. Which company actually pays her—or whether she gets paid at all—is not a résumé issue.

Here's another example: John was the manager of the mailroom at his company. The company outsourced the mail function, which means that it was now being handled by an outside firm. John stayed in exactly the same place, doing exactly the same job, working with exactly the same people as he had in the past. However, his paychecks now came from the outsourcing company instead of the place where he worked. Do not disrupt your résumé just because your company decides to handle its finances in a certain way. What if the company John worked for now decided to use a different outsourcing firm? Should he list three different companies on his résumé when he hasn't moved at all? Of course not.

In the same vein, many people gain experience by doing volunteer work. Sydney wanted to learn a new programming language. He received a severance package from his former employer and decided to quickly get some real-life experience by doing exactly this kind of work for a major corporation—for free. He said to the hiring manager: "There is no risk on your part. You get someone to work for free for a few months, and I get new experience to put on my résumé." Sydney was "hired." On his résumé, Sydney noted in his summary that he was using the new programming language and stated that he was doing consulting work for this major corporation. In fact, Sydney did the work just so he could put it on his résumé. (If you feel funny saying that you are doing consulting work when you are not getting paid, then ask the company to pay you a token amount.)

This holds true for other volunteer work you may have done throughout your life. For example, I ran The Five O'Clock Club for many years without getting paid (by my choice, all the money went to other workers). Even though I did not get paid, the experience still counted, and I happily put it on my résumé.

If you have had a number of short-term consulting assignments during a given timeframe, it is still usually better to list the companies for which you did the work rather than the company that paid you. The sample below shows how one very successful job hunter did it.

By the way, you can use this same technique if you had a number of short-term on-payroll jobs. Just combine them so you don't have a long list of dates.

TIME WARNER, REUTERS, ADP　　　　　　　　　　　　　　　2011-present
Project Manager

For the **REUTERS** Training and Education Department:

- **Implemented Gyrus database:**
- Department had owned database for 2 years but had given up on implementing it.
- Identified steps necessary to implement, convinced management of plan's feasibility.
- Wrote procedures manual. Trained staff.
- **Had system up and running in two months.**

For the **TIME INC.** Corporate Finance Department:

- Member of team implementing Essbase system (a state-of-the-art financial database).
- By creating simple control procedure, **credited with saving project.**
- Cited for providing **fast turnaround time**.
- **Provided smooth transition** in coverage for employee on leave.
- Assumed all duties, including preparation of annual plan, monthly consolidated financial statements, cash flow statements, and analysis of ROI.

For the Controller of **ADP BENEFITS SERVICES**:

- Audited the very disorganized books of four acquired companies. (Books had already been audited twice, to no one's satisfaction.) **Recommended final purchase price.**
- **Revamped** the company's **billing, planning, and analysis systems.**

If you wish in this world to advance, Your merits you're bound to enhance; You must stir it and stump it,
And blow your own trumpet, Or trust me, you haven't a chance.

WILLIAM SCHWENCK GILBERT, *Ruddigore*

If you do a number of consulting or freelance up the way such experience is presented in the assignments where the names of the organizations are not significant, you may want to write it up the way such experience is presented in the next

example. Be sure to use numbers as much as possible to show the significance of what you did.

Employment History

Consultant   Dec. 2010-Present

- Alliance for the Development of Salt Lake City
  Conducting market/**feasibility study for a 6,000-square-foot center** for arts organizations.
- Nonprofit Technology Today, Inc.
  Writing **newsletter for CEOs** of 1,000 United Way agencies. Improves use of technology.
- Other clients include Center for Mediation and Law, Foundation for the Arts.

Imagination rules the world.

Napoleon Bonaparte

The Steps to Follow in Developing Your Résumé

You've already made a great deal of progress in the development of your résumé. However, let's take a break so you can see an overview of the entire process. That way, you will know where you are heading.

These steps are one way to approach the development of your résumé. They show a thought process. They are simply guidelines; you will see that even the résumés in this book do not adhere to them completely. When you know the guidelines, you will be better able to do what is appropriate for your situation. Each step is covered in much greater detail in this book.

Step 1. Use Your Old Résumé or Develop a Work History

Use your current résumé, if you have one, as a shell for the development of your new résumé. If you don't have a résumé, write up your work history, starting with your most recent position and working backward.

Now put this information aside until later. We don't want it to ruin your creativity.

Step 2. Determine the Target Market (Industry and Position) in Which You Next Want to Work

If you are at the very beginning of your search and have no target, you can use our book *Targeting a Great Career* to figure out what kind of job you want to have next. Otherwise, you can develop a tentative résumé, which you can revise after you have identified a target market.

You will be developing a résumé for a particular target market (or perhaps closely related markets). You may need to revise your résumé for other markets. After you have completed your résumé with one market in mind, you will reexamine it to see if it works for each of your other targets. But don't worry about that now. Just focus on your first target.

Step 3. Write Out Your Most Important Accomplishments

Write out your most important work-related accomplishments from your Seven Stories Exercise—*without* looking at your current résumé. (Be sure to see the section "How to State Your Accomplishments.") Polish up these accomplishments and make them the best you can. They were important to you, so chances are, you will want to have them on your résumé.

If you want the reader to value these rewritten accomplishments as much as you do, then they should take up more space on your résumé than those that are less important to you.

Step 4. Put These Rewritten Accomplishments into the Proper Place in Your Old Résumé

Now take your old résumé or the work history that you developed in Step 1, and put these accomplishments in their proper place in it. Your résumé will look a little strange right now because some of it will be in your old format and some of it will be rewritten.

Chances are, you now have rewritten a sizeable part of your résumé. At this point, *do not worry about the length of your résumé*. We'll take care of that later.

Step 5. Rewrite the Jobs of Which These Accomplishments Are a Part

Each of your rewritten accomplishments is part of a job. Rank the accomplishments within each job. You will usually put the most important first, rather than placing them in a chronological sequence.

Step 6. Write the Summary

The very first line in your summary should make it easy for the reader to figure out what you can do for him or her. For example, the first line can simply point the reader on the right track: **Accounting Manager** or **Website Designer**.

The second line should separate you from all the other accounting managers or website designers out there. Take a look at two later chapters, *Writing the Summary at the Top of Your Résumé* and *Sample Summary Statements*. Also be sure to see the sample résumés in the accomplishments section of this book and the sample summary statements in that section.

If you do not use a summary statement, you will be positioned by your most recent job. If you are going after exactly the same kind of position, or if the most recent position sets you up

perfectly for the next one, then you may not need a summary.

But chances are you do need one. A well-crafted, attractive summary catches the eye and allows you to make all of the essential points about yourself up front, in those crucial first 10 seconds. You will especially want to use a summary if there are accomplishments early on in your career that you want to make sure the reader does not miss.

We can't stress enough that the average résumé is looked at for only 10 seconds. Regardless of the length of your résumé itself, the summary makes it easier for the reader to see the most important points, to *get it*.

Step 7. Polish the Rest of Your Résumé

So far, you have:
- written out the accomplishment statements that appeared in your Seven Stories Exercise
- reworked the jobs of which those accomplishments were a part
- written the summary of your résumé to make you look appropriate to your target market.

There is only a little bit left to refine on your résumé. For the remaining parts, refer again to *How to State Your Accomplishments*.

Use what talents you possess: the woods would be very silent if no birds sang there except those that sang best.

HENRY VAN DYKE

Step 8. Fix Up Your Job Titles

Now review your job titles and company names to see how they fit in with your overall positioning. You may replace company-dictated job titles with ones that better reflect what you actually did and that may be better understood by your target market.

Step 9. Check the Message of Your Overall Résumé

Scan your résumé to make sure the theme you stressed in your summary runs throughout. For example, if you positioned yourself in your summary as having great sales ability, make sure the reader can easily see sales-related accomplishments in your résumé. Ask a friend to tell you what he or she sees in the first ten seconds.

Step 10. Adjust the Appearance and Length of Your Résumé

Now you can think about the length of your résumé. To shorten it, consider the following:

- Do you have excessively wide margins? It's fine to have one-inch margins all around—or even 3/4 inch. You can also edit the line spacing. (See *Andy: His Seven Stories Made the Difference* for a more detailed explanation.)
- Get rid of words that have overflowed so that they are on lines by themselves. You may have to rewrite a sentence slightly so that the statement does not overflow onto another line, but that rewrite will save you one line on your résumé. These changes can add up.
- **Get rid of anything that lowers the average weight of your résumé**. If you're a senior vice president, you don't need to mention that you once worked in the mail room. If you have saved a company $1 million, there's no reason to mention that you saved them $10,000 earlier. You don't have to tell the reader everything you've ever done—only the important things. However, do not mindlessly cut out the first 10 years of your worklife if they may be of interest.

Cut if you're getting rid of wordiness, but *don't cut* if you're sacrificing content that helps build your case. Don't obsess about keeping your

résumé to two or even three pages. One of our most successful Five O'Clock Club clients, a senior executive, received six amazing job offers after a very short search, and she was using a *six-page résumé*. It had a great summary statement and was formatted in The Five O'Clock Club style, but even I thought it was too long.

However, when she contacted companies (through a targeted mailing, which you can read about in our book *Shortcut Your Job Search*), they called her in. Her résumé was effective in her target market. She felt that all the experiences she recounted were important. And she did not want to cram the accomplishments to fit on fewer pages, making them unreadable.

Make your résumé as short as you can, but still make sure it is readable and scannable and doesn't omit anything important.

Your primary concern is not the length of your résumé. Your primary concern is: Does it position me correctly?

Step 11. The Final Scan

Sometimes, a job hunter tells me an important accomplishment, and I look for it on the résumé. If it's there at all, often I cannot find it. When I ask the job hunter, the response usually is: "Let me look for it. I know I can find it." And only with a great deal of searching, can the job hunter unearth this accomplishment. If even *you* have trouble finding important points on your résumé, surely the reader will also.

When someone does a 10-second scan of your résumé, what does the person see? Make sure readers see what you want them to see.

Step 12. Test Your Résumé in the Marketplace

You have formed a hypothesis of how to present yourself on paper. You have decided what you think will be important to readers and what you want them to know about you. Now you have to find out how others actually see you when they see your new résumé. You may find that certain statements are being misunderstood or that people see you in a way that is different from what you had planned. Adjust your résumé accordingly.

Step 13. See the "Résumé Checklist" Later in This Book

Quotes to Inspire You

I made a commitment to completely cut out drinking and anything else that might hamper me from getting my mind and my body together. And the floodgates of goodness have opened upon me— spiritually and financially.

DENZEL WASHINGTON, IN "SPOTLIGHT: DENZEL," *Essence*

Discoveries are often made by not following instructions, by going off the main road, by trying the untried.

FRANK TYGER

And Peter O'Toole told me not to play small parts, even in vehicles that would get a lot of exposure, because that would make me a small-part actor. He advised me to play leading parts anywhere—in rubbishy scripts, if need be—but play leading parts.

MICHAEL CAINE, *Acting in Film*

The Five O'Clock Club®

Writing the Summary at the Top of Your Résumé

Greatness is not measured by what a man or woman accomplishes, but by the opposition he or she has overcome....

Dr. Dorothy Height, president,
National Council of Negro Women

Feel stuck in your present position? Peel off your old label, slap on a new one, and position yourself for something different.

Whether you're an accountant who wants to go into sales, or an operations person who dreams of being a trainer, the challenge you face is the same: You have to convince people that even though you don't have experience you can handle the new position.

It's a little like show biz: You play the same role for years and then you get typecast. It can be difficult for people to believe that you can play a different role. To move on to new challenges, you have to negotiate into the new job by offering seemingly unrelated skills as an added benefit to the employer. The key to these negotiations is *positioning* yourself.

Positioning

Simply put, positioning yourself means stating your skills and qualities in a way that makes it easy for the prospective employer to see you in the open position or in other positions down the road.

You may want to stay in your present organization, in which case you are positioning yourself to the person in charge of hiring for the particular department you want to enter. Or, you may want to go to a new organization or even a new industry. In this case, you are positioning yourself to a new employer. Either way, the steps are the same:

1. Determine what skills and qualities your prospective employer wants.
2. Search your background to see where you have demonstrated skills and qualities that would apply.
3. Write a summary at the top of your résumé to position yourself.
4. **Use the same summary on your LinkedIn page** and to sell yourself in an interview.

Your summary says it all. It should sell your ability, experience, and personality. It brings together all your accomplishments.

The rest of your résumé should support your summary. For example, if the summary says that you're a top-notch marketer, the résumé should support that. It's completely within your control to tell whatever story you want to tell. You can emphasize certain parts of your background and de-emphasize others.

> You can get typecast. To move on, you have to negotiate into the new job... by positioning yourself.

Thinking through your summary is not easy, but it focuses your entire job hunt. It forces you to clarify the sales pitch you will use in meetings.

However, many people *don't* put a summary that positions them on their résumés or on their LinkedIn page. They say they want "a challenging job in a progressive and growth-oriented organization that uses all my strengths and abilities." That doesn't say anything at all, and it doesn't do you any good.

Résumé: Your Written Pitch

Make sure the first words on your résumé position you for the kind of job you want next, such as *Accounting Manager*. Line *two* of your résumé, also centered, should separate you from all those other accounting managers. For example, it could say, "specializing in the publishing industry." These headlines in your summary could then be followed by bulleted accomplishments that would be of interest to your target market.

Most people write boring résumés. To avoid this, keep in mind to *whom you are pitching*. Tell readers the most important things you want them to know about you. List your most important accomplishments right there in your summary.

It all starts with the Seven Stories Exercise. After you have done this exercise, you will talk about your accomplishments very differently than if you just sit down and try to write a résumé. The Seven Stories Exercise is the foundation for your résumé. Write out your work-related stories in a way that is *expressive* of you as an individual. Brag about yourself the way you would brag to the people in your family or your friends. Put *those* words at the top of your résumé to make it much more compelling.

Let's consider a few examples of summaries that *will* work for you:

Pursuing the Dream Job

Jane, a client-relationship manager at a major bank, has handled high-net-worth clients for more than 20 years. She is taking early retirement and thinking about a second career. Two directions are of interest to her: a job similar to what she has done but in a smaller bank; or, the job of her dreams—working as one of the top administrative people for a high-net-worth family (such as the Rockefellers), handling their business office and perhaps doing things that involve her interests: staffing and decorating.

If Jane were to continue on her current career path and go for a position as a relationship manager at a smaller bank, she would highlight the years she has worked at the bank. Her summary, if used in her résumé, would look like this:

More than 20 years handling all aspects of fiduciary relationships for PremierBank's private banking clients. Successfully increased revenue through new business efforts, client cultivation, and account assessment. Consistently achieved fee increases. Received regular bonus awards.

However, to pursue her dream job, Jane's regular résumé won't do. She has to reposition herself to show that her experience fits what her prospective employer needs. Her summary would read like this:

Administrative manager with broad experience in running operations

- In-depth work with accountants, lawyers, agents, and others.
- More than 20 years' experience handling all aspects of fiduciary relationships for bank's private banking clients (overall net worth of $800 million).
- Expert in all financial arrangements (trust and estate accounts, asset management, nonprofits, and tenant shareholder negotiations).

Her résumé would also focus on her work *outside* PremierBank because these activities would interest her prospective employer: first, her work on the board of the luxury apartment building of which she was president for 14 years, and then the post she held for 10 years as treasurer of a nonprofit organization. Finally, Jane would highlight accomplishments at Premier-Bank that would be of interest to a prospective employer, such as saving a client $300,000 in taxes.

Ready to Take Charge

Robert had worked in every area of benefits administration. Now he would like to head up the entire benefits administration area—a move to management. His summary:

14 years in the design and administration of all areas of employee benefit plans
- 5 years with Borgash Benefits Consultants
- Advised some of the largest, most prestigious companies in the country
- Excellent training and communications skills
- MBA in finance

From Supporting to Selling

Jack wants to move into sales after being in marketing support. His prior résumé lacked a summary. Therefore people saw him as a marketing support person rather than as a salesperson—because his most recent job was in marketing support. He has been an executive in the sales promotion area, so his summary stresses his internal sales and marketing, as well as his management, experience:

Sales and marketing professional with strong managerial experience
- Devise superior marketing strategies through qualitative analysis and product repositioning
- Skillful at completing the difficult internal sale, coupled with the ability to attract business and retain clients
- Built strong relationships with the top consulting firms
- A team player with an enthusiastic approach to top-level challenges

Notice how he packages his experience running a marketing department as *sales*. His pitch will be, "It's even more difficult to sell inside because, in order to keep my job, I have to get other people in my company to use my marketing services. I have to do a good job, or they won't use me again."

If you do not have a summary, then, by default, you are positioned by the last job you held. In Jack's case, the employer would receive the new résumé with the new summary and say, "Ah-ha! Just what we need—a salesperson!"

Sophisticated Positioning

Here are how some people repositioned their backgrounds in a sophisticated way. Jeff had been in loan-processing operations in a bank. Outside of financial services, not many organizations do loan processing. To position himself to work in a hospital, Jeff changed his positioning to say transaction processing because hospitals process a large numbers of *transactions*, but not loans. Otherwise, they would look at his résumé and say, "We don't need to have loans processed."

In fact, many people who work in banking see themselves as working for information services companies. Money is sent via computer networks and wire transfers. They are passing information, not currency.

Nydia had worked at both banks and pharmaceutical companies. Because of her target, she positioned herself as having worked in *regulated industries*.

David saw himself as an international human resources generalist, but was having difficulty with his search. Since there were no international jobs in his field, he should not have positioned himself as *international*.

Finally, on the next page is an example from one of our coaches, Bill Belknap.

"Before" Summary: The entire résumé for this senior executive lacked quantifiable results. The "amped up" version got tremendous traction in the market. It so impressed the CEO of a well-known publisher that Bill's client was hired as a senior marketing executive there.

MEDIA INDUSTRY EXECUTIVE
with expertise in

- **Corporate Finance**
- **Strategic Planning & Analysis**
- **Product Development**

- Recognized hands-on, pro-active individual with <u>**excellent project management skills**</u> and the ability to drive multiple projects to completion in complex, deadline-driven environments
- <u>**Skilled financial modeling and operational analyst**</u> on both division and corporate operating levels, as well as the development of detailed <u>**plans for the integration of acquisitions and divestitures**</u>
- <u>**Strategic thinker who can identify risks and opportunities**</u> within served markets and quickly develop and implement operating plans that account for such conditions

SENIOR FINANCE EXECUTIVE
With experience growing brands, creating high-level partnerships, and increasing profit margins

KEY RESULTS

- Managed launch of a new marathon training business for *Competitive Runner*, including digital products and physical events that <u>**generated over $900k in incremental profits**</u>.
- Initiated and negotiated a strategic partnership with MultiHealth, where Wiley provided custom editorial content and branded ancillary products to insurance customers of MultiHealth. <u>**Program generated profits of $640k in first year**</u>.
- Managed the development of more than a dozen new print and digital ancillary products that <u>**drove revenue and earnings growth by 18% and 20% over 12 months.**</u>
- Negotiated a new DVD distribution agreement for *Oxygen* magazine that <u>**reduced existing expenses by 50%**</u> and provided guaranteed minimum payments for a 3-year period, while improving national retail distribution coverage.
- Produced a co-branded workout DVD for *Wheaties* cereal that was featured in onpack promotions across three product lines and was the <u>**key feature in securing a $2.5M advertising program for *Oxygen* magazine.**</u>
- Key player in successful M&A transactions aggregating <u>**more than $500M in value**</u>.

EXPERTISE

P&L Management	New Product Development
Brand Strategy	Strategic Partnerships
Cash Flow Management	Mergers, Acquisitions, & Divestitures
Cost Control	Global Product Development
Financial Planning & Analysis	Global Licensing

RECOGNIZED FOR

Driving Financial Performance – Hands-on Approach – Change Agent – Strategic Thinking

Now, think about *your* target market and how you should position your background for your target.

Elliott: Getting Back into a Field He Loved

Elliott had been in sports marketing years ago, and had enjoyed it tremendously. However, he had spent the past four years in the mortgage industry, and was having a hard time getting back into sports marketing.

The sports people saw him as a career changer and a mortgage man. Even when he explained how marketing mortgages is the same as marketing sports, people did not believe him. He was being positioned by his most recent experience, which was derailing his search.

When job hunters want to change industries—or go back to an old industry—they cannot let their most recent positions act as a handicap. For example, if a person has always been in pharmaceuticals marketing, and now wants to do marketing in another industry, his or her résumé should be rewritten to highlight generic marketing, with most references to pharmaceuticals removed.

In Elliott's case, the summary in his new résumé helps a great deal to bring his old work experience right to the top of the résumé. In addition, Elliott removed the word "mortgage" from the description of his most recent job; his title at the mortgage company now stands out more than the company name. And he removed company and industry jargon, such as the job title *segment director*, which is not easily understood outside his company. He also updated his Linkedin profile to represent his new positioning of himself as a sports marketing person.

Notice that Elliott's description of what he did for the mortgage business is now written generically—it can apply to the marketing of any product. With his new résumé, Elliott had no trouble speaking to people in the sports industry. They no longer saw his most recent experience as a handicap, and he soon had a terrific job as head of marketing for a prestigious sporting-goods company.

If you want to move into a new industry or profession, state what you did generically so people will not see you as tied to the old.

For a thorough discussion of how to change careers, see our book *Targeting a Great Career* to figure out what you want to do and our book *Shortcut Your Job Search* to tell you how to do it.

Bring Something to the Party

When it comes down to negotiating yourself into a new position, seemingly unrelated skills from former positions may actually help you get the job.

For example, some of my background had been in accounting and computers when I decided to go into coaching and my CFO (chief financial officer) experience helped me ease into this new career. I agreed to be CFO at a 90-person career-coaching company provided I was also assigned clients to coach. My ability to create a cost-accounting system for them was what I "brought to the party." I was willing to give the company something they wanted (my business expertise) in exchange for doing something I really wanted to do (coaching executives).

Combining the new with the old, rather than jumping feet first into something completely new is often the best way to move your career in a different direction. You gain the experience you need in the new field without having to come in at the entry level. Equally important, it is less stressful because you are using some of your old strengths while you build new ones.

Coming from a background different from the field you are targeting can also give you a bargaining chip. If you are looking at an area where you have no experience, you will almost certainly be competing with people who do have experience. You can separate yourself from the competition by saying, "I'm different. I have the skills to do this job, and I can also do other things these people can't do." It works!

This book contains dozens of additional positioning (summary) statements. In addition, you will see how the positioning statements are used to set the tone for the rest of the résumé.

"Before" Résumé

ELLIOTT JONES

421 Morton Street Chase   Fortune, KY 23097

SEARS MORTGAGE COMPANY   2012-present
Vice President, Segment Director, Shelter Business

- Director of $4.6 billion residential mortgage business for largest mortgage lender
- Organized and established regional marketing division for largest mortgage lender, including first and second mortgages and mortgage life insurance

SportsLife Magazine   2009-2012
Publisher and Editor

- Published and edited largest health/fitness magazine. Increased circulation by 175%. and so on...

ELLIOTT JONES

421 Morton Street, Chase Fortune, KY 23097 · ejones@yahoo.com

Fifteen years: domestic and international marketing management in the *leisure/sporting goods industry*

- Multibrand expertise specializing in marketing, new business development, strategic planning, and market research.
- Identified customer segments, developed differentiable product platforms, implemented communication strategies, managed sales, oversaw share growth, and generated profit.

SEARS MORTGAGE COMPANY　　　　　　　　　　　　　　　　　2012-present
VICE PRESIDENT, BUSINESS DIRECTOR
Residential Real Estate Business

- Business Director of a $4.6 billion business. **Managed strategic planning, marketing, product development, and compliance**.
- Consolidated four regional business entities into one; doubled product offerings. Grew market share 150 basis points and solidified #1 market position.
- **Developed and executed nationally recognized consumer and trade advertising, public relations, and direct-response programs**.
- Structured a product-development process, integrating product introductions into the operations and sales segments of the business.
- Organized and established regional marketing division.

SPORTSLIFE MAGAZINE　　　　　　　　　　　　　　　　　　　2009-2012
Publisher and Editor

- Published and edited largest health/fitness magazine. Increased circulation by 175%.

and so on...

The Five O'Clock Club

Sample Summary Statements

I know what pleasure is, because I have done good work.

ROBERT LOUIS STEVENSON

What are the most important points you want your target market to know about you? State them in your summary. Take a look at the summaries in this chapter.

Try not to be too intimidated by what you read here. You are seeing people with their best foot forward. They may have struggled for days to some up with these summaries. Don't be discouraged. Remember that though this is the most

difficult part of the résumé to write, it is also the most important. Try it, and see how well you can show off what you have done.

And be sure to look at the summaries in the résumé sections of this book. Plenty more are there, many with "before" résumés – the initial attempts people made.

Don't forget that it (your product or service) is not differentiated until the customer understands the difference.

TOM PETERS, *Thriving on Chaos*

PC Development and Support Technician

Support and advise senior management on computer needs and implementation. **Experience in all areas of project management**. Work well with people with varying computer abilities. Take initiative. Place high value on accuracy.

Marketing Professional
with honors degree in Marketing (**magna cum laude**) and **four years of experience**

- Solid history of **successful projects, promotions and awards**.
- Coordinate the efforts of many to meet organizational goals.
- High in energy, with strong interpersonal skills.
- Hands-on experience includes: Market Research, Marketing Support, Project Management, Public Speaking, Training, Computers, Vendor relations.

Planning and Policy Professional
with experience in <u>international and government affairs</u>

- Planned and prescribed courses of action to achieve the objectives of **corporate, government, and non-profit organizations**.
- Developed policies for company's domestic and foreign businesses.
- Work effectively in a variety of environments and cultures.
- Excellent research, communications, and interpersonal skills.

Four years as an Executive Assistant
coupled with continuing college education

- Take on **major projects from initiation and planning through to implementation and follow-up**.
- **Very computer literate**: Excel, database software, Powerpoint.
- A solid history of **excellent work relationships**, both with the public and with internal personnel at all organizational levels.
- **High in initiative and energy** with strong ability to exercise independent judgment.
- Excellent writing skills. Trustworthy and discreet.

A podiatrist in private practice
with a reputation for being professional, courteous, and knowledgeable about state-of-the-art treatment modalities

- Give my best to both project and patient.
- Set high standards. Thorough and detail oriented.
- Build **excellent rapport with colleagues and patients** alike.
- Superior oral and written skills.
- From a family of doctors.
- Member, **Board of Directors**, American Red Cross, South Central L.A. Service Center

Experienced television journalist
with both national and international experience

- **60 MINUTES** • **VISNEWS LIMITED** • **CHARLIE ROSE** • **THE FORD FOUNDATION**

Particular expertise in:

- Proposal drafting and presentation for special events and projects.
- Coverage of Capitol Hill and White House news events.
- Newsgathering, packaging, and editing.
- International satellite feed coordination.

> **If you've worked for brand-name employers, highlight their names in your résumé.**

Fluent in English and Portuguese with working knowledge of Spanish.

Facilities and Support Services Manager

- Managed and developed **3 service departments** with a **staff of 40**.
- Reorganized and set quality standards to reduce costs and lower turnover.
- Implemented training programs, improved morale and the respect of workers for one another.
- Strong negotiation skills. Work with high-technology applications.
- In 50,000 sq. ft. building, managed **office planning, telecommunications, maintenance, and record retention.**

Customer Service and Operations Manager

- Over 20 years' experience with Uniroyal.
- Successful in **managing and store operations**. Also **international** business experience.
- Speak Portuguese, Spanish, and some Italian.
- Excellent computer skills (Uniroyal has one of the most modern computer systems).
- College degree. Establish a good rapport with clients of different socioeconomic levels.

20 years' experience in TV Production

- Network and Local, Daytime and Primetime Dramatic Series. New York, Miami, Los Angeles.
- Intimate **knowledge of scripts** and work with writers.
- Strong **production administration skills** interfacing with and supervising crew, staff, and budgets.
- **Decision-maker** responding to fast-paced quality production demands **with a spirit of creative compatibility, stability, dedication, and ease.**

Program Developer and Administrator
with experience in virtually every area of counseling, education, and research
Specialize in work/family issues
- Director of a counseling center serving **over 1,000 clients yearly** with $500,000 budget.
- Expert in computers, quantitative and qualitative analysis.
- Supervised the implementation of hundreds of research studies.
- Published articles on aging and trauma, and children and trauma.
- Clinical Psychology, **Ph.D.**; Personnel Psychology, **M.A.**

Understand the impact of change on the employee's productivity.
Gained experience through thousands of referrals to myriad agencies for every imaginable difficulty.

A *tagline* at the bottom of your summary can be a personality statement that balances your opening headline.

Finance and Accounting Systems Manager
with a CPA/MBA and 14 years' combined experience

- Seven years' experience in the agricultural services industry.
- Manage, organize, streamline, and automate administrative, operating and financial functions.

---

11 years' experience in
Juvenile Justice/Child Welfare Advocacy

- Managed **staff of 60**; 150 volunteers; 3 departments; budget of $2.2 million.
- Designed programs, facilities and information systems.
- Managed quality of service programs.

Set the tone for the quality of service provided by staff and volunteers.
Achieve organizational goals while maintaining excellent relationships.

Seven years' experience in all areas of
Kitchen Management
in a variety of established restaurants.

• Chez Marguerite • Saxony Hotel • Hyatt Hotel • The Square Plate

- Resourceful and organized manager; accepted additional responsibilities that easily fit into an already coordinated schedule.
  - Managed staff of 7
  - Trained and developed staff
  - As a motivator and teacher, inspired staff to be reliable and organized
  - Responsible for hiring
  - Conscious of food costs
- Worked closely with owners and management to develop menu items that fit in with overall scheme. **Resulted in higher sales**.
- Can provide a **variety of cuisines and methods for preparation**:
  - various ethnic orientations: French, Italian, American and so on
  - various levels of complexity; from simpler pasta dishes to foie gras and truffles
- Developed and implemented systems in all areas of kitchen:
  - Operate **on schedule** regardless of interruptions or problems
  - Quickly take over any area to keep production going
  - Create a satisfying kitchen atmosphere
  - Institute systems to maintain good sanitation habits

Degree, Culinary Institute of America
Eight years' business experience

Twenty-five years with
local, regional, and national not-for-profit organizations
developing and administering **self-supporting programs for members and the public**.

Primary areas of interest:

- Designing programs and service-delivery systems
- Identifying and cultivating funding sources
- Recruiting and training volunteer leaders

Clinical Nutrition Specialist
in pediatrics and public health

- 8 years' experience in basic **laboratory research**.
- Provide **consulting services to 15** nonprofit, community, and academic **institutions**.
- **Widely published** to lay and scientific audiences.
- Experience ranges from care of individuals (infancy to middle-aged) to planning of **national programs.**
- Have worked with all the major nutritional disorders.
- A specialist in the rehabilitation of failure-to-thrive children.

Resourceful, persuasive, diplomatic, constructive and goal-oriented.

Consumer Electronics Executive
with 17 years' hands-on experience in Information Systems and Technology for Financial, Multimedia, and Manufacturing businesses

- Operated as Technical Due Diligence Manager for **$30 million long-term co-marketing deal between GE and Facebook**
- Project Management: **budget of $1+ million;** multinational technology and marketing staffs of up to 50 people
- Special Consultant to $6 million General Electric Venture Fund
- Established first-ever **Enterprise Content Integration** platform within company for global rollout. Would be available to all 180,000 employees worldwide.
- Ran SIG for Time Warner worldwide (50 people; 5 countries)
- Liaison between Systems and Finance groups for 3 major global banks: **JP Morgan Chase, Bank of New York, and Bankers Trust**
- Proficient in Chinese, German, Spanish, French, Japanese, Italian

> The tagline at the bottom answers the questions "How **do you do your job?** If I hire you, what kind of person can I expect?"

Many years of hands-on business experience coupled with a scientific background.
A natural liaison between technical and business groups.
Have easy-going relationships but an intense work ethic.

18 years' experience in Project Management

PC computer systems, training and education, PC-based business solutions
A PC problem solver, developer, and troubleshooter

- Designed, developed, and managed **state-of-the-art CBT and Web-based** programs that significantly enhance training experience and performance of participants.
- Managed the development of unique, highly marketable **real-time computerized simulation**.
- 18 years of teaching, training, and adult education.
- During two-year period, managed company's first PC Center devoted entirely to learning a fundamental new technology.
- Hired and managed instructor staff by matching needs of business unit to skills of instructors.
- Trained over 500 professionals of all levels in first year of operation.
- Taught classes in every software the company used.
- Managed company's **first-ever worldwide video conference** for Chairman and President with 18,000 employees.

You will see more summary statements in the résumé sections of this book.

13 years' experience developing
Corporate Trademark Promotions, Special Events and Licensing Campaigns

Substantially increase revenues through the development of creative and unique concepts as well as detailed attention to follow-through. Extensive national, international and multinational exposure. Interaction with CEOs of major corporations.

20 years' international business experience in

• international trade   • sales and marketing   • management
Specialize in the **Asia/Pacific region**, especially Taiwan and Hong Kong

Strong **business negotiation skills with Asians**. **Established Asian subsidiaries** for three major U.S. corporations. **Strong company representative** for trade and operations both in Asia and the U.S. Speak nine Chinese dialects, English, and Japanese. Establish easy rapport with all levels of professional people. U.S. citizen.

18 years in **Corporate/Public Affairs** specializing in **international programs**
Work with top levels in corporate, government, international, and philanthropic organizations.
Routinely assigned sensitive and "impossible" major projects.

Creative Executive
specializing in the new media and entertainment industries
with more than 20 years' experience in:

• Product Development   • Project Management   • Content Development

- **Content Provider**: For **Internet** company providing commercial video search engine service, developed characters and concepts for corporate branding.
- **Website Developer**: For **online community/retail website**, creating content, marketing strategy, interactive game.
- **Brand Director**: As **Editor-in-Chief of Pluto Group**, Plutonium Entertainment, oversaw the
- **#1 best-selling comic-book character** in the country, producing annual revenues of **$46 million**.
- **Product Innovator**: As **Creative Director**, Porter and Sklark, initiated and developed new product category, producing **wholesale grosses of $90 million** over 5-year period.

Team leader and troubleshooter with proven ability to bring together ideas and talent to create imaginative, commercially successful, high-quality products.

INTERNATIONAL HUMAN RESOURCES EXECUTIVE

Policy Development   Organizational Planning   Management Training

Over 15 years' experience in international human resources environments. Solid capabilities in strategic planning, policy formulation, management development, succession planning, and recruitment. Major accomplishments in improving productivity through executive development, management training, business development, and strategic planning. Additional skills in providing technical and professional assistance to start-ups in international markets.

Marketing Manager
specializing in major fund-raising/development/marketing activities/special events
for not-for-profit agencies and small companies

Areas of Expertise
- Telemarketing   • Broadcast Fund-Raising   • Direct Mail
- Media-Stimulated Calling   • Major Special Events
- Membership/Customer/Constituency Development

- Created integrated campaigns including direct marketing, television, fund-raising, and so on.
- Managed **telemarketing programs** for organizations such as:
  - GTE   • The United Way   • UNICEF   • The Ford Foundation
- Conducted **major television fund-raising campaigns**.
- **Managed all communications for the 2012 Democratic National Convention**
  - Coordinated the work of 300 to 1,000 people.

CONSUMER SALES AND MARKETING MANAGER

Areas of Expertise

- Sales Management
- Merchandising
- Telemarketing
- Brand Management

- Trade Shows/Sales Meetings
- Sales Incentive Programs
- Pricing, Packaging, Promotions
- Excellent Speaker

- Managed **staff of 12; $1.1 million budget**.
- Took a brand with no exposure in the Michigan market: Grew it to **$4 million within 3 months**.
- Coordinated 2 key sales meetings and 2 retail trade shows.

Aggressive in the marketplace. Consistently a top performer.
Effectively organize and manage staff.

An innovative strategic marketer, manager, and research scientist
with 10 years at IBM.

- Launched new products in a highly competitive market.
- In-depth understanding of business, customers, competitors and the resulting products.
- Ph.D. in Chemistry; undergraduate in Pre-Med.
- Technical consultant to U.S. Navy.
- Six years in Research, Development, and Manufacturing.

Senior-level technology manager
specializing in health care and financial systems

- Managed multiple projects concurrently, with **staffs of up to 30** per project.
- Developed **in-house hospital systems** to replace vendor-supplied systems.
- Turned a system that cost millions annually to deliver into **a revenue generator** of $1.5 million per year with a potential of $15 million.
- **Strong technology background**: large mainframe systems, PC, microcomputer applications, automated operations, customer support, large-scale social media.
- **Designed and developed a large transaction processing system servicing 22 countries**.
  - Served as **user interface** to all 22 countries.
  - Handled millions of transactions per day.
- Often **present to most senior levels of management** from marketing and technical perspectives.
- A strong leader and motivator who establishes excellent user relationships.

Never missed a deliverable.
Never installed software that was defective.

INTERNATIONAL BUSINESS JOURNALIST
With more than 20 years of experience in

- Writing and editing   • All forms of media   • Developing top-level contacts

<u>Experience includes:</u>

- Founding global magazine
- Setting news agendas
- Managing worldwide network of reporters
- Ties with government / business leaders
- Reporting from six continents
- Public speaking

An **<u>editorial strategist at three prestigious publications</u>**, with extensive knowledge of key economies, markets, and industries.
<u>Articulate communicator</u> to members of editorial team and the wider world.
Dedicated **<u>team player and keen competitor</u>** in tough media markets.

Senior Human Resources Executive
Recognized as authority on employment law and policy, problem resolution, conflict and crisis management

- Have handled hundreds of difficult/sensitive cases.
- Successfully restructured over 1,000 employees with only two external actions resultant.
- Developed one-day seminar "Employee Relations and the Law" for Human Resource Professionals. 100 Human Resource people trained.
- Administered Employee Relations Programs to 40,000 employees nationally.
- An idea generator and manager, troubleshooter, and resourceful problem solver.

Fifteen years' management experience with the State of California in Information Technology, Telecommunications Networking, Computer Technology, Data Center facilities planning and construction.

- Managed a network of over 300 lines, over 3,000 terminals, communicating with all major State buildings.
- Coordinated reconstruction of 10,000-square-foot data center that met corporate standards.
- Planned security and implemented encryption for critical data communications lines.

Conduct timely implementation of new lines, new technology,
equipment installation, and follow-up.
Excellent rapport with other managers, end users, clients, and staff.

In the following résumé, the job hunter does not like his present job.
Therefore, in the summary he highlighted jobs he had 6 and 10 years earlier:

Manager of Financial Planning and Analysis
with a public accounting background

<u>Industry Experience Includes:</u>

• Retail   • Financial Services   • Transportation   • Communication   • Chemicals

<u>For Macy's:</u>

- Wrote business plans for **store openings**,
- Supervised and performed financial projections and **analysis of sites, competitors and demographics**,
- **Coordinated five-year** and annual plans and quarterly and monthly budget,
- **Wrote business plan** of a home-center chain.

<u>In public accounting:</u>

- Selected to develop new audit techniques, which reduced costs of major audits,
- Taught national and regional audit seminars.

MBA, Finance; BS, Finance and Accounting

Accounting/operations executive
with over 18 years of steadily increasing diverse management experience.
Complex and sophisticated environments.

- Business experience ranges from securities and credit cards to travelers' checks and mortgage servicing.
- Quantitative and analytical orientation-CPA.
- Managed both line operations and staff units from 5 professionals to over 50 people.
- Extensive user involvement in development of PC-based and mainframe-resident applications.
- Developed innovative strategies and methodologies to solve major problems.

PROFILE

Regional Sales Manager
Technology-Based Industries

- **Staff of 20**   • Revenue of $30 Million
- **Consistently exceeds plan**.
  - In three years at Wal-Mart, **doubled worldwide sales** of certain core products.
  - Obtained enthusiastic support from 16 internal organizations.
  - In Houston during oil bust, managed major account sales group.
  - **Took it from last place to #2 in Xerox**.
  - Brought leadership, direction, and focus to a disintegrating situation.
  - Achieved **11 President's Clubs**.
- Formally recognized for assembling **the most talented sales teams**.
- Strongly believe in results-centered management.

*Develop imaginative, profitable solutions consistently
delivered with the support of challenged, committed colleagues.*

A corporate trade finance and marketing executive
with 10 years' international and domestic experience.

- Proven **generator of fee revenue** via financial advisory mandates.
- Structure and market cross-border trade finance solutions which **open foreign capital markets**.
- Experience in both the trading and financing of commodity trade flows.
- Identify, originate, structure, and close **innovative and resourceful financial structures** for countries burdened with debt:

  - commodity/asset-based trade   • commodity swaps
  - debt swaps/liquidation   • barter/countertrade/offset
  - hedging techniques   • unblocking of currencies
- Foreign sales management, product introduction, and marketing experience

---

CFO and General Manager
*Directed companies ranging from $100 million to over $1 billion.
Divisional as well as Corporate Management experience.*

Industry Specialties

- Pharmaceuticals/Health Services   • Publishing   • International
  - Consumer Goods   • Manufacturing

Chief Financial Officer
Specializing in turning around/growing medium-sized companies.

- A key member of the management team developing growth strategies while keeping the company under control.
- Set up the corporate structure for new subsidiaries.
- Rebuilt the financial organizations of two medium-sized companies, enabling them to raise significant capital.
- Attract and retain top-quality people.

Areas of expertise:

- Finance
- Administration
- Real Estate
- Banking Relationships

Industry experience includes:

- Service Businesses
- Sports
- Construction
- Chemical/Manufacturing
- Perfume
- Retail

Business Manager
with strong **customer-service management expertise**.
Over 20 years in financial services and not-for-profit

- **Created** and directed **new business** opportunities and **turned around** performance.
- As Business Manager, **increased profits 294%** over two years. Improved service 41%.
- As Customer Service Consultant, measurably improved service in **60 locations**.
- As Branch Manager, increased revenue 37% in one year; significantly improved service.
- As Board member for **three not-for-profit** organizations, directed programs that provided services to children, families, and people with AIDS.

Focus simultaneously on increasing revenue and improving service.
Noted for forming exceptionally strong relationships, motivating staff,
providing leadership, direction, and spirit to get the job done.
Energetic, articulate, resourceful.

Chief Legal Executive
specializing in communications, information, and entertainment.

A General Counsel:
manage internal lawyers; supervise outside counsel.

A deal-maker and senior legal advisor:
key member of the management team;
sophisticated in legal, financial, and business dealings.

Human Resources Generalist
• Financial Services   • Health Care   • Manufacturing

Developed new programs/services. Achieved significant cost savings. Improved and enhanced existing services. Excellent presentation, negotiating and consulting skills. High standards of integrity, professionalism and team-play. M.B.A.

Areas of Expertise

- Organizational Development
- Training and Development
- Employee Relations
- Agency Relationships
- Succession Planning

- Compensation
- Performance-based Management Systems
- Staffing and Mobility
- Employment Management
- Affirmative Action

Financial Services Technology Head
regularly selected to manage large, challenging development efforts.
Domestic and International

- Manage staffs of 150; budget of $25-30 million.
- Successful experience with large, "from scratch" development efforts:, both domestically and internationally. Responsible for:
- management of all projects dealing with front-end systems **worldwide**.
- development and maintenance of **all systems throughout Middle East and Africa**.
- complete redevelopment of all product processing and administrative systems.
- **Saved $60 million** by renegotiating major purchasing agreements

A "hands-on" senior manager with very firm technical grounding.
Lead and motivate technical staffs while developing excellent user relationships.

SENIOR CORPORATE LEGAL MANAGER
for global organization with 100+ attorneys and annual profits of $1 billion.

GTE   DUPONT   NBC

Industry experience includes:
• consumer products   • information business
• media   • communications/R&D   • chemicals, pharmaceuticals

- Senior legal advisor, **reporting directly to President and COO**.
- **Instituted and led** what culminated in a **judicial victory for entire industry**.
- **Successfully prosecuted copyright-infringement suit against major competitor**.
- Achieved strategic goal of maintaining customers and revenues.

Recognized for reflective and open analytical methods, astute business-counseling skills and ability to provide strategic focus with respect to company's domestic and international consumer businesses.

Project Manager specializing in service businesses

- Managed projects of up to **120 people**; **budgets of up to $30 million**; both domestically and internationally.
- Expert in the use of project-management software tools and techniques.
  - Built diverse applications on multiple software and hardware platforms.
  - Built and implemented $20-million **integrated customer information system**. Hired and trained highly skilled project team.
  - Developed a **generic package** that satisfied the needs of companies in **28 countries**.
  - Managed relaunching of proprietary **credit card**. Total responsibility for all specifications, hardware, code development, and implementation.
  - Experience as both a line and matrix manager.
  - CASE-tool experienced.

Start projects from scratch, build strong project plans and strong, loyal teams.
Known for being able to resolve "impossible" problems
and motivate demoralized staff.

Audit Executive—Multinational Environment

Involved in auditing all aspects of the Corporation including Technology.
Managed Multicurrency Audit Budgets up to $20 million.
14 years' experience in interfacing with Audit Committees, Secretary since 1991.

- Managed multinational, multilingual global audit staffs—up to 340 people.
  - Able to deal with any audit issues
  - Resources, expertise and technical skills were shared globally.
  - Put in streamlined audit processes and automated audit systems.
- Have reported directly to Chief Auditor or CEO continuously since 1978.
- Developed Audit Strategic Plan focusing on Business and Audit Risk.
  - Encouraged auditors to take prudent risks.
- Regularly address audiences of up to 200 people on Auditing Topics.
- MBA, CPA and Chartered Auditor.

Senior Sales
and Client Management Executive
with a track record of creating substantial new business income.

• AMBRACK   • HAGEN-ROGERS   • WILDE-LORD

- A generalist, with a current specialization in **Telecommunications, Publishing, and Information**.

- Significant domestic and international market experience: in corporate, not-for-profit, and government agency client markets in both wholesale and retail.

- Management experience in both short- and long-range planning, corporate development, risk management, project management, and building new lines of business.

*Manage the start-up, turn-around, and enhancement
of corporate finance relationships and lines of business.*

GENERAL COUNSEL
with a staff of 40 lawyers
specializing in health law, environmental law and public policy

- Key member of management team of 2,000-person organization with $500 million budget.

- Intimate knowledge of **important State and Federal government agencies** responsible for Health, Insurance, Social Services, and Environmental Conservation.

- **Negotiated a dozen landmark health laws of national significance**, major consent agreements and intra- and interagency agreements.

- Organized, led, and reported on **major investigations of government corruption** and mismanagement. Resulted in major legislation, dismissals, and program improvements.

- Serve as public spokesperson for State Department of Health on key health issues including medical malpractice, government reorganization, and regulatory reform.

*Excellent judgment, high integrity.
Able to organize and motivate large groups.*

Electronic Résumés, Online Company Applications, Answering Ads Online, and Having Your Own Website

For this chapter, we asked a group of Five O'Clock Club coaches to give us their opinions on this topic, and included coaches who have their own search firms, coaching businesses, or work in human resources. Their comments should give you a rounded perspective on the use of electronic résumés in your job search. The coaches are: Anita Attridge, Bill Belknap, Chip Conlin, Celia Currin, Rob Hellmann, Peter Hill, Laura Labovich, Mark Moyer, Bernadette Norz, and Damona Sain.

Perhaps you've heard the story about the Philadelphia-area human-resources executive who applied anonymously for a job in his own company as an experiment. He didn't make it through the screening process. Employers are starting to use ridiculous computer programs that screen applicants—and very few applicants can get through.

So what do job hunters do in response to this new software? They spend endless hours trying to get *around* those systems hoping their résumé can be selected. Give it up! Job hunters' time would be better spent trying to figure out the name of the person to contact and then contacting them directly. Contact *anyone* in that organization and get in to see them. We call it "surrounding the hiring manager." See our write-up on that topic in the chapter, "How to Answer Ads" just a few pages back.

If you are getting lots of meetings this way, continue on that same path. But if you are not getting meetings, please change what you are doing.

Insanity: doing the same thing over and over again and expecting different results.

ALBERT EINSTEIN

Ten years ago, the prediction was that computer-scanned résumés would be the driving force in the selection process of the future. The career press talked of nothing else. As of this writing, however, electronic résumés have had little impact on the job searches of Five O'Clock Clubbers. Let's put electronic résumés in perspective. In this book, you will read that there are four basic ways to get interviews in your target market: through search firms, ads, networking, and direct contact. Five O'Clock Clubbers learn to consider all four techniques for getting interviews and then to assess which approach produces the most meetings for them. You should consider using search firms and ads in your job-search mix. In your particular field, they may be an important source of meetings. However, these approaches are passive: you have little control over the process. The search firm or the company that placed the ad must call you in. The use of electronic résumés is also a passive approach to job search. You must wait for someone to call you in.

On the other hand, networking and directly contacting companies are proactive approaches: you decide whom to contact and you contact them. While we encourage job hunters to consider every technique for getting interviews in their target markets, we want them to measure which techniques result in meetings with hiring managers. Those are the techniques you should use more. If electronic résumés result in meetings for you, then use them.

What is an electronic résumé?

In this chapter, we are no longer talking only about the résumés that get scanned into a company's database. Here we will cover everything from the way you attach your résumé to an email to the way you upload your résumé in company websites.

> **In spite of an online application, you are more likely to get the interview because of your résumé and your initiative in contacting the hiring manager.**

"Sorry, Ralph, but I'm replacing you with Johnson here. I got him off eBay."

Making Your Résumé Scannable

Every time an online application asks you to cut and paste your résumé, a scannable version of your résumé is required. The guidelines that follow will help you to create a powerful scannable résumé.

If you have been using The Five O'Clock Club approach to developing your résumé, you are almost there. First of all, you have gotten rid of company jargon so the outside world can understand what you have done. You have also changed your job titles to reflect what you actually did, rather than using company-dictated titles that may not be as accurate. And you have made your résumé accomplishment- oriented (a good approach no matter what kind of résumé you have).

Electronic résumés are scanned into a database. They do not need to look pretty. In fact, you cannot have any hard tabs, underlining, bolding, bullets (use "*" or dashes instead of bullets), or other characters that may confuse the scanner: just use plain, straight text. In Word, save the résumé as plain text format, then edit it that way.

In addition to having a plain text format, your résumé must contain keywords that the hiring manager is most likely to search for regarding the kind of work you want to do. Therefore, at the top of your résumé, where you may have put Operations Manager, for example, add a string of words that would also be appropriate for you, such as:

operations manager, administrative manager, accounting manager, general manager, strategic planner, inventory control manager, materials manager, customer service manager, management consultant.

Important nouns should be included and repeated in various contexts. One recruiter whom we consulted uses only 34 keyword sorts; most use far more. She advises that an analysis of the ad will let the astute applicant know what the important keywords are for the résumé.

If you have prepared your résumé The Five O'Clock Club way, the body of your résumé should be fine. Again, choose words they are likely to look for. If you are adept at computers, list the hardware and software you know. Only list software that is generally available, not the company-specific systems you may have used. For example, you may list IBM, MAC, Lotus 123, or

WordPerfect. But don't list ACS, your company's Accounting Control System. That's a name that would not be recognized in the outside world.

The rest of your résumé would be the same as what you have already prepared, but without any highlighting.

But remember that only 3 to 6 percent of all jobs are found through recruiters, so please don't go crazy. One coach noted that all these bells and whistles don't mean that recruiters are more successful in getting the right person into the right job. In fact, they may be less successful because they are not figuring out the human element from the onset and are missing out on terrific candidates.

Some companies have equipment that scan thousands of résumés. A large company may get a million résumés a year! Theoretically, when someone in that company wants to hire a new employee, the manager asks to see only those résumés that fit the experience he or she is looking for. In real life, Five O'Clock Clubbers are getting jobs with companies that happen to use scanning equipment, but they are not getting many interviews through this technology. Instead, Five O'Clock Clubbers are getting in to see the hiring managers through networking, direct contact, search firms, or even answering ads. When you contact a company through its résumé-scanning technology, it is usually a dead end. If a company asks for a scannable résumé, provide one, but be proactive: find some other way in. That's what Five O'Clock Clubbers do. The interview is most likely to come from the "other way," not from an uploaded résumé.

> **Use the one-two punch: apply online, then contact the hiring manager or someone who works closely with that person. That's the Five O'Clock Club way.**

Online Company Applications

Companies commonly ask you to fill out an online application. However, as one coach warned,

"Company applications are unforgiving. One online application disallowed any words in the 'salary required' box. So, my client could not write 'negotiable.' Of course, she researched her market value in her area and figured out a range. Then it wouldn't take a range, and only a 5-digit number!"

Another coach suggests that you avoid the questions involving references or income. If the application requires an income figure to proceed, try to select $1 or $100, etc. We're teaching you to play the odds here: you are more likely to be screened out when you state your actual salary than if you provide no salary number. On the application, keep referring back to your résumé so you don't need to be repetitive on the application. Leave references blank or "available upon strong mutual interest" (which is the Five O'Clock Club approach to references). The application is often a bureaucratic formality. You are more likely to get the interview because of your résumé and your initiative in contacting the hiring manager.

Another coach, who also works as a Human Resources executive, gave this example:

This whole trend toward electronic résumés and online applications reminds me of a few years ago when we first did a beta test on our new online application system at the company where I work. I pretended to be applying for an administrative assistant position and for each of the questions regarding my background experience and qualifications I doubled or tripled those required.

For example, when asked if I had a minimum two years college, I replied I had a graduate degree, and asked if I had a minimum five years related work experience, I replied I had 20 plus years.

However, one question asked in a multiple-choice fashion what would be the correct steps in sending out a merged mailing. Now, although I'm pretty good with computers, I had never performed a merged mailing, so I basically guessed at the answer.

Well, I guessed wrong on that one question and never made the first cut of having my application move forward for further review. The moral of the story is that no matter how qualified a person may be, and even if that person is the best possible fit for a job, answering applications online is all about acing the application, not the job.

A much more successful approach is what I call the one-two punch: a job hunter goes through the online application process because most companies will not even consider a person's candidacy unless they do so. But then network your way into the company. This is what The Five O'Clock Club suggests in general: answer the ad or fill out the application, then forget about it and find some other way in.

Some of our members are able to identify someone in their network (such as through their LinkedIn contacts) who then refers them to someone in the hiring department of the company with whom they had also applied online. In turn, hiring managers can quickly move their applications and résumés to the top of the pile, and generate an interview once they have more information on someone. Some will even go to the mat with HR if they want to see someone badly enough.

Remember that companies have specific ways that résumés need to be submitted (often as uploads onto their web portal for applications). As one coach notes, oftentimes an ad will state the preferred way of sending the résumé, so do what is required, but also network your way in or contact someone directly! And another coach notes: "It is quite clear that we coaches are all on the same page (after all, it's part of the methodology!) regarding the huge advantage an individual has by contacting the right person at the right level vs. online submission. All of our stats back that up."

Most coaches agree about the effectiveness of the one-two punch: apply online, then contact the hiring manager or someone who works closely with that person. That's the Five O'Clock Club way.

A majority of positions are filled without the outside world ever knowing about the opening. For example, the hiring manager could run into someone at the health club who talks about a neighbor's dog that bit a guy whose brother turned out to be a great candidate for that job.

Cartoon Courtesy © Jerry King

"Excuse me, Mr. Pomplin, but there's a gentleman here who says he's concerned because you haven't responded to not one of his 12,000 spams."

The Recruiter's Point-of-View

Executive search consultants prefer Word documents because they often do some light editing, perhaps tweaking the format to fit what their client companies expect and removing your contact information and adding their letterhead. But don't forget that the executive recruiter is a go-between.

One coach, who has been an executive recruiter for the past twenty+ years, says this:

I can safely attest to the ebb and flow over the years of how companies source their candidates, and yet the overriding truth remains that networking and direct contact get the job done far better and more efficiently for an individual job seeker than any other mode, including recruiters! Now that I have stated the obvious . . .

From my experience as an executive recruiter dealing directly with HR and internal recruiters, there are inefficiencies involved with the online application process, and these often restrict pulling in those candidates that would make the best fit for the role. As other coaches have noted, companies will ask specific multiple choice questions that are meant to pre-screen candidates before their résumés are seen. Data from the online application is assessed, and the search criteria are prioritized, which again may knock out qualified candidates who may match up quite well otherwise.

In their defense, most of my client companies insist that they eyeball many résumés of candidates who may not make it through the initial filter, or they simply read all of them, time permitting. Yes, you should attach a Word document or insert additional information in the space provided to help justify your candidacy if you lack the experience or skills for a specific job. However, do not rely on the online submission as the way into a company.

I agree 100% with the one-two punch recommendation, as I always suggest the same when coaching. A majority of positions are filled without the outside world ever being alerted about the opening. Typically, an unsolicited résumé arrives on the manager's desk and happens to be at the top of the pile, or the person who the hiring manager ran into at the health club talks about a neighbor's dog that bit a guy whose brother turned out to be a great candidate for that job.

Most of the HR professionals with whom I work often regard the online application process as a necessary evil, and they tell me to make sure my candidates apply online. But at the same time I email their résumés directly to the hiring manager and HR, as a failsafe to make sure they get in front of the right eyes.

Another coach noted that Applicant Tracking Systems (ATS) have moved from scanning to "parsing" content from a résumé into a standard format based on the employer's preferences. But he warns that this technology merely reinforces the "screen out" mentality, instead of creating any kind of a meaningful platform to really find the best fit for any given position.

One of our coaches, who works with clients earning $200,000 and above, said:

I have had only two or three clients in the last two years who have had to deal with requests for an electronic résumé and they just removed the bolding and changed the bullets to asterisks. In terms of applying online, most corporate sites either have their own format or just ask you to attach your Word Doc résumé. I have not had a single client who has ever had trouble answering an online ad.

> **In most cases, an online résumé is not worth it.**

So, use your judgment about relying too heavily on electronic résumés. We all would like something magical to save us from the grueling work of searching for a job, but many of the ideas you may come across are not effective.

And a friendly reminder from yet another coach: "The downside of relying too much on company websites and online postings is that only 10 to 12% of jobs are found this way. Increasingly these postings are consuming more time to complete. Since 80% of jobs are found though networking and direct contact, job hunters will realize a far greater payoff if they spend 80% of their job search time on these activities. Most jobs are not posted. In fact, to avoid job postings, many companies are now offering monetary rewards to employees who refer a person who is selected for the job. Several clients have been told they would not have been hired if someone within the company had not recommended them."

Online and Multimedia Résumés for Creative and Technical Positions

Depending on your profession, you may want the hiring manager to see examples of your work. Some job hunters create a multimedia résumé, with extensive background information; it may include video clips or samples of work, all packaged to be transmitted electronically. This method may be appropriate for creative and technical positions because it demonstrates use and understanding of the technology.

Then, there is the Web-Résumé, which is done in HTML formats and benefits a viewer who needs to see a broader, visually-oriented portfolio. Web pages can include photographs, links to other websites, design/layout graphics, streaming video, and other high-tech features. The benefit of having an HTML résumé is its presence on the Web 24/7, its universal compatibility, and its appealing appearance. At present, there is still a site called VisualCV that allows you to do a Web-type résumé. For a while it was the gold-standard for web portfolios, but technology changes so quickly, there may be a better site by the time this article is published!

VisualCV and other résumé websites help people to create their own résumé pages and video résumés. The issue with all of these is that résumés generally need to be positioned for a specific job target, so you need multiple versions—one for each target. This is a limitation with LinkedIn as well: you are allowed to have only one profile. In addition, Web-Résumés may be hard to update in some cases, particularly where video is involved. Remember, people are able to constantly make small revisions to their résumés, but changing a video requires real work. So **most coaches agree that the conventional résumé is not going away.**

One coach noted that posting using Box.net appears to be a useful tool since it integrates with LinkedIn: "VisualCV is fine for a static résumé, and has worked well as a simple static website for me. They have many samples to show you how it might look: www.visualcv.com. And if anyone is interested, here's mine: http://www.visualcv.com/phiconsulting."

The consensus of our coaches is that you should have an online résumé if you have only one job target or a consulting practice (and it therefore requires very little in the way of changes). Or, if you want to be a web developer and don't have any work yet to show online, developing your own website / résumé could showcase your work. Or, if

you are in the visual arts or graphic design, having a website / résumé showing your designs is more powerful and can strongly complement, or even a substitute for, your résumé.

Other than those special cases, if you want to have an online résumé, consider using LinkedIn instead. As one coach said, "Sure your own personal résumé/website can be impressive—but is it worth the time—and the lack of flexibility in being able to have multiple résumés for each target? I would say in most cases an online résumé is not worth it."

"I'm sorry, Roberts, but as a traditionalist, I'm just not ready to buy into this 'computer' fad. However, I'm still considering your 'voicemail' suggestion."

Cartoon Courtesy © Jerry King

Your Positioning on LinkedIn

Be sure to read the article in the Members Only section of our website (www.fiveoclockclub.com), "Social Media: Using LinkedIn to Advance Your Career." Below is additional information from our coaches, specifically regarding how LinkedIn relates to your résumé.

In general, our coaches suggest that job hunters put their efforts into LinkedIn instead of other outlets for their résumé, making their LinkedIn profile top notch. As one said: "I am among the many coaches who believe that LinkedIn is currently a 'must have' for anyone seriously job hunting at a professional or managerial level and above."

Another shares a similar opinion: "LinkedIn is the number 1 professional networking site. The summary section, which is limited in the number of characters that can be used, needs to be compelling and should differentiate you from others in your field. After completing your résumé in The Five O'Clock Club style, it's time to update your LinkedIn profile."

One coach notes says that "'Profile' is a misleading word because on LinkedIn your profile should be your full-blown résumé. Both internal and external recruiters have told me they often ignore candidates when they see just a profile. They want to see the companies you have worked for, your results, and your key skills."

Another coach warns of the complexities: "On Linkedin, there are opposing views. But, to differentiate yourself from the now 100 million Linkedin users, you need to add some personality, humor, and stories to your profile, and give it a different feel than you give your résumé. The jury is still out on whether you should write your profile in 3rd or 1st person, but recently Linkedin (the company) gave celebrity blogger Guy Kawasaki's profile—an extreme makeover and put it in the 1st person. [www.linkedin.com/in/guykawasaki] You can see that Linkedin endorsed it. This fits his irreverent personality and it is highly readable and engaging."

One coach had these details to add:

LinkedIn is definitely the big gorilla in the room. I am of a school of thought that a LinkedIn profile should not be just a "cut-and-paste" of a résumé in its entirety. I see LinkedIn profiles as a bit of a teaser to hook an employer or recruiter with just enough information to contact the individual, who can then send the full résumé later. Attention spans online tend to be very, very limited, so I advocate the following strategy to my clients, which has been working quite well:

1. The SUMMARY section is written in the first person in conversational tone. This is by design as it personalizes this portion of the profile. I typically aim for one to three paragraphs, each containing one to three sentences.

2. The WORK EXPERIENCE & GOALS section is written in résumé language. Again, this is by design. A good formula here is one (maybe two) pithy sentences about responsibilities, and two or three very brief bulleted accomplishments for each entry. This gives the readers a snapshot of the most important things you want them to know about each experience. The further back you go in your employment chronology, the less information needs to be included.

Of course, keywords should be included for search engine optimization.

> Since fewer people are using snail mail, it is more likely to get the hiring manager's attention, especially for more senior-level positions.

Most coaches recommend that job hunters consider including a LinkedIn profile URL in the contact section of their résumé, and also on business cards they can hand out at networking events. You could include other links on your résumé as well, if it helps to sell yourself. These would include links to websites you designed, a video you created, and so on.

Just another reminder from yet another coach to bring us all back to real life: "Direct contact and networking still seem to be the best way to reach people, as stated in the current books. My clients reply to ads and never hear anything (and then they come to me for help!). But when reaching out directly to the hiring managers via networking or direct contact, everything changes, and they get meetings. This is what we've been saying in our books, and it's true."

This coach also notes that while LinkedIn profiles are essential, they are not a substitute for résumés in many (or most) cases, because:

- You can have only one profile, so that requires that you position yourself more generally than you would like if you have multiple targets.

- If you are currently employed, you have to be careful what you put on your profile in terms of what you are going for. If it is very different from your current job, your boss might get suspicious.
- You might have to make your profile less accomplishment-oriented because it is so public. Actual numbers might work on a résumé that will be seen by a very targeted audience, but might not be appropriate for a LinkedIn profile. Be sure to discuss this with your coach or small group.

In sending your résumé via email, should you include your résumé in the body of the email or as an attachment?

The prevailing opinion seems to be that résumés should always be **attached** because formatting can really help in delivering your pitch/message. The cover letter, however, should always be in the body of the email, so it's more likely to be read. A good cover letter/email will stimulate enough interest so that the résumé will be opened.

Most coaches agree that the attached résumé should be in PDF format so that all recipients will see the same thing you see (different versions of Word, or Mac vs. PC, display résumés differently, such as inserting strange page breaks). You can even attach PDFs to online applications.

These days, most job hunters are contacting hiring managers via email. The reasons for using email are these:

- It works. Email is the language of business these days: everyone reads email.
- It's much easier on the job seeker to send an email—important from a time management perspective and psychologically.
- It's easy for the recipient to just hit reply.
- You may look outdated by sending a letter.

That said, you will need a compelling/relevant subject line to get people to open it, so it doesn't go into spam (e.g., "referred by", "saw your article", etc.). You also need an email address that has your name in it—it's a marketing opportunity and makes it less likely to go into spam. And you gen-erally need to follow up with a phone call—unless you really are spamming people.

Snail mail letters do have an advantage in that they can stand out (if they are read in a timely way, not always the case these days), show care and effort, and may appeal to "old school" hiring managers who don't consider this spam. What's more, since fewer people are doing it, it is more likely to get the hiring manager's attention, especially for more senior-level positions.

One person who coaches only the most senior executives said, "Whenever there is a chance that the firewall may knock the email into junk mail, my clients send it by both email and snail mail."

How much time should a job hunter spend on posting résumés online or answering ads?

This is a trick question in case you've missed our warnings throughout this chapter! As one coach said, "Very, very little time should be spent on this: less than 10 percent of a job hunter's time, for all the reasons we know as Five O'Clock Club coaches. This channel is more competitive, passive, and very time consuming. It is the 'passive' element that bothers me the most: I am a huge advocate of clients taking control of their searches—and maintaining control. **The big downside of relying too much on company websites and online postings is that opportunities will be lost if job hunters are not doing more productive things such as networking and direct contact.**"

A final warning. We have written this chapter only because *job hunters* want to know about the subject *and* waste too much time posting their résumés online, developing their own websites (that no one will see), and filling out online company applications. **Spend only ten percent of your job-search time that way**. Become more pro-active in your search through networking and direct contact. However, be sure to read the chapter on *Using Social Media in Your Search* (especially LinkedIn).

Good luck. Be wise. Follow the methodology. And thanks to all of our coaches who contributed to this chapter.

Using the Internet as a Job-Search Tool

The essence of the high-risk society is choice: the choice between embracing uncertainty and running from it.

MICHAEL MANDEL, *The High-Risk Society*

The Internet is a great research tool and may even help you connect with people. However, it does not provide the benefits of personal contact and valuable perspectives that one-on-one information-gathering meetings provide. Consider the Internet as simply another job-search tool to be added to your repertoire of Five O'Clock Club techniques. The following hints will help you make it an effective complement.

Develop an Internet Plan to Coincide with Your Job-Search Marketing Campaign

One of our biggest challenges at The Five O'Clock Club is to convince job hunters to spend less time on the Internet, primarily answering ads, or drifting off into irrelevant areas such as scrolling through databases, accessing career centers, looking at job postings, or chatting in newsgroups. Be very focused while you are online. The Internet can be interesting but it can also be somewhat addictive and can distract you from your real mission of targeted research, learning about an industry, field or person (such as through LinkedIn), and developing your target list of organizations and people to contact. It can also help you in your follow-up after a job interview. Or you can see job postings that tell you the correct words to use in your resume for the kind of position you're seeking. It may seem like productive time because a few hours online can generate a lot of information.

However, the time may be better spent elsewhere. Be sure to balance the time you spend on the Internet (or in library research) with the time you spend talking to real people, writing letters and emails and following up after a job interview.

The best way to develop your Internet plan is to define specific tasks you will need to accomplish in your allotted Internet time. Include the Internet as part of the research component of your target list and then as a further source when obtaining information about specific companies. Consider online job postings as a great source of companies that are hiring, ones you can then contact directly in the departments or divisions that are appropriate for you.

The Internet has become another means of obtaining meetings to be added to the list: networking, direct mail, search firms, ads, and now the Internet. Also, keep in mind that there continues to be a lot of hype and media articles about the effectiveness of online campaigns as compared with other job-search methods. Be wary of those "research studies" that show the techniques hiring managers use to find job hunters, which can bear little resemblance to the techniques job hunters should use to get interviews. For example, at The Five O'Clock Club, we may post on Craig's List and use that as our primary source of back-office personnel. For one job opening, we will get 300 to 500 resumes within a couple of hours. That's good for us, but the odds are against all of those people who answered the ad. After all, we're going to hire only one person – not 500. Even those who are supposed to be helping job hunters, such as other outplacement firms, continually quote research on how employers find candidates. Remember that is a good market, only 6% of all jobs are found through job postings of all kinds and only 6% of all jobs are found through search firms. Therefore, spend only that percentage of your time on those techniques.

Choose the Websites Appropriate for Your Search

Finding the right websites to review online postings should be part of your initial campaign as you develop your target list. In the same way you'll find periodicals the movers and shakers in your industry read, you'll also find industry-specific websites. These websites often contain job postings or have links to affiliate job sites. More importantly, they will bring you up-to-date on what's happening in your field or industry so you do better in your meetings. During the course of your information meetings, ask about industry periodicals and industry websites, too. Check the website of industry organizations and associations as a source for leads through job postings, not to mention activities in your field for networking contacts. Be sure to visit LinkedIn to find out the background of every person with whom you will meet. Also Google those people to find out whether they have been quoted or mentioned in the business press.

Career sites often contain job postings for a company that are not listed on the firm's own corporate website. If it appears there are no open positions at a company, it may be because their jobs are listed elsewhere or not listed at all, so check through career sites for company-specific listings of your target firm. Keep in mind: Not all open positions are posted to websites and not all positions posted to websites are open.

Search firms often have sites allowing users to complete a profile then included in the candidate database. Complete the profile if you consider the firm reputable but make sure there's a notation about privacy so your résumé is sent out only with your permission. And, remember, you can spend hours on this, but your chances are slim.

Responding to Online Job Postings

Before responding to the online posting, verify whether the format you're using to send your cover letter and résumé is correct. Some companies want your résumé included in the body of the email with no attachments. Other firms want two attachments, the cover letter and your résumé. Some companies request responses in text format only, so sending a word-processed document is not appropriate. In that case, convert the word-processed document (.doc or .docx) into a text format (.txt) before sending. Some want .pdf only to avoid the risk of viruses. This may seem trivial but you don't want your response eliminated before it is even reviewed.

When sending your résumé as an attachment, include your last name as part of the document name. For instance, don't call the attachment "My Résumé." If the attachment gets separated from the email or if there is internal email correspondence about a number of candidates, you don't want your documents to be easily confused or misplaced. On the subject line of the email, try to include a notation that will address the topic but will also encourage the reader to open the email. For instance, instead of just "My Résumé" include a notation about your area of expertise (from the first line of your Two-Minute Pitch). Try to keep this line to a minimum as this field is not uniform across all Internet service providers.

Consider online job postings in the same way you would want ads in newspapers and trade periodicals Position your response by matching your background to their requirements. Your response may be scanned by a computer so be sure your résumé contains the appropriate buzzwords for your industry.

Before sending your email response to the company, send it to yourself first. Check the "From" box. **If you have a cutesy online name, change it to a more business-appropriate name**, even if it means signing on to a new online service or expanding the existing membership with your current Internet service provider. Check your Subject line to see if all the characters you intended are included in this space. And refrain from using all lower-case, which will make you seem less serious.

There's often a tendency to be less formal when sending email than when sending written documents. Remember: This is still a job search so spell-check your email before it goes out. If your browser does not have a spell-check feature, cut and paste a word-processed document that you've verified off-line into the body of the email. Always add the email address as the last item so you don't accidentally send an incomplete letter while you're still working on it.

Posting Your Résumé Online

Many of the Internet career websites provide an area in which job hunters post their résumés for access by potential employers. However, access is not limited to just potential employers. Do you want your current boss looking at your résumé online? Who else has access to your personal information, credentials, and employment history? Would you tack up your résumé on a public bulletin board or hand it out to strangers just because they asked for it? And how can you follow up effectively if you don't know who has viewed your credentials?

However, some job hunters have found posting their credentials helpful in their search and there are ways to minimize some of these concerns. For instance, you can post only a portion of your personal information so interested respondents can call you for further details, allowing you to screen them. Online posting is certainly an option but is not recommended and removing or replacing an online résumé is rarely as easy as posting it.

Remember, the Internet is another tool to supplement your Five O'Clock Club techniques. If you need a quick reminder of this methodology, simply check out our website at **www.fiveoclockclub.com.**

Jobholders do not see the organization as a shifting pattern of needs. The only "opportunities" they recognize are the jobs that are currently posted on bulletin boards down at Personnel. And they grumble about how damned few of those there are, failing to note all the while the expanding range of unmet needs all over the organization.

WILLIAM BRIDGES, *JobShift: How to Prosper in a Workplace Without Jobs*

Social Media: Using LinkedIn to Advance Your Career

We asked a group of Five O'Clock Club coaches to give us their opinions on Social Media in general and LinkedIn in particular. The coaches were: Damona Sain, Win Sheffield, Celia Currin, Mary Anne Walsh, Anita Attridge, Bill Belknap, Rob Hellmann and Chip Conlin.

Technology changes, and you have to change with it, but the basic techniques and thought processes for career development don't change. As one of our coaches said, "I constantly give my clients this advice: even if you do not embrace social networking, you need to understand how business is using it because it will come up, sooner rather than later, in business conversations.

"So, please, for self-preservation, avail yourself of the data. By the way, www.mashable.com is one of the best sites for keeping pace with the business uses and business trends involving social media."

Yes, times have changed. In the 1960s and 1970s, if you left your house and the phone rang, you missed the call. People did not have home answering machines. Nowadays, people are connected to their cell phones everywhere they go.

Twenty years ago, the Internet did not exist. Today, it can dominate our lives. We think that the new Social Media are meant to extend our relationships, but there are perilous risks, as well as benefits.

We can all build lots of connections, but let's be smart about it. Facebook is the cause of many relationship break-ups. A 2009 study makes the claim that "increased Facebook use significantly predicts Facebook-related jealousy" in romantic relationships.

While Facebook tends to be more of a personal medium, LinkedIn is more for professional relationships. Used correctly, it can help you to improve your current career, find a new job, or build a consulting practice.

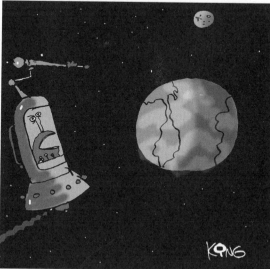

Cartoon Courtesy © Jerry King

"I've located the source of all that annoying spam we've been receiving...preparing to destroy."

Social Media in General

Keep up your contacts while working

Before Social Media came into being, we urged our clients who had landed jobs to make sure they had two networking meetings a week— no matter what—to keep up their contacts, keep up with what was happening in their fields and industries, and to already have developed contacts if they needed information to help them in their careers or wanted to search again.

> **Be smart about building your connections.**

Social Media can help you to keep up your contacts, particularly given how busy everyone is these days, but our coaches caution that "nothing substitutes for face-to-face contact. Don't ever forget the value of a phone call over an email." Meeting people virtually does not replace meeting people directly—either in person or via telephone. One coach advised, "Make sure that 20 to 30 percent of your time—whether in your job or job hunting—is 'in the field' meeting and connecting with people face-to-face."

Social Media *are* a serious part of the resources and tools that help people in their jobs and in job search. The basics of managing your career, looking for a job, or building a consulting practice have not changed—just *the tools* that help people to connect have changed—ranging from email, online search, to LinkedIn, blogs and Twitter.

> **Use Social Media as one tool to develop your career, build a consulting practice, or find a new job.**

These tools help you to stay in contact with your network of people and companies, and to continue to build your network. You can use social networking tools to build your reputation as an industry or subject expert by blogging and tweeting—or every bit as important—responding and commenting on other people's blogs and tweets.

As one coach said: "Social networking should not be viewed as just a job-search tool. That's wrong and inefficient. This would be the equivalent of going to just one interview with the belief and expectation that it will produce a job offer. It's a resource for managing and navigating your career. Yes, you use social networking to conduct a dynamic job search, but it's so much more than that. Use it to expand your network, as a resource for information, and to build a community of like-minded people who will support you both on the job, as well as in job search."

Social Media Can Waste Your Time

Whether you are employed or not, we all know that anything on the Internet (or computer or handheld mobile devices, especially Smartphones) can suck up too much time. One coach advises that for one or two weeks, you should assess how much time per day you spend online. Track how often you click on interesting links and *surf to unrelated topics*. Then cut all your time in half for two weeks. Use that extra time to meet with people directly via phone and in person, rather than relying on virtual meetings alone.

As one coach put it: "Let's face it, it takes a lot of time and care to build Stage 1 and 2 contacts (getting to know people who know about your industry and field and then those who are more senior than you). It's easy to avoid the sometimes intimidating and anxiety-producing effects of reaching out to people in person. Social Media are also pretty much a '2-D' interaction. That can increase miscommunication possibilities."

Comparing Various Social Media

Facebook is generally for social purposes, rather than career development. Twitter can be very time-intensive and the tweets move so quickly that you can lose track of them easily if you stay away for a couple of days (even hours sometimes!).

Blogs are labor intensive, but can be effective if you like to write and *write well*. But check out the blogs you return to time and again, and figure out why they are appealing. Being too wordy with no graphics or other media (such as a short video) can be a recipe for a lack of traffic. Other media include verbal podcasts, but you need good recording equipment or no one will stay to listen. This coach notes: "I think well done video podcasts (NOT amateur YouTube versions!) on Twitter, Facebook, blogs, and whatever else there is, would likely appeal to more people—but ONLY if they are well done and if you are photogenic or a natural in front of a camera."

All of the above can take up so much of your time! Be sure to track the amount of time you are on the computer and what you are doing there. It is very easy to waste time digging through news-letters, blogs, junk mail, and it is important to keep the time invested *under control*.

What's more, Social Media can be a new way of "hiding out" instead of actually making contact with real people. The Internet in all of its forms is a great research tool. But as we used to say, if you are spending all of your time in the library (or on the Internet), get out more. If you are spending all of your time meeting with people, research more. You need both for a successful career today.

Finally, Social Media are used more heavily in certain industries and professions than others. Here's one coach's thoughts on the subject: "Social Media are a tool to support your career. Like any tool it's best used when the audience you're target-ing has embraced it and believes in it.

"Know whether your audience uses it so you don't waste a lot of time using the wrong tools to advance your career or your search. If everyone in your desired target is heavily invested in social networking then you should be, too. For example, I have a client who just became the president of a digital ad agency. He's on Facebook and LinkedIn to keep his universe of contacts—both profes-sional and personal—apprised of his whereabouts and plans. He also uses and promotes other technologies to demonstrate his commitment to being 'wired.'"

LinkedIn

Every professional needs to be on LinkedIn. We have over 1,000 members in our Five O'Clock Club LinkedIn Group. LinkedIn has gotten rave reviews at The Five O'Clock Club. Wrote one Clubber to his group: "LinkedIn is a terrific tool that can help extend a person's network and sim-plify the process of identifying members of your network in target companies and industries. It's free to join so I've tried to recruit lots of other Five O'Clock Clubbers. As a quick anecdote, I received a cold call this morning from a distant contact in my LinkedIn network who is looking for help on a number of his projects. I was the perfect fit. A perfect lead! I wish you the same good luck, and pass it on. If you join, make sure you connect to me; the bigger your network the more effective it will be."

From one coach's point-of-view: "LinkedIn is being described as 'the best' online career-man-agement guide around; and rightly so. There is a huge WOW factor knowing that at least 45 million others are on LinkedIn.

"Remember more than 85% of recruiters are trying to find you daily. Just a few years ago we thought of career management as a ladder: Get that first job and hang on that rung until you or someone else decides it is time to go. The current thinking is to visualize your career as a ramp where you are consistently, conscientiously, and concisely moving forward up this ramp using all the tools available to you, especially the art of building and maintaining relationships on an on-going basis throughout your career. What better vehicle than LinkedIn to assist you in accomplish-ing this lifetime project of managing yourself?"

Another coach offers comfort to concerned employees: "Clients sometimes worry that their employer will see their activity on LinkedIn and assume they are looking for work. You can update your status on a quarterly basis, or at a minimum, when you complete each major project. You can even mention to your boss that you are tracking your accomplishments using LinkedIn."

Our coaches tend to agree that LinkedIn is

simply a tool. As one said, "The key is to build relationships; to some extent LinkedIn can nurture or even extend a relationship. I think of LinkedIn as a fancy Rolodex and I rely on it as I would a Rolodex. It is not a substitute for developing the relationships. It is a *medium*, a sophisticated medium, but in the end, a medium."

> Would you like to see a great LinkedIn profile? Look at Guy Kawasaki's.
> www.linkedin.com/in/guykawasaki

Get the Professional Headline and Profile Right!

One coach represented many of our coaches when she said, "Mainly, I work with two categories of people" those high-potential clients who are on the cusp of promotion and are ripe for business coaching, and those individuals who are interested in transitioning into a new career. The most important first phase of coaching is assessment or identifying one's career distinction, which is a cornerstone piece to crafting a dynamic profile. I strongly suggest working with a Five O'Clock Club Coach at this assessment-stage to help you identify your professional reputation or positioning. Keep in mind that it is hard to do these alone and much more fun to do in concert with a professional coach."

Before writing your LinkedIn Heading and Profile, re-read the section of our *Interviewing* book on the Two-Minute Pitch. As we say at the Club, "if your pitch—the way you're positioning yourself —is wrong, everything is wrong." As one coach said, "Whether you are looking to advance your career, build a consulting practice, or are looking for a new job, it's extremely important that your profiles on LinkedIn and other social networking sites be consistent in how they position you professionally. It's amazing *how many disconnects* we see between a member's profile on LinkedIn, the Summary Statement on their résumé, and even they way they talk about themselves in their

pitch." Says another coach, "You can create an effective LinkedIn profile by following many of the same principles that we would recommend for your résumé. For example, focus on accomplishments, have a summary section, use keywords that resonate with your audience, and so on."

The LinkedIn Professional Heading is a small field, but the most important. As one coach noted: "It is your positioning statement and is the reader's first impression of your perceived promise of value —and we all know how difficult it is to change a first impression! Remember your positioning lives in the hearts and minds of others for a long time." This same coach developed the following list for you to consider:

Coaching questions to ask yourself:

1. What is the impression I want to create in the Professional Headline?
2. What do others say about my Professional Headline?
3. Are these congruent thoughts?
4. What is the feeling you want it to evoke?
5. What is the feeling others get when they read your Professional Headline?
6. What does it say about your career distinction that you bring to an organization?

Compare the feeling you get when you read these two very real Professional Headlines—Joe: "In career transition" vs. Jill: "Big picture visionary who gets the job done using creative non-traditional tactics." Which person would you want to get to know?

Most people decide they want to reposition themselves depending on where they want their career to go. A Clubber who had worked for the big consulting firms her entire life wanted people to instead see her as a "Communications Executive with 10 years of international experience." How do you want to be seen?

Would you like to see a great LinkedIn profile? Look at Guy Kawasaki's:
www.linkedin.com/in/guykawasaki

I know: Social Media are his job. The Internet is his life's work. But he is a good example of someone who has taken full advantage of what LinkedIn has to offer. Pay special attention to his summary statement. You can see that he's put a lot of thought into his. If you have been working closely with your coach, you may be able to simply insert your résumé summary statement onto your LinkedIn page. Every Five O'Clock Club coach would tell you that you want to consistently communicate your pitch in all of your communications: résumé, cover letter, your verbal pitch about yourself, email messages, and all other Social Media.

> **Develop your LinkedIn heading and summary after you've completed your résumé. That way, they both position you the same way.**

By the way, if you are proud of your LinkedIn profile, be sure to list your LinkedIn address (see Guy's address, above) in all of your email correspondence, at the top of your résumé, and so on. If you've done a good job on your LinkedIn profile, you want others to see it. And, rather than using the address that is assigned to you, you will want to change your LinkedIn address and use Guy's format (with his name as part of the url).

All of our coaches echo the same thought: Complete your LinkedIn profile *after* you have completed your résumé. The Headline, 120 character limit, should define who you are and what differentiates you from others. The summary, 2,000 characters, should position you strategically for your career development, consulting business or job search. Start with the summary section from your résumé. Use bulleted points or short paragraphs so that it can be read easily. LinkedIn doesn't give you the option for bulleted points, *but* you can get them by using a copy/paste of bulleted points from Microsoft Word into your profile, or simply use dashes or asterisks.

Another coach suggested: "I understand that people who have completed most of their LinkedIn profile *are more successful in attracting*

employers through the LinkedIn service that finds people for employers."

Only one LinkedIn Profile, so you need to choose

It is impractical and confusing to spread your network across multiple profiles (unlike your résumé, where you can and should have a different résumé for each job target). Having only one profile means that you will have to decide whether to go more general, to encompass multiple job targets, or to focus your profile on your primary job target only.

Your decision will depend on your specific situation. By focusing on one job-target, you maximize the likelihood that someone from your target audience reading your profile will quickly grasp how you can help them. Try writing your profile for your primary job target, IF the "cost" doesn't outweigh the benefit. Remember that your boss or colleagues may wonder why your profile says something very different from what you are currently doing!

Warning: In case you accidentally open up more than one profile (search under your name if you are unsure), close one down to avoid major confusion in building and updating your network (Note: You cannot transfer connections from one profile to another).

Also remember that your LinkedIn Profile has a broader viewing audience than your résumé. Your résumé is targeted for a specific industry or position, and you may decide to have more than one résumé. However, you should have only one LinkedIn profile, which means you may leave out certain specific accomplishments because of the profile's broader viewing audience. You will need to be the judge of when that's the case.

Recommendations

We asked our coaches about the number and kinds of recommendations a person should have. Here's what they said:

- Have at least three or four. Be careful not to have too many "reciprocal" recommendations (i.e., if you recommend me, I'll recommend you).
- People usually get a little suspicious about too many recommendations. (Even Guy Kawasaki has only six.) On this subject, when you ask people for a recommendation, it can be very helpful if you tell them quite specifically what you are hoping they will be comfortable in saying—to the point of writing a "draft" of a recommendation that they might want to use as a sample and change or adjust in any way that suits them. This takes the hassle out of the process for the recommender and helps you get the recommendation you really want.
- Recommendations should ideally be from previous managers or colleagues. As with references, if there are key points you would like them to include, let them know.
- Many of my clients have been contacted by both internal (company) recruiters, as well as external. Several were told they were being contacted because of the quality of their references. This is because I try (not always successfully!) to have my clients:
  1. Create a script for what they want said.
  2. Make sure the content from the reference is performance-based or behaviorally worded, NOT just a rave about the person. For example: "When Mary led the XYZ project team we met all of our committed delivery dates and came in under budget. I don't think we could have done this without her leadership."
  3. Choose the same people who are your job references; this makes the process much more efficient.

> **Too many recommendations make you look insecure.**

Why Update Your LinkedIn Page?

Some people—especially consultants—regularly update something on their LinkedIn page so that a notice will be sent to everyone in their network and keep them top-of-mind. Whether or not you are a consultant, you can let people know what projects you are working on. What our coaches say:

- Check your profile regularly to see if there's anything you can add that will keep your name and expertise showing up via status updates. Also, LinkedIn keeps adding features. Make sure that you take advantage of any that will showcase your skills.
- Like all updates (e.g., on Facebook), it can be overdone.
- People change their headline and summary as they become clearer about what is important to their target markets.

Using LinkedIn to Build a Consulting Practice

You can use LinkedIn to build a consulting practice by contacting companies or key people of interest to you.

Said one coach: "One financial client who wanted to work with small companies contacted all the smaller CPA firms on LinkedIn in his target market. He then met with them to let them know about his skills, since many small businesses contact the CPA firms to ask about recommendations for financial people." Excellent idea.

Another coach suggested using LinkedIn regularly to record your accomplishments and advertise your events.

Your LinkedIn Photo

I've seen some photos that were not professional looking. They were way too sexy. This is not a dating service. Our coaches say:

- Use a plain background, have a warm

smile, use solid colors for background and clothing. Have your hair under control. Preview your photo and ask others for their input. If you have your own consulting business, it's best to have either a studio photo or one at high resolution so it can be reduced or enlarged for this and other purposes.

- The photo needs to be professional—ideally, professionally done. The photo is your business picture and should be as professional as your image and presentation would be at an interview.

> **Don't use a sexy photo.**
> **This is business, not a dating service.**

Should you put Personal Information on LinkedIn?

To repeat what we say at the Club, if it helps your search, put it in. If it doesn't help, leave it out. If you're interested in skiing, for example, a reader could have a positive or negative reaction to this information. Our coaches say:

- Be strategic about personal information.
- Don't think of LinkedIn as a place for any personal information. It seems out of place there—it's more appropriate on Facebook.
- The Club rule is right.

Joining Groups

Joining as many groups as possible increases your network base. Groups that can be most helpful are professional (industry and function), alumni groups, special interest groups and, of course, the Five O'Clock Club group. What else do our coaches have to say?

- Joining groups is a great idea, especially when you can participate in their discussions. Not only do they help you to

showcase your knowledge and skills to a very targeted audience, but you can keep up-to-date in your field as you read others—posts. However, if you join too many groups, you can waste time with status updates; so prioritize the ones you think will be best for your purpose. Searching is all about finding the right keywords. I remember trying to help a client find groups related to accounting and the results were not what he was looking for. That might have been a keyword issue or simply that typical accountants don't set up these groups. (There were plenty of groups for CPAs, for example.)

- A footnote to the advice about not joining too many groups: If you are going to join a group try to be active in it and get to know the people in it. That's the point—not just having a laundry list of groups. As in all career development activities, you should be conscious of whether it is working for you. Are you seeing real results? Building a network? Study the metrics.
- Again, Club rules apply: if it works, do it; if not, stop.

> **Use LinkedIn the same as**
> **you would any other medium.**
> **Use it in a professional manner.**

How to Contact People through LinkedIn

I get requests all the time. The standard request that LinkedIn provides does not help me to figure out who this person is. Here's what our coaches have to say:

- Always customize your invitation to others you ask to join your connections list. The standardized invitation is very impersonal and shows you don't care enough to reach out personally.
- I absolutely agree that if you are building

your network, you should personalize all correspondence—this is the chance to reach out and touch, and make it personal and leave an impression in someone's mind. Don't blow it to save two minutes.

- I am not offended if someone I know sends a standard request. Even so, I appreciate a custom note. If the custom note is from someone I don't know well, I feel it is a little pushy. In the end, I will only connect with those I know.
- Personalizing your LinkedIn request helps to make your request stand out from many other requests that the person may be receiving.

> **The standard request that LinkedIn provides does not help me to figure out who this person is.**

How to Build Your Network on LinkedIn

- Be sure you know the people you LinkedIn with—whether you are going to them or they are coming to you. Make sure that your network is full of people who actually know you and you know them.
- Check out the connections your connections have. If you find someone you'd like to reach out to, first check with your connection to find out how they know the other person, just as you would in a live networking situation. Then customize (always customize) your request appropriately.
- I stick to my contacts' contacts. I tried to go further and it fizzled out—no relationship, so no result.
- It's important to be selective in the invitations to accept. On most sites, as soon as you accept someone's invitation you become part of their network, and may get invitations from people who may really not fit within your network. If they

cannot really help you, or you cannot be of help to them, why do it?

How to Contact Someone in a Targeted Organization

Should you simply contact that person directly (direct contact) or should you ask someone else for an introduction (networking)? Is contacting someone via LinkedIn any different from our typical advice?

- Most of our coaches agree: This is just like the Club's advice with other mediums: Contacting the person directly will provide you with the most control in connecting with someone. If you are trying to connect with a very senior person, you may want to contact a person you know before contacting the senior person. LinkedIn is the same as with any other medium.
- At The Five O'Clock Club, we advocate both ways to contact others. I'd look at the person's level. Unless you're a high-level executive, don't approach a CEO of a medium to large company directly. Remember our phrase, "contact people one to two levels higher than you are."
- Most job hunters I have observed are more successful when using LinkedIn and other sites to develop contacts and generate informational meetings. It's really about going after those Stage 2 contacts (people one or two levels higher than you are who are in a position to hire you or recommend that you be hired), then following up with a targeted mailing, and good old-fashioned phone calls.
- I have observed a trend among some job hunters using LinkedIn to identify the hiring manager, or someone of influence within the company for which they have applied online for a position. It's what I call the "one-two punch"—the same as if you were answering an ad, but also get

your résumé bumped up because of your effective use of direct contact or networking.

Some General LinkedIn Suggestions

- I think it is important to regularly spend some time on LinkedIn and to be thoughtful about extending your network before you might really need to. LinkedIn makes networking quite easy and it lets you reach out and touch lots of contacts before you need the favor—and when you might be able to put some money in the favor bank.

- As for the time you might spend on LinkedIn, review it as you would ads, maybe look at it after the workday, once a day or look at it once a week.

- LinkedIn should be used as any other resource on an as-needed basis and with a purpose. It's important to build your LinkedIn network by including groups. With a rich LinkedIn network, you can then use it to source candidates and companies. Like any of the social networking tools, it should be used with a purpose in mind.

- Check your privacy settings. Look at your progress bar and try to have it at least 75% complete. Look for groups pertaining to your industry/profession and join them. Follow discussions and contribute whenever possible.

Getting a Job Interview Through LinkedIn

We asked our coaches whether any of their job hunters have ever gotten a job interview through LinkedIn ads. Here are some of their answers:

- One group member did and was surprised to be hired for a position overseas.
- None of mine, but I have heard of people getting interviews through it.
- I have clients who have gotten interviews through recruiters. As many have noted, recruiters regularly troll LinkedIn for candidates.

- One client today said a recruiter called her about a position that he had posted, since her skills fit the profile. It appears that recruiters—both independent and for companies—are more aggressively using LinkedIn to identify candidates.

Having a LinkedIn Profile doesn't mean you're looking for a job

One coach reminds us of the following: While your résumé equals "job search," the same is not true for your LinkedIn Profile. If you are actively looking, you may want to indicate that somewhere on your LinkedIn profile (assuming you don't have a current employer who will care). This way, potential employers may be more likely to contact you.

We say "may" because some potential employers may be more interested in you if you appear to be employed. And, if you are going out and getting what you want in a job search, as we recommend, rather than waiting for the recruiter to call, indicating on your profile that you are looking becomes less important.

Nevertheless, some clients have gotten responses by indicating an openness to new opportunities on their profiles, which is why some coaches suggest that you consider it. If you think that it makes sense, in your case, to let people know that you are looking, do one or more of the following:

- Edit "Contact Preferences" (bottom of your profile) to include career and job opportunities. Some coaches say that you should do this even if you are currently "happily" employed. Since so many employed people check these boxes, it will likely not be looked at askance by your current employer.
- Since the Contact Preferences section is buried at the bottom of your profile, you may want to enter near the top of your Profile Summary Section "looking for my next great challenge," "Open to new opportunities," or something similar.

NEVER put "unemployed" or "looking for a job" on your profile—these phrases have negative connotations and will turn off a potential employer.

- Alternatively, if you are not working, you could enter one of the phrases in the bullet above as your current job title.

However, most coaches agree that you should not put these phrases in the "headline" at the top of your profile, under your name—making it the first thing a potential employer sees. Since your headline can only be 120 characters, it is better to use this limited space as an opportunity to share a "mini-pitch," that is, a concise statement about how you can help a potential employer.

> **If you're not using Google Alerts, you're not a player in your organization, industry or profession.**

Some Cool Advice

One coach suggested this very powerful LinkedIn technique:

"Use the counterintuitive approach of typing in your target company's name in the People box. If you type in Medco, as an example, the search engine brings up the names of all the people 1, 2 and 3 degrees of separation from you who work [or used to work] at Medco. Very powerful.

"You can also do this on Twitter and Facebook. For those who are social-network challenged or cynical (believe it or not many of my clients are...but not for long!), this will quickly tell you if some of your targets are social-network savvy. For example, Medco and WebMD (and hundreds of Fortune 500 companies) pay for Twitter ads. Currently, many of the world's largest companies and consulting firms use Twitter as part of their recruiting strategy.

If you do the above on Facebook (e.g., type Medco in the people search box), it will give you a list of people who work or have worked at Medco

and are on Facebook. It also give a hotlink so you can make Direct Contact! How cool is that?

Keeping Plugged into Your Industry and Profession

One problem is that we tend to focus on the next hot thing, but spending your time wisely matters! Whether you are employed or not, you need to conduct research to stay up with what's happening in your industry or field. Don't forget the basics that we teach at The Five O'Clock Club. If your only source of research is LinkedIn, that's not good. Consider the following basics for starters:

- Many members **use Google for industry, company or people information**, even if they're going after esoteric industries such as social service agencies, ethics, education policy, think tanks and nanotechnology. Key any industry name into Google and see what comes up. You may have to look through a few pages of information, but there will probably be a site that is a key one for your industry or field. Key in the people you are trying to research. Chances are, you'll find them.

- Make sure you **use Google alerts** for the organization you work for and your main competitors. If you're not doing that, you're not a player. Just go to Google, key in the word "alerts" and it will take you to the Google alert page. Key in the words you would like an alert for, see a preview of the kind of results you would get, modify the word if you don't like the results, and note how often you would like to get alerts on these keywords. You've probably already Googled yourself to see what the world would see. If not, you really ought to.

- **Go to the Google Blog page** and see what comes up. You might get some really good (but not necessarily trustworthy) information about a person or organization.

- Take a look at our **Extensive Bibliography** in our book, *Shortcut Your Job Search* and in the Members Only section of our website: www.fiveoclockclub.com.
- **Subscribe to online journals about your field or industry**. You'll get their newsletters with the hot topics of the day.
- And, one of our tried and true favorites: **Join professional or trade associations**. You really do need to get out there and see real people.

There are fundamental differences between training and education. If you are trained you become the employee, if you are educated, you become the employer. If you are trained you have a J.O.B. (if you're "lucky"), if you are educated you have a career. If you are trained you have been taught to memorize, if you are educated you have been taught how to think.

JAWANZA KUNJUFU, *Countering the Conspiracy to Destroy Black Boys*

It isn't possible to win high-level success without meeting opposition, hardship, and setback. But it is possible to use setback to propel you forward.

DR. DAVID SCHWARTZ, *The Magic of Thinking Big*

The
Five
O'Clock
Club®

PART FOUR

Résumés for Making a Career Change

Carol: Moving Toward Her Dream

Carol had been in traditional bank marketing for many years. Now she wanted to think about the next move in her career. She completed all of the assessment exercises in our book *Targeting a Great Career*.

In her Forty-Year Vision, Carol could imagine herself 15 years from now in her own small company representing independent filmmakers and serving as the agent for actors. She imagined 10 people working for her. She also imagined that her business would be international.

This exercise result was a complete surprise to her. However, years ago—before she took a sensible job in banking—Carol had worked in the arts and had even hosted a television show in Japan. In fact, it turned out that all of her friends were in the arts—not in banking. I asked Carol to give this scenario some deep thought before dramatically changing her career.

At work the next week, she was astonished to find that her coworkers were talking about someone they knew who was making an independent film

and needed help. She could not believe her ears; she asked if they thought she might volunteer to help promote the film. To add to the felicity of the situation, the lead actor was an African American—as Carol was. Part of her long-term plan was to change the image of African Americans in films so they are not just cast as being people of color, but are cast in parts that would ordinarily go to whites.

So she volunteered to publicize this independent film, and she accomplished a lot. In fact, the film won an award at the Cannes film festival, which was partly attributed to her efforts.

Carol decided to move her career in the new direction. Perhaps she could get a day job in the entertainment industry that would mesh with what she was now doing at night.

We redid her résumé to highlight her extensive marketing experience in both banking and in the entertainment industry. She is now conducting a search aimed at the entertainment industry, and will move her career in a completely different direction.

Carol Franklin

234 Mercy Douglas Drive
Drysdale, TX 44555

cfranklin555@netscape.net

Home: 555-555-1234
Work: 666-555-2312

International Marketing Executive
in the finance and entertainment industries

- Manage a P&L and the marketing function for $30 million business.
- Publicist for Yours Truly, an independent film. Won award at Cannes.
- Set up regional processing centers in Europe and Asia.
  - Dramatically improved customer service.
- Appeared as a regular host on Japanese television and radio.
- Speak Spanish, Japanese, and French.
- Master's in Business Administration in the Arts.

Possess a combination of business sense and artistic awareness.
Known for meeting the goals at hand.

Howard: Repositioned for a New Industry

Howard had spent his entire working life in banking. Now he needed to look for a job, but banking was retrenching. (In fact, 78 percent of the people who lost their jobs in his bank ended up leaving the banking industry.) Therefore, he decided to target a growth industry—health care. But he hedged his bets by targeting banking as well.

Howard got rid of the banking jargon in his operations background and highlighted those areas that would interest managers in hospitals and other health care claims-processing centers.

In addition, Howard seriously targeted health care by meeting lots of people in the field, joining health-care administration associations, subscrib-ing to health-care trade journals, and networking into lots of hospitals.

The changes in his résumé may seem subtle, but they made all the difference in the world. For example, the term "financial services" is dropped in the headline of the health care summary. The first bullet on the banking summary lists opera-tional areas specific to banking, while the health-care summary emphasizes generalized transaction processing, with no specifics.

To make it simpler, we have included here only the summaries. The body of each résumé stayed the same.

By the way, Howard ended up in an exciting job in health care.

Banking Summary

Financial Services Operations and Control Executive
with a uniquely strong data processing and systems background;
experienced in turnarounds and conversions.

- Managed **every aspect of operations**: check processing, security processing, lockbox, charge card processing, ATM and POS settlement.
- Controlled every major financial services application: deposit accounting, trust accounting, cash management and electronic funds transfer.
- **Turned around failing operations**. Built management teams.
- Managed **large-scale systems conversions and consolidations**.
- Designed management information and **quality improvement systems**.
- **Assessed entire operations** designing new workflow and control processes.

Areas of Expertise

- Transaction processing management
- Workflow analysis
- Starting up operations

- Accounting and control
- Team building
- Planning/Restructuring

- A participative manager who builds consensus.
- As a senior manager, work effectively with top management and boards.
- Experienced and successful in turning around and starting up operations.
- A strong planner, having successfully managed large system conversions/operation consolidations.

Health Care Summary

Operations and Control Executive
with a uniquely strong data processing and systems background;
experienced in turnarounds and conversions.

- Managed numerous **transaction processing** operations, all high volume and computer based.
- **Developed claim tracking systems** and management information systems that cut costs, reduced risk and improved customer service.
- Led major technical conversions, managing both systems analysts and operations personnel, in multimillion dollar computer projects.
- Implemented accounting and control methods that corrected major financial control problems.
- Assessed entire operations, designing new work flows and control processes.
- **Turned around failing operations** by building management teams and eliminating fundamental problems within the operation.

Areas of Expertise

- Transaction processing management
- Workflow analysis
- Starting up operations
- Accounting and control
- Team building
- Planning/Restructuring

- A participative manager who builds consensus.
- As a senior manager, work effectively with top management and boards.
- Experienced and successful in turning around and starting up operations.
- A strong planner, having successfully managed large system conversions/operation consolidations.

The Five O'Clock Club®

Stephen: Moving from Nonprofit to For-Profit

Even if Stephen were not trying to change careers, his is a good case study of how to restate one's accomplishments better and reposition oneself for the future. Like many people, Stephen wrote a résumé that was simply a listing of what he had done in each job, without regard to what he would like to do next.

Following the steps we recommend, Stephen did his Seven Stories Exercise and Forty-Year Vision. He thought he might like to look for work in the for-profit sector, after having spent his working life in not-for-profit. Therefore, we would need to use the jargon of the for-profit world.

When Stephen wrote out his Seven Stories, his top accomplishment was his most recent job. Here is how he related that accomplishment to me:

I turned around a fragmented, demoralized network of 13 volunteer-run chapters, estranged from the national organization, into a vigorous and activist network of 37 chapters. The network that I formed became the driving force for 100 percent growth in national membership over 8 years.

As Stephen spoke, I took notes. He was verbally positioning himself very differently from the way he had positioned himself on his old résumé. The résumé was dull, whereas the story he was telling me now was alive and dramatic. We needed to capture that drama on paper so people would understand what he really did: He turned around an organization. To dramatize the accomplishment, we showed the situation he was presented with and the result he achieved. The accomplishment statement is centered, bolded, and italicized so it pops out:

Took an organization that consisted of 13 dispirited and disorganized chapters and made it into a vibrant, profitable 37-chapter organization.

On his new résumé, this sentence is the central statement in the rewrite of that job. Take a look at the rest of that job, and see how it is presented in the "before" and "after" versions.

Since his most recent job was the biggest accomplishment he had, we wanted to highlight it more than anything else on his résumé. We also made sure that the top of page 2 started with an important accomplishment. When the reader turns the page, that is the first thing he or she sees.

In working on his summary, Stephen decided that he most enjoyed starting up, growing, and turning around organizations, so we made that the key subpoint in his summary statement. To make him marketable in the for-profit market, we can't use the term Associate Director. Instead, we called him a general manager, which was a job title he had held previously in a very small organization. He thought that that title would work for both the for-profit and the not-for-profit sectors.

The first bullet in the summary tells the reader more about the general manager role he played in his most recent position: He was part of a three-person team that controlled the budget for this organization. Note that, as much as possible, we use numbers in his summary so the reader can quickly see what he has done.

Because Stephen comes across in person as very relaxed, we needed to let the reader know that, in his own way, he gets a lot done. So the italicized portion at the bottom of the summary tells us how he operates despite his laid-back demeanor.

Stephen was doing consulting work to earn money while he continued to look for the right job. Because he had been doing this for a while, he needed to put it on his résumé or it would look as though he had been doing nothing since he left his last full-time job. Again, numbers help to stress the importance of the work he did. For example, simply saying that he wrote a newsletter would not be as impressive as saying that he wrote a newsletter for the CEOs of 1,000 United Way agencies to help them improve the use of technology in their organizations. Although all of this work was for nonprofits, we stated it to appeal to for-profits.

STEPHEN CROWN

33 West South Street
Central City, Utah 99025
444-555-9814 (h)
444-555-1990, ext 234 (w)
E-mail: stcrown@aol.com

EMPLOYMENT
2006-Present

American Institute of Design Engineers
Associate Director, Membership and Chapters

The AIDE was founded in 1918 and is the major engineering design membership organization in the U.S., with 9,000 members and an operating budget of $2,300,000.

Developed and managed a nationwide network of 37 incorporated, volunteer-run chapters, with an annual budget of $160,000. Organized the creation of 24 new chapters since 2006, including incorporation, board formation, by-laws, tax-exemption, fund-raising and committee and program development. Developed orientation and other support materials, including a management handbook, for chapter board members and volunteers. Acted as ombudsman between chapters and the national organization. Provided on-site consultation to chapters on management, planning and program development.

Responsible for long-term membership growth, from 4,500 to 9,000 since 2006, and a membership budget which grew from $600,000 in 2006 to 51,400,000 in 2014. Managed production of recruitment materials; direct mail campaigns; database installation and maintenance; and delivery of membership benefits. Wrote and produced quarterly membership newsletter.

Introduced and organized annual three-day retreats for 150 chapter leaders and national board members. Originally created to provide technical assistance to chapter leaders, the retreats evolved into the major forum for broad-based discussions of national issues and examination of the future direction of the organization.

Involved in all aspects of national conferences, including site selection, marketing, and production of events for up to 1,500.

Member of three-person management team, with staff of fifteen, responsible for all aspects of organizational development and direction, including long-range planning, strategy, and policy. Personally supervised staff of three.

(Example continues)

2001-2006	**Affiliate Artists, Inc.** Associate Director, Residency Operations Ran national multidiscipline performing artists residency program, involving major corporate sponsors, local arts institutions, and emerging artists. Also managed $100,000 statewide program serving local arts councils, funded by the State Council on the Arts. Created and developed showcase programs in the state and elsewhere. Responsibilities included artist selection and training for residency work; selection and preparation of local presenting organizations; grant writing; and reports to granting agencies.
1998-2000	**Orchestra and Chorus of St. Louis, St. Louis, MO General Manager** Founding manager of small professional orchestra and chorus with $100,000 budget and eight-concert season, specializing in rarely performed music, presented at the St. Louis Art Museum.
1997-1998	**Repertory Theatre of St. Louis and Opera Theatre of St. Louis, St. Louis, MO** House Manager
1992-1997	**International House, Paris and Rome** Teacher of English as a second language
EDUCATION 1990	**St. Andrew's University, Scotland** BA, French and German

STEPHEN CROWN

33 West South Street
Center City, Utah 99025

444-555-9763
E-mail: stcrown@aol.com

General Manager
**specializing in high-growth, start-up and turnaround situations
in cause-related or cultural service organizations**

- Part of three-person management team controlling a **budget of $2.3 million**.
  - Doubled membership from 4,500 to 9,000.
  - Grew membership income from $600,000 to $1.4 million.
  - **Created 24 incorporated chapters**.
  - Served as in-house consultant to all 37 locations.
- **Founder and general manager** of a professional orchestra and chorus in St. Louis.
- Cultivated **strong contacts with corporations** such as Mobil Oil, GE, Alcoa, Westinghouse

Conceive the vision. Develop the plan. Implement all details.
Coordinate diverse constituencies. Motivate and lead all levels to operate toward the organization's goals.

Consultant   Dec. 2014-Present
- Alliance for the Development of Salt Lake City
  - Conducting market/**feasibility study for a 6,000 sq. ft. center** for arts organizations.
- Nonprofit Technology Today, Inc.
  - Writing **newsletter for CEO's** of 1,000 United Way agencies. **Improves use of technology**.
- Other clients include: Center for Mediation and Law, Foundation for the Arts.

American Institute of Design Engineers   2006-Dec. 2014
Associate Director

*Took an organization that consisted of 13 dispirited and disorganized chapters
and made it into a vibrant, profitable 37-chapter organization.*

- Part of three-person management team, with a staff of fifteen, responsible for all aspects of organizational development and direction, including **long-range planning, strategy, and policy**.
- **Increased membership from 4,500 to 9,000**
  - and membership **income increased from $600,000 to $1,400,000**.
  - Implemented infrastructure for a nationwide network of 37 incorporated chapters.
- Created 24 new chapters, including incorporation, board formation, by-laws, tax-exemption, fund-raising, and committee and program development. Conceived of **national conference approach where all could attend**, regardless of distance.
  - Became a "town meeting" and highlight of the year for 1800 attendees.

Stephen Crown - Page 2

Associate Director, *contd.*

- Supported/directed chapter management.
  - **Introduced systematic training** including board and volunteer training.
  - Wrote and produced orientation and other support materials for chapter board members and volunteers. This included a **130-page management handbook**.
  - Conceived and organized annual three-day orientation and planning meetings for 150 chapter leaders and national board members.
  - Provided **on-site consultation** to chapters on management, planning, and program development.
- Acted as ombudsman between chapters and the national organization.
- Managed production of recruitment materials and direct-mail campaigns.
- Supervised database installation and maintenance, membership processing, and delivery of membership benefits.
- Wrote and produced quarterly membership newsletter.

Affiliate Artists, Inc.   2001-2006
Associate Director, Residency Operations

- **Ran national multidiscipline performing artists residency program**, involving major corporate sponsors, local arts institutions, and performing artists.
- **Managed statewide program** serving local arts councils, funded by the State Council on the Arts.
- Created and developed showcase programs in the state and elsewhere.
- Responsible for artist selection and training for residency work, selection and preparation of local presenting organizations, grant writing, and reports to granting agencies.

Orchestra and Chorus of St. Louis, St. Louis, MO   1998-2000
General Manager
- **Founding manager of professional orchestra and chorus** with eight-concert season. Specialized in rarely performed music. Presented at the St. Louis Art Museum.

Repertory Theatre of St. Louis   1997-1998
Opera Theatre of St. Louis, St. Louis, MO
House manager, responsible for all front-of-house activities.

EDUCATION
BA, French and German, St Andrew's University, Scotland, 1990

MEMBER
American Society of Association Executives
Technical Assistance Providers Network

The Five O'Clock Club

Alana: Making a Major Career Change

By Laura Labovich, Certified Five O'Clock Club Career Coach

You miss 100% of the shots you don't take.
WAYNE GRETZKY

What lies behind us and what lies before us are tiny matters compared to what lies within us.
RALPH WALDO EMERSON

Alana was a superstar in sales, but wanted to transfer into a Human Resources generalist role. While her HR experience was, understandably, limited, we needed to create a résumé that positioned her for that type of role; a "sales" résumé would not suffice. In order to do this, we relied heavily on the examples she uncovered from her Seven Stories Exercise, and placed them throughout her résumé as "proof" that she can do what she says she can do (HR). For example, it was clear from her Seven Stories that she really enjoyed training and conducting performance reviews, so we gave both of these stories a bigger role in her résumé. The training example, for instance, is highlighted at the very top of the résumé, so a hiring manager will not have to survey the entire résumé to get a snapshot of her HR-related experience.

In addition, we reviewed the details of several job descriptions that she felt were a good fit for her, and we peppered key words of the industry throughout her résumé: performance appraisal, new hire, training, etc. That would be crucial in getting interviews for one of these HR jobs. Because she had spent a good part of her career in retail and in sales, in a line leader role, we wanted to make it obvious why that's important: a keen understanding of bottom-line results. As a cost-center, HR must have a strong understanding of return-on-investment (ROI), so by positioning her as an expert in the hiring manager function, as someone who has, in essence, run her own business, she was able to share how that was important to HR decision-makers.

In pulling it together, we had to keep some elements of sales and retail in her résumé because it was so prevalent in her history, but we highlighted in those jobs the relevant HR duties and responsibilities she held. Thus, it was clear immediately what value she offers a prospective employer, in the role of an HR professional. By placing the title she's targeting right at the very top, big and bold, it's easy for a manager to see what she's looking for.

Alana Fritz

22158 Mayfair Court
Ashburn, VA 20147
703-221-3958

OBJECTIVE

To utilize my extensive management experience and hospitality training to obtain a management position

SUMMARY OF QUALIFICATIONS

- Accomplished manager with over 7 years of experience.
- Strong interpersonal skills; proven ability to work well with individuals at all levels.
- Dedicated individual; achieving a reputation for consistently going beyond what is required.

PROFESSIONAL ACCOMPLISHMENTS

Management

- Oversaw four store openings. Responsibilities included coordinating advertising, hiring, training, and exceeding new store sales quotas.
- Started as a store manager and was promoted to a Training Store Manager and finally a District Manager in Training.
- Supervised a staff of 20 in my store while being responsible for the training of all new management in the district.

Customer-Service

- Demonstrated excellent knowledge of the local area helping our hotel rank 13th (in the company) in GSS.
- Work well under pressure in fast-paced environments.

WORK HISTORY

2007-present	Company X, Chantilly, VA	Guest Representative
2002-2005	Company Y, Fredericksburg, VA	Customer Service Assoc.
1996-1998	Company R, Woodbridge, VA	Department Manager
1995-present	Fritz Family	Full-time Mom
1992-1996	Company T, Northern VA	District Manager in Training
1991-1992	Company U, Clinton, MD	Soft-lines Manager

EDUCATION

Bachelor of Business Administration, University of Michigan, Ann Arbor, MI 1991

ALANA FRITZ

22158 Mayfair Court | Ashburn, Virginia | 20147 | (703) 221 3958 | alanafritz223@aol.com

HUMAN RESOURCES: ADMINISTRATOR • GENERALIST • TRAINER
Industry Specialization: Hospitality • Retail • Consulting

- Creative and compassionate client service professional with <u>**10+ years' experience leading people and driving momentum of processes and initiatives in the hospitality and retail industries**</u>.

- Demonstrate passion for serving the customer, both internal and external, by understanding unique business and personal issues and offering a better solution.

- Diligent and focused--tackle tough problems and follow them through to a satisfactory conclusion.

- <u>**Respected as the calm and stable "anchor of reality" in crisis situations**</u>; possess consistent ability to develop team and turnaround poor performers.

- Dedicated, client-focused, professional with career hallmarked by ability to consistently go beyond what is required and expected to get exceptional results.

SELECT CONTRIBUTIONS

- <u>**Implemented an effective training program successfully arming associates for store opening**</u> (Company X).

- Bring valuable line leader experience to HR role and <u>**can rapidly and naturally connect programs to the bottom-line**</u>; rapidly promoted through the ranks for commitment to operational excellence, customer service and thorough understanding of retail as entertainment…<u>**oversaw four retail store openings; coordinated advertising, hiring and training efforts while exceeding new store sales quotas**</u> (Company Y).

CAREER RELATED COMPETENCIES

Employee Benefits and New Hire Orientation • Talent Acquisition • People Management • Performance Reviews
Client and Employee Issue Resolution and Escalation Process Management

CAREER TRACK & CONTRIBUTIONS

COMPANY X—Chantilly, Virginia   2006-present
Company X Hotels & Resorts are the most trusted name in hotels; renowned for its "commitment to people" quality, and genuine care.

Concierge (promoted from Guest Representative). Supervise concierge services for elite guests (Silver 10+ nights, Gold 50+ nights, and Platinum 75+ nights)…expert in local attractions and the overall area…deliver high-touch customer service to elite clients.

- Gather, summarize and provide information to guests about property and surrounding area amenities, including special events and activities. Answer, record and process all guest calls, messages, requests, questions, or concerns…contact appropriate individual or department as necessary to resolve guest call, request or problem.

Contributions

- Awarded Associate of the Month (12/2008) in recognition of increasing guest satisfaction survey (GSS) numbers for categories of Guest Experience upon Arrival and Elite Recognition. Nominated for company-wide award (2012) for "stellar service."

COMPANY Y—Westborough, Massachusetts   1998 - 2002
Leader in wholesale distribution of plumbing and heating supplies to the wholesaler; holds 5 patents and employs 14 full time employees.

Sales/Account Representative. Developed business in new territories…increased sales by 25% year over year…created and implemented marketing plans and managed an ongoing customer base of 15-20 accounts.
Contributions

- Catapulted existing account revenue 65% through local account growth and implementation of marketing and sales initiatives.

COMPANY T—Fredericksburg, Maryland
Founded in 1946, Company T operates more than 1,300 women's apparel specialty stores in 31 states.

District Manager (promoted from Store Manager and then to Training Store Manager)
Oversaw four store openings…led human resources function including sourcing, recruitment, interviewing and selection efforts; and new hire benefits training and ongoing training efforts.
Contributions

- Developed, **implemented, and rolled out various HR new hire policies** and procedures in accordance with federal, state and local laws, increasing productivity 25% and creating finely-tuned orientation process.
- Ensured highest performance of team members, and **enacted an employee performance review** and rewards system incorporating self-assessments and succession planning.

FORMAL EDUCATION

Bachelor of Business Administration, George Washington University - 1991

The Five O'Clock Club

J. E. Bean: Cashing in on Volunteer Work

J. E. was lucky: When she lost her job as a bank accounting clerk, she received generous severance pay and an education grant. She used her time and money wisely. She went to school to study medical billing and then volunteered full-time in a hospital as a medical biller. Although she was not paid, work is work, and she knew it was the experience that counted.

With six months of volunteer experience under her belt, J. E. launched a search for a full-time paid position. The important things she wanted to say about herself were described in her current volunteer position, so she didn't need an elaborate summary. The rule of thumb is this: If you do not have a summary, you are positioned by your most recent position.

In her summary, she simply listed the most important things she wanted her readers to know: her medical billing as well as her accounting background. She also included a few statements that describe her personality—the way she approaches her job. Then the reader knows not only that she accomplishes a lot but also *how* she does it.

Because J. E. is already in the field that interests her—and because she wants more of the same—she has a relatively simple story and can tell it in a relatively small amount of space.

J. E. Bean
1346 Commonwealth Avenue
Dobbs Ferry, New York 99999
(999) 555-6544
jebean489@prodigy.net

Medical Biller
with strong background in accounting and proof control
A hard working team player with a perfect attendance record

Holly Oak Medical Center   2014-Present
Medical Billing
- Currently a volunteer in the OB/GYN
- Accurately enter patients 'demographics into the Medical Manager System, as well as post payments and make changes when necessary.
- Verify patients' insurance eligibility.
- Abstract information from patient files for reimbursement.
- Code CPT procedures as well as diagnosis ICD'9 CM.
- Abstract demo information from ADT system for billing purposes.

Citibank
<u>Senior Accounting Clerk</u>   2003-2013
- Handled basic accounting functions. A/P, A/R, billing.
- Performed 2-way proof of debits and credits.
- Performed "back-value" calculations on mutual funds and private banking.
- Conducted heavy research.
- In securities area, worked with PaineWebber, Salomon, and other broker-dealers.
- Handled securities deliveries, fed wires and government securities, etc.
- Reconciled daily department transactions.
- Computer skills include: Windows, Word, Excel, Lotus Notes.
- An exceptional team player with great communication skills. Supported fellow co workers.

Bankers Trust
<u>Foreign Exchange Department, Claims Processing</u>   2002-2003

Ralston-Purina 1995-2000
<u>Inventory Clerk</u>
Handled billing and collections of all incoming and outgoing merchandise and quarterly inventory.

EDUCATION

<u>Springhurst College</u>, 2014
Currently studying advanced medical billing

<u>American Institute for Career Learning</u>, 2013
Certificate in Medical Billing

<u>International Career Institute</u>
Merit courses in Recordkeeping, Office Practice and Procedures, and Computer Literacy

Paul: He *Thought* He Was Making a Career Change

Think of it like Camus's Sisyphus—he keeps pushing the rock up that hill, pushing and pushing and pushing. It never ends. But the thing you must realize is, Sisyphus is happy.

Roman Polanski, filmmaker, quoted by Robert
Goldberg in The Wall Street Journal

You get moving very quickly and you end up in the wrong place.

Marshall McLuhan, quoted by Pico Iyer,
The New Business Class

Paul had worked in the not-for-profit world his entire life, and he was now 62! He was the head of the direct-marketing arm of a major not-for-profit. (As with all of our résumés, the real name of his former employer is not used in the sample résumé). He felt that he was undervalued and suspected that he was about to be squeezed out. He wanted to go into the for-profit world.

To learn more about this target area, his coach and group at the club suggested he read trade journals, join direct-marketing trade associations, and get to know people in the field. Paul learned so much in his intensive research that he went a few steps further: He *spoke* at the association meetings, began writing for trade journals, and even appeared on the cover of a prestigious trade magazine.

When he first developed his résumé, Paul thought of himself as a not-for-profit specialist. But his best recourse now—whether he wanted to stay in nonprofit or move into for-profit—was to emphasize what he had done in bottom-line business terms. After all, nonprofits today are run like businesses.

Paul de-emphasized the name of his former employer and even replaced his official title (which did not work well outside his present organization). He played up the actual work he had done and made it much more bottom-line oriented.

The biggest mind-set change for Paul was to stop presenting himself as a career changer trying to make a *break* into a different realm. The more he stressed *transition*, the more prospective employers saw it as a problem. Paul tried a new approach: He had learned so much he was able to come across as an insider. When prospective employers mentioned that all of his experience had been in the not-for-profit world, he feigned surprise. He emphasized that his presentations were primarily to those in the for-profit sector and emphasized how those in both the for-profit and nonprofit worlds were following his lead.

The weakest approach is to *say* that you are trying to break into a field. The strongest approach is to show that you have already *been* in that field and simply want to get another job in that same field.

127

PAUL A. DORFMAN

777 Riverside Drive
Oswego, CA 99999

padorfman321@yahoo.com

Business: (555) 555-2594
Home: (555) 555-4736

Industry-Recognized Direct Marketing Executive
with extensive database systems experience

Currently managing programs raising over <u>$25 million annually</u>

- <u>Reversed a declining catalog mail-order business</u>, increasing revenue 12% in the first year and 30% in three years.
- Improved profitability of a $15 million direct-mail program after a five-year decline.
- In one of the most dramatic direct-mail successes in many years, developed computer software and database support for an increase in presidential-year revenue from $2.5 to $12.5 million.
- Recently interviewed by *Time Magazine on Air* and quoted in *Time* magazine. Also featured in *Direct Marketing News* and *U.S. News and World Report*, all both online and in print.

National Public Radio
DIRECT MARKETING DIVISION HEAD
2012-Present

- <u>Created a new direct marketing department</u>. Changed direct response agencies. Improved acquisition effectiveness more than 50% and increased retention.
- Initiated acquisition investment models, subsequent value analyses, and retention benchmarks.
- Increased revenue by improved segmentation and targeted mailings.
- Selected to direct an $11 million product marketing business including catalog mail order, retail, and volunteer consignment.

VICE PRESIDENT, SYSTEMS & OPERATIONS
2004-2012

- Directed a $3.6 million catalog mail-order business, <u>**increasing revenue to $6.5 million in 3 years**</u>.
- In three months, turned around a troubled computer facility, and installed database software saving $250,000 annually.
- Built a stable and effective systems & operations department (35 staff) supporting an increase in direct-mail revenue from $4.3 million to $14 million in seven years.
- Negotiated corporate grants from Digital Equipment Corporation to purchase over $1 million in computer equipment for half the retail price.
- Appointed acting Chief Financial Officer.

REPUBLICAN NATIONAL COMMITTEE
Director, Management Information Systems
2000-2004

- Prepared business plans and developed computer database support to increase direct-mail revenue fivefold.
- Initiated, planned, and implemented a new direct-marketing computer center, reducing automation costs by $30,000 per month.
- Invited by IBM to address their President's Assembly on the effective use of IBM systems.

Paul A. Dorfman - Page 2

LIBRARY OF CONGRESS

Chief, Copyright Planning and Technical Office   1992-2000

- Planned and directed the complete automation of the U.S. Copyright Office of 600 staff including implementing widespread organizational and workflow changes.
- Reduced the time to process routine copyright claims from six the three weeks, while improving service.
- Appointed Acting Executive Officer.
- Received award for Outstanding Performance.

Previous Assignments

- In a single year, planned and implemented an online automated retrieval system to track the status of all legislation introduced in the **U.S. Congress**.
- Directed management information and business systems consulting, first in Amsterdam and then in London for Auerbach Associates, Inc.
- Managed programming and software development projects for IBM's Federal Systems Division.

EDUCATION

- Harvard Graduate School of Business, Executive Education Program
- Princeton University, B A. Mathematics

PROFESSIONAL RECOGNITION

Invited to speak at numerous Direct Marketing conferences in the U.S. and Europe:
  Direct Marketing Association:
        Annual Catalog Conference (Chicago, June 2012)
        Annual Conference (Dallas, October 2012)
        Non-Profit Conference (Washington, DC, January 2013)

National Public Radio:
  Direct Marketing Fundraising Seminars (2011-2013)
  Paris, London, Madrid, and Geneva

PROFESSIONAL ASSOCIATIONS

- Direct Marketing Association:
    Board Member, Nonprofit Council Operating Committee
    Computer/Information Technology Council
- International Society for Information Management (SIM):
    Board of Directors and Executive Committee
    Past Chairman, Greater New York Chapter

PART FIVE

Résumés for Executives

Donald: Repositioned into a New Industry

*In making our work a gift to the world, in making it
an expression of our love for life, for God, and for our
fellow man, we fulfill our highest potential, our most
beautiful destiny as human beings.*

MICHAEL LYNBERG, *The Path with Heart*

---

*Summing up her career in her autobiography, she said:
"My attitude had never changed. I cannot imagine
feeling lackadaisical about a performance. I treat
each encounter as a matter of life and death. The one
important thing I have learned over the years is the
difference between taking one's work seriously and
taking one's self seriously. The first is imperative and
the second disastrous."*

DAME MARGOT FONTEYN, OBITUARY IN
The New York Times

> **This résumé has served as one of the
> most popular examples for executives at
> The Five O'Clock Club.**

Donald had become known as a guru in
the record business, a relatively small industry.
The chances of finding another position in that
industry were slim, and even if they had not been,
Donald was ready for a change. He had worked
many years, expected to work many more, and
so wanted to reposition himself as someone who
could work in different kinds of businesses.
Therefore, his résumé *does not mention the industry in which he worked.* In addition, he got rid of
all industry jargon, including the names of the

celebrities with whom he had worked. Except for
the company names themselves, which he cannot
change, a reader cannot tell that his experience
was actually narrowly focused.

Before Donald went on interviews, he studied
in depth the industries of the people he approached—he came across as an insider. He was
extremely knowledgeable in his conversations
with senior management. He sounded so authori-
tative that it never became an issue that Donald
had not worked in those industries.

The following résumé is on three pages. It has
served as one of the most popular examples at The
Five O'Clock Club, and hundreds of clients have
used this format for their own résumés. The entire
front page of this résumé is a summary so that the
reader cannot possibly see the specialty companies
Donald worked for (on pages 2 and 3). Instead, it
presents him as a marketing executive who can
work for virtually any company.

On the other hand, if Donald had wanted
to present himself as a specialist in the record
industry, he would have placed that specialty in
the headline of his summary. It's as easy as that.

By the way, Donald ended up with three
concurrent offers—none in the record industry.
He did an excellent job of developing his Targeting Map (see our book *Shortcut Your Job Search*),
and he contacted every company on his target
list. He always had 6 to 10 things in the works,
kept his spirits up, and served as a role model for
other clients. He had private counseling sessions
in addition to the group and landed the right job
within 10 weeks.

Donald Garafalos

334 Lexington Blvd.
Mansfield, TX 00997

555.789.5448 (day)
garafalosxx@aol.com

Global Strategic Marketing Executive
with extensive Management Consulting experience

*Global expert in domestic / international business services,
marketing strategies, and performance improvement.
Grow businesses in emerging markets. Focused on top management strategy-related issues.*

Strategy Development   **Market Assessment**   **Organizational Effectiveness**

Brought cutting-edge technology solutions in strategy analysis to a $6 billion company:
- Assessed **38 offices around the world**. Defined **strategic business plan** for company worldwide, including Europe, Southeast Asia, Latin America. Recommended informed solutions.
- **Maintained growth**. Created value. Used networked-based "industry information clearinghouses."
- Developed a uniform and creative global approach for marketing issues and information technology critical to the **long-term competitiveness** of this industry.
- Contributed to moving the company **from #5 to #2** in its sector within 3 years.

Member of 5-person steering committee reporting directly to chairman:
- Oversaw **global implementation** of company priorities. **Traveled extensively** to all markets. Monitored progress, reviewed targets, and reported back to the board on a **quarterly basis**.
- Supplemented **strong growth in North America** by even stronger results in **Europe** and truly exceptional performance in **Southeast Asia and Latin America**.

Took a product that did not sell internationally and moved sales from 150,000 units to 5 million within 18 months.
- Motivated **hundreds of marketing executives** around the world.
- Helped company executives understand **electronic commerce** and the effect on the industry.
- Worked with TV networks, local governments. Developed brand into **household name**.

Managed budgets of $10 million plus; staff of 20:
- Created and staffed highly successful marketing and sales divisions at **major companies**.
- Quickly built **trust and credibility** with business associates.
- **Resolved issues** based on cultural differences.

*Resourceful problem solver, quickly identifying problems.
Recommend timely and effective solutions.*

Donald Garafalos - page 2

Business Management Inc.   2012 till present

Increasing worldwide sales through targeted marketing.

- Implement marketing strategies market by market, maximizing product sales in major countries.
- Build licensing teams around the world.
- Create distribution networks and seek opportunities in emerging markets.
- Monitor marketing activities at local level, acting quickly on resolving issues.

Maintain highly productive working relationships and provide a creative platform that enables our business associates to be a driving force in the global arena. Help shape our clients' global impact as well achieve long term profitability.

Bertlesman North America   2009-2012
Vice President Global Strategy and Communications, West Coast

Established company's division as a global leader in its field, making that division the most profitable business of the group, with $10 million in annual international income.

- Directed company's marketing team in 64 countries, achieving 40% sales increase.
- Traveled around the world leading priority projects.
- Oversaw multimillion-dollar advertising budget.
- Member of company's executive committee, advising board on strategic international-related issues.

General Electric USA   2007-2009
Vice-President International, Amazon Records Group

Created the company's international marketing division: now the #1 profit center for the Group, generating over $50 million in annual foreign income.

- Hired staff including senior sales positions; conducted sales and marketing training.
- Designed and implemented priority system and marketing planning procedures to optimize margins, market share, growth, and volume and reduce operating costs.
- Created marketing strategies, understanding the needs and nuances of all cultures, producing extraordinary sales, capturing the full international potential.
- Managed advertising, promotion and sales initiatives, securing great deals.
- Introduced product development techniques, increasing sales through targeted marketing and producing brand identification for new lines.
- Introduced international artist development techniques, increasing sales through targeted marketing, producing brand identification for new products and recorded goods.
- Consolidated reports including sales figures, competition performance, and market share data for the chairman, covering over 100 projects on a monthly basis.
- Demonstrated great fiscal responsibility while evaluating marketing budgets.

Donald Garafalos - page 3

CBS / WORLDWIDE   2002-2007
Vice President, International, CBS Records Group, 2005-2007

*Delivered 120% international sales increase and established CBS-USA as
a major player around the world. Guided marketing, sales, and promotion in 46 offices.*

- Created and delivered high-impact sales presentations motivating extraordinary performance by creative teams around the world. Produced 20-minute infomercials and electronic press kits.
- Guided quarterly strategy meetings on site in Europe, Asia, and Latin America to focus on company-wide priority issues.
- Designed and implemented an International Product Release System that is marketing-driven and creatively led, facilitating local manufacturing, streamlining operations, and promoting corporate communications. This system enables a simultaneous global release schedule and prevents costly import of records by the local companies.
- Improved profitability by reducing departmental costs and monitoring marketing expenses.
- Represented the chairman effectively at international corporate events and conventions. Conducted acquisitions and identified viable business opportunities.

Director, International Marketing and Communications, CBS Worldwide   2002-2005
- Headed marketing and sales for the territories outside of North America and Europe.
- Increased Southeast Asia regional sales from 15% to 25% in one fiscal year.
- Directed international marketing efforts for North American properties, supervised staff of 10, including the London office that was in charge of European marketing.

Columbia Records   Paris and New York   1993-2002
Manager, International Promotion, Columbia Records

- Handled all media communications for Columbia-US clients. Organized all global media events for the corporate affairs department.

International Label Manager, Columbia/Chrysalis France Paris

- Approved and scheduled all international releases originating from UK/US. Supervised marketing department for local products.

EDUCATION

Fluent in French and Spanish
UCLA—Legal course in Business Affairs (2007)
The EFAP school of Marketing and Public Relations (Paris, 1987)
Lycée Bergson, graduate (Paris, 1988)

Louis: Making the Jump from a Technical Role to Executive Management

By Peter Hill, Certified Five O'Clock Club Career Coach

The brick walls are there for a reason. The brick walls are not there to keep us out. The brick walls are there to show us how badly we want something.

RANDY PAUSCH'S BOOK AND LECTURE, *The Last Lecture*

There are two ways to live: you can live as if nothing is a miracle; you can live as if everything is a miracle.

ALBERT EINSTEIN

Louis was a mid-level construction project engineer who was decidedly not just a technical professional. He saw himself as leader of people and teams who happened to be a project engineer. He wanted to market the transferable skills that would help take his career to the next level, in a new industry, where he could eventually be accountable for regional operations, profitability, and strategic activities for a multi-national corporation.

What Was His Situation?

Louis was a career changer. He had worked for 18 years in construction project engineering for a huge French multi-national company. Holding French citizenship himself and living in Vietnam, he operated on the global stage wherever his company happened to send him. His role on paper was very technical and he was highly rated by the company for leading and working on multiple projects across Southeast Asia and Europe: bridges, earthworks, viaducts, an Olympic sta-

dium, and a nuclear power plant. Because he did his job so well, he felt his career advancement within the company was very limited. His company viewed him as technical leader, and Louise saw himself as extremely under-utilized.

Louis wanted to try something different from construction by moving away from engineering and into a more general management role. He decided to target growing companies in manufacturing, defense, aeronautics / aerospace, renewable energies, or oil and gas. His strategy was to get in as a project manager, but eventually advance to a higher management position (Managing Director) where he would be earning 120-150k Euro + bonuses. His target geographies were Asia, US, Australia.

The Challenge

His old résumé positioned him as technical project engineer, his old role, but didn't reflect the skills that qualified him for the new role to which he aspired: a business leader who leads people, creates and develops effective teams, manages business risks, and maximizes profitability. Specifically, Louis needed to position himself as having a track record of systematically improving the financial outcome of all projects in which he has been involved. He is very well organized, has a taste for perfection, and focuses on the human aspects of the work rather than just the technical aspects (like so many engineers). Lastly, Louis is passionate about environmentally friendly business practices and sustainability. He wanted his résumé to reflect this so that it would appeal to companies that held the same values.

What We Did

The summary section of the résumé is now written in a way that positions Louis as a management executive who operates on the international stage. The scope of his work is clearly laid out in the sub-headline explicitly stating that he drives meaningful business results for "Multi-Million Euro Projects in France, The UK, Turkey, China, Hong Kong, & Malaysia." By including specific country names, we add color to the story Louis is trying to tell.

The summary section highlights his business skill (new target!) not technical skills (what Louis used to do). Also, notice that the word "Engineering" only appears once in the summary when mentioning his education. A powerfully targeted quote from a credible source further positions Louis as an international business leader, rather than just a project engineer.

The employment section of the résumé is called "Management Experience & Results." Here we took his very technical background and positioned it as having meaningful business impact, which of course it did! When mining for relevant accomplishments, Louis was asked to create CAR stories (Challenge/Action/Result) then link the outcomes of each story to business results rather than technical accomplishments.

The content that is bolded and underlined showcases his business acumen and capabilities. This draws the reader's attention away from the technical aspects and gives a stronger impression that Louis understands and drives business results.

The Community Activities section further solidifies his positioning as a people person and a thought-leader.

Results

Louis is being very well-received. He has been actively using his new résumé in discussions with recruiters in France and Australia. It is also posted on Blue Steps, where he has also received very good feedback.

His résumé has generated interest from several companies, which have led to three very serious offers:

- One with a French firm based in Kuala Lumpur, which, after two months of interviews and negotiations, has finally offered him a local package. He declined the offer because the package was too local (too low!)
- One with a French firm based in Bangkok that first said that his level/salary was within the range of what they were willing to pay, but finally said that they were looking for somebody younger/ cheaper.
- A major Korean technology company (he was approached through a NYC head hunter).

Adapting the Approach

Louis also adapted this résumé writing strategy for his LinkedIn profile. Soon after doing so, he was contacted by four different recruiters (3 Russians and 1 Italian) for the exact same job position, a management role in St. Petersberg, Russia.

Louis Moreau

10, rue Jacques Prevert - 56890 Saint Ave - France

tel/fax: +33 5 55 55 45 42 (parents) - cellular: +60.55 555 1234 (Malaysia) - email: louis@moreau.name

Highly motivated and goal oriented Project Manager with an extensive experience on large-scale international construction projects. Has applied successfully modern management techniques to complex and time-constraining projects in order to deliver the works to the satisfaction of the clients, while generating substantial cost savings. Excellent team leader, well organised and down to earth with a passion for excellence. Excels in using his personal skills to inspire and energise others. Now seeking a new and challenging opportunity to further apply these skills within another industry sector.

Frazzier International; Hanoi, Vietnam   **Feb 2006 to date**
Project Manager
[Frazzier, a leader in concessions, construction and related services; 1,000 business units and 100,000 employees; €12,000 millions turnover].

- Responsible for the replacement of all the stay cables of the existing 12km long Paifing Bridge while keeping the traffic (95,000 vehicles per day) un-interrupted, including 41 staff and 120 labours
- Established relationships of trust with the Authorities, the Client, the local partners and all other parties in the aim of running that very challenging project in a spirit of collaboration for the benefit of all.
- Organised the engineering and construction activities to the highest level of safety and quality, keeping non-conformities and accidents to a minimum level.
- Implemented a rigorous risk management policy in order to systematically eliminate intangible cost factors.
- Successfully implemented a Six Sigma scheme that allowed to save 63 working days.
- Introduced innovative environment measures that resulted in reducing the project carbon footprint by half.
- Significantly improved the profit margin of the project by administrating it in a systematic and rigorous manner.

Frazzier International; Hanoi, Vietnam   **Nov 2004 to Jan 2006**
Project Manager

- Responsible for the construction of a 2.7km cable stay bridge, including 28 staff and 116 labours.
- Organised the contractual and financial negotiations for extension of time and compensation for loss and expenses while preparing for arbitration with the Client.
- Successfully re-programmed the project's activities, reduced the cycle times and the completion date.
- Re-structured the purchasing, the accounting and the cost control resulting in a substantial cost reduction.

Vincent-McDonald, Channel Tunnel Rail Link, London, UK   **Dec 2001 to Oct 2004**
Section Manager

- Responsible for the administration of two of the five sections of works (Earthworks and Viaducts) for the construction of the new high-speed rail link (Eurostar) in East London. Head of a team of 37 staff (including 24 engineers and quantity surveyors) and 144 labour, for a budget of £45 million.
- In charge of co-ordinating the works, managing technical issues and resources, preparing work programmes, implementing the company's policies in terms of Safety, Quality, Environment and risk management, supervising budgets and cost control, preparing progress reports.
- Successfully merged two sections of works, recovered the delay and reduced the staff.

- Successfully reduced costs by £4.5 million by using recycled materials, implementing a scientific method for the treatment of contaminated land and by improving the productivity through the Six Sigma method.
- Subsequently received two environmental awards (the CTRL Sustainability Award and the UK Green Apple award).
- Restructured the process of hand over to the Client by creating a computer database that saved considerable time on compilation of documents.

Ankara Stadium Constructors JV, Ankara, Turkey　　　　　　　　　**Jan 1998 to Nov 2001**
Deputy Construction Manager
Construction of an 80,000 seats Olympic Stadium, Istanbul, Turkey

LOUIS MOREAU

88, rue Jacques Premier
54322 Main Street, Paris, France

■ ■ ■

Vietnam Tel: +84 12 555 9876
Email: louis@moreau.name

INTERNATIONAL MANAGEMENT EXECUTIVE
18 Years Experience Securing Profitability & Enhancing Corporate Image
for Multi-Million Euro Projects in France, The UK, Turkey, China, Hong Kong, & Malaysia

- Drive **profitability** and **substantial cost savings** for large, highly complex projects valued up to €72 million by…
  - efficiently **organising teams**,
  - systematically **managing physical and financial risk**,
  - innovatively **adapting modern management techniques,** and
  - consistently **meeting deadlines**.

- Help establish an **environmentally friendly company image**.
  - Results known to boost financial performance and marketability.

- Have successfully **built and led teams** of up to 150 people.
  - A collaborative leader who shares successes and credit.
  - Have a **passion for excellence**.

- Foster **solid relationships with all stakeholders**—corporate senior man-agement, staff, labourers, sub-contractors, government agencies, clients.

- Degreed in **Civil Engineering**. Trained and experienced in Six Sigma.
  - Member of Association of Project Management.

- **Multi-lingual:** fluent in French, English, Spanish; knowledge of Turkish.

> "Louis is a highly motivated, down-to-earth, culturally sensitive project manager, a creative and contemporary thinker. His has a unique combination of skills, leadership abilities and positive application of the latest management best practices. He effectively manages challenging projects and multicultural teams repetitively delivering cost effective results."
>
> – Jim Smith, Independent Risk Consultant for XYZ Bridge cable-stay replacement project.

A CHAMPION OF SUSTAINABILITY

Build, train, and lead teams to execute more environmentally friendly practices.
Also work on the social side of sustainability by improving social benefits
of employees and engaging companies in charitable initiatives.

MANAGEMENT EXPERIENCE & RESULTS
18-year tenure within various companies and joint-venture projects of XYZ GROUP,
a global leader in concessions, construction, and related services.
1,350 business units; 99,000 employees; €15 billion turnover.

PROJECT MANAGER, Frazzier International JV—Hanoi, Vietnam   2006 – Present

Built and currently leading a **team of 41 staff** and **120 labourers** for this **€32 million project** that is **highly unpredict-able** in terms of productivity, completion date, and profitability. Comprised the replacement of all stay cables of the existing 8 km-long Hanoi Bridge, while maintaining 24-hour/day bi-directional flow of 135,000 vehicles per day. **A global first in innovation** for both technical and human challenges.

- **Doubled the profit margin** by thoroughly managing risk during stage 1. Improved project deliverables by applying Six Sigma techniques—saved 63 days.
- Ensured **smooth execution** and **on-time completion**.
- Achieved a **50% reduction of the carbon footprint** by introducing novel environmental measures.

- Created a robust risk management policy that eliminated intangible cost factors.
- Established trusted relationships with local authorities, the client, and local partners.
- Solidified an image of the company with government departments as "a contractor that can be trusted."
- **Set up a team to research and develop** a vital piece of machinery for the project.
  - Used Six Sigma to optimise the machine's performance.
  - Resulted in **significant reduction of risk**.

PROJECT MANAGER, Frazzier International—Hanoi, Vietnam   2004 – 2006

Directed a **€9.5 million project** for the construction of the 2.7 km-long Pan Metro cable-stay bridge. Led **28 staff** and **116 labourers.** Project was delayed 3 years due to poor performance of a third party—selected as the 5th project manager to attempt to finish the assignment.

- **Completed the project** and secured **profitability despite delays** and non-payment from the client.
  - Met quality targets while managing a tenuous contractual situation.
- Restructured purchasing, accounting, and cost controls. **Substantially reduced costs.**
- Organised contractual and financial negotiations for the extension of time and compensation for loss and expenses while preparing for arbitration with the client.
- **Reduced cycle times and completion date** by re-programming project activities.

STATION MANAGER, Vincent-McDonald, Channel Tunnel Rail Link—London, UK   2001 – 2004

Programmed and coordinated **€60.3 million worth of environmentally sensitive projects**—two of five sections (earthworks and viaducts) for the construction of the new high-speed Eurostar rail link in East London. Led **37 staff**—including 24 engineers and quantity surveyors—and **144 labourers**. Established safety, quality, environmental, risk management, and cost control policies.

- Despite having no experience in the technical area:
  - **Saved €5 million** by using Six Sigma methodology to boost productivity.
  - Ensured on-time completion to the satisfaction of the client.
  - Spearheaded a **recycled materials programme**.
  - Company received the Controlled Sustainability Award and the UK Green Apple Award.
- Recovered a lengthy delay—merged programming of two sections into one.
- Used Six Sigma methodology to **boost efficiency** of lorries and excavators **by 50%.**
- Designed a land contamination map which **saved €1.1 million** in logistics costs.
- Secured a reputation as the **most efficient and proud team** on the project.
  - Eventually integrated another section of works (bridges) under the same leadership.
- Restructured the client handover process by creating a computer database that saved considerable time on the compilation of documents.

DEPUTY MANAGER, Ankara Stadium Constructors JV—Ankara, Turkey   1998 – 2001

Set up the main project management tools and systems for the Turkish construction manager of an 80,000-seat Olympic-standard stadium—included quality assurance, document control, method of works, selection of sub-contractors, budget and cost control, and KPI's. **€145 million project.**

- **Saved €1.4 million**—changed the design of external works.
- Became a key link between the French and Turkish groups (staff of 200+) by using a friendly, optimistic style and learning to speak Turkish.
- Developed a technical document and mail management database that was adapted by the parent company to be **used at sites company wide**.

LOUIS MOREAU

PROJECT ENGINEER, The Hillson Group—head office in Paris, France　　　　3/19

Coordinated a gas power plant project **in Guangzhou, China**. Partnered with the American group Willet Energy. **Spearheaded problem solving** and the smoothing out of contractual issues.

SITE ENGINEER, Hillson-Franklin JV—Hong Kong　　　　1994 – 1997

Fully accountable for a team of **5 senior staff** and **70 labourers** for the construction of concrete piers for the Central Kowloon viaduct. Also served as Assistant to the Construction Manager for the preparation of works programming, equipment ordering, cost controls, and KPI's. **€62 million project**.
- Achieved targets by **establishing strategic business relationships** with the other sections of works and the sub-contractors—included planning, budgeting, and contractual issues.
- Put a **late section of the project back on schedule** and **completed within budget** when selected to take over and restructure the section. Saved 3 months.

CONSTRUCTION ENGINEER, HCCM JV—South Hangzhou Bay, China　　　　1992 – 1994

Managed sub-contractors for the finishing stages of a nuclear power plant. Organised large-scale safety tests that facilitated the handover to local authorities. **Trained the Chinese maintenance contractor**.

COMMUNITY ACTIVITIES

Author/Speaker, *Enhancing Project Team Roles and Responsibilities in Project Cost Management*
Pan-Asia Construction Cost Control and Management Conference 2009—Singapore
Founder, *Paddle for Hope* dragon boat rowing relay charity event in 2009—Hanoi, Vietnam
Member, Management Committee of the Alliance Francaise (a tuition and arts centre)—Hanoi, Vietnam
Board Member, Rotary Club—Hanoi, Vietnam
Founder, *Umit 2000* earthquake charity project ("Umit" means "hope" in Turkish). Managed a
volunteer team to raise €138,000, and design, build, and equip a health clinic at the epicentre.

EDUCATION & TRAINING

BSc, Civil Engineering and Town Planning, 1992
National Institute of Applied Sciences (INSA)—Paris, France
Baccalaureate (General Certificate of Education), 1986
Lycee A-R Lesage—Vannes, France
- Six Sigma Performance Based Leadership (Yellow Belt)
- Planning & Management Course　　　　• Mind Mapping Brainstorming Course

---

PERSONAL

- **Birthdate:** 8th March 1964　　　　• **Nationality:** French

Tom: What Did He Really Do?

Tom Warren's old résumé is pretty standard: He states the jobs he's had and what he did in each one. It's the same old historical approach.

The problem is that his résumé leaves out all of the important parts. For his new résumé, we simply added four parts: the all-important summary and three introductory paragraphs that state what Tom *really* did in each job. (For the purposes of this example, we have reproduced only the first page of Tom's two-page résumé.)

For example, in the last job on the page of the old résumé, he states that he managed eight Manhattan branches. We had already completed his Seven Stories Exercise, so I knew there was more to his personality than this implied. Here is how our discussion went:

Kate: "Tom, do you want to manage bank branches?"

Tom: "Not a chance. I hate branch management."

Kate: "But this résumé positions you, among other things, as a branch manager."

Tom: "That's what I did in that job."

Kate (I try to provoke him): "But to me this sounds so boring. What did you really do in that job? What is it you brag to your wife that you did?"

Tom: "Kate, you don't understand. That job was important. I turned around the largest problem-ridden branch business in the company."

Kate: "Oh, excuse me, Tom. How could I have known? I don't see that on your résumé. Let's put it on there. Now, what kinds of things would you like to do next?"

Tom: "I want to build major businesses or turn around problem brands."

Kate: "Have you done those things before?"

Tom: "Yes, I definitely have."

Kate: "Then let's put that in your summary. It will dramatically increase your chances of getting to do those things again. "

That's what you have to do, too. For most people, the problem is not that they stretch the truth on their résumés; the problem is that they unwittingly fail to tell the truth: They don't say what they *really* did.

Figuring this out is much more difficult than simply reciting your job description. That's why it's important to do the Seven Stories Exercise (which you will find in the front of this book and in our book *Targeting a Great Career*). It helps you step back from a résumé frame of mind so you can concentrate on the most important accomplishments of your life. Then the exercise helps you to think about each accomplishment: what led up to it, what your role was, what gave you satisfaction, what your motivation was, and so on.

We added those parts to Tom's résumé and left the rest alone. In fact, the parts we added are the only parts that really matter, so those are highlighted and the rest becomes the background.

Now Tom has a good sales piece—one that truly reflects what he did.

This new résumé is a *strategic document*. It *looks ahead, not back*. It thinks about what he would like to do next and then finds those experiences in his background that support what he wants to do. In addition, it highlights those areas that were the most satisfying. Now he has increased his chances of finding a new job where he repeats or builds on those satisfying experiences.

THOMAS WARREN

2343 Fifth Avenue   thomas.warren@aol.com   Home: 212-333-4444
New York, New York 11000   Business: 212-555-1111

PREMIERBANK   2002-Present
International Institutions Group   2011-Present

Director of Electronic Banking
Responsible for support and development of all interbank payment and information systems.

- Developed and market tested a new off-line funds transfer product.

- Upgraded and repositioned existing worldwide online payment system.

- Created line-wide repricing plan to maximize target customer penetration.
Developed strategy to integrate payment, information, and securities products.

New York Retail Bank   2009-2010
Director, Special Marketing Group

Responsible for growth and profitability of the New York bank's $13 billion consumer portfolio. Managed new product development, pricing, and sales promotion.

- Developed, positioned, and introduced the PremierBank Investment Portfolio, PremierBank's first mass-market integrated investment product. Created new portfolio-selling concept to incorporate it into the branch sales process.

- Established more efficient PremierBank core-account promotion tactics.

- Developed new investment savings product.

- Created unique research method to guide new product development.

Senior Area Director, Financial District   2004-2009

Managed eight Manhattan branches with $31 million net revenue and $1.2 billion total footings. Responsible for total branch performance, including sales, service, control, revenue, and expenses.

- Put new management team in place in three key branches.

- Reversed balance declines by revitalizing business-account marketing.

- Established distribution strategy and plan for World Trade Center marketplace, including customer and business offsites.

- Developed a high-net-worth tailored credit program for area with $2 million-$3 million annual revenue potential.

- Initiated regional staffing efficiency analysis, which significantly improved branch productivity.

THOMAS WARREN

2343 Fifth Avenue
New York, New York 11000

thomas.warren@aol.com

Home: 212-333-4444
Business: 212-555-1111

Innovative financial services marketer
with 10 years at PremierBank and heavy package-goods product-management experience.

- Created new products, such as a new off-line funds-transfer.
- Built major businesses, such as a $13-billion portfolio.
- Turned around problem brands, such as the turnaround of a major branch system.
- Strong strategic thinker and team builder.

Areas of Expertise

- Product Management
- New Product Development
- Sales Management

- Electronic Banking
- Branch Banking
- Market Analysis

PREMIERBANK
International Institutions Group
Director of Electronic Banking

2002-Present
2011-Present

Created a multiyear business plan to **restore PremierBank's leadership** in interbank electronic payments through the worldwide rollout of superior off-line payment products.

Responsible for support and development of all interbank payment and information systems.
- Developed and market tested a new off-line funds-transfer product.
- Upgraded and repositioned existing worldwide online payment system.
- Developed strategy to integrate payment, information, and securities products.

New York Retail Bank
Director, Special Marketing Group

2009-2010

Created the New York Retail Bank's **first effective way to package and sell its diverse investment product line**.

Responsible for growth and profitability of the New York bank's $13-billion consumer portfolio. Managed new product development, pricing, and sales promotion.
- Developed, positioned, and introduced the PremierBank Investment Portfolio, PremierBank's first mass-market integrated investment product. Created new portfolio selling concept to incorporate it into the branch sales process.
- Established more efficient PremierBank core-account promotion tactics.
- Developed new investment-savings product.
- Created unique research method to guide new product development.

Senior Area Director, Financial District

2004-2009

Reorganized and redirected a large, problem-ridden branch business to restore balance and revenue growth.

Managed eight Manhattan branches with $31 million net revenue and $1.2 billion total footings. Responsible for total branch performance including sales, service, control, revenue, and expenses.

The
Five
O'Clock
Club

David: Handled His Fear of Discrimination

No spring nor summer beauty hath such grace,
As I have seen in one autumnal face.

JOHN DONNE, *The Autumnal*

At thirty, man suspects himself a fool;
Knows it at forty, and reforms his plan.

EDWARD YOUNG

If man is to vanish from the earth, let him vanish in
the moment of creation, when he is creating something
new, opening a path to the tomorrow he may never see.
It is man's nature to reach out, to grasp for the tangible
on the way to the intangible.

LOUIS L'AMOUR, *The Lonesome Gods*

(The secret of how) to live without resentment or em-
barrassment in a world in which I was different from
everyone else... was to be indifferent to that difference.

AL CAPP, "MY WELL-BALANCED LIFE ON A WOODEN
LEG," *Life*, MAY 23, 1960

As long as you keep a person down, some part of you
has to be down there to hold him down, so it means
you cannot soar as you otherwise might.

MARIAN ANDERSON, WHO SANG AT THE
LINCOLN MEMORIAL IN 1939

David was worried that he would have difficulty finding a new position because he was an
older man and lacked formal schooling. Yet, using

the following résumé, he received four excellent
offers within a very short time.

In creating the résumé, we concentrated on
the assets; his strengths—properly stated—
allowed us to position him effectively.

David has steadily advanced in his career. To
those within his industry, every line on his résumé is impressive. In his summary, David notes
how he is different from others in his field.

The résumé is compact and clear — eliminating
any accomplishment that would be considered routine.

No one even noticed that David had not gone
to college. What's more, no one could have accomplished what David had without having been around
a few years. His age actually became an advantage.

Don't Be So Sure Your "Weakness" Is Showing

Most job hunters have something that they
think will keep them from getting their next
job. It could be that they feel they are too young
or too old, have too little education or too
much, are of the wrong race, creed, nationality,
sex, sexual orientation, weight, or height, or are
very aware that they have a physical disability.

While it is true that there is prejudice out
there, job hunters who are too self-conscious
about their perceived handicaps will hold themselves back.

In addition, they may inadvertently draw attention to their *problem* during the interview. Your attitude must be: "What problem? There is no problem.
Let me tell you about the things I've done."

DAVID WALTERS

942 Cherry Hill Road   david.walters@msn.com   Business: 222-555-3907
Los Angeles, CA 99125   Home: 222-555-1074

Treasury Executive
with over 20 years of international as well as domestic experience.

- Possess a clear understanding of the basic interrelationship of all aspects of the financial markets.
- At the forefront of simple, innovative solutions that are easily acceptable to others and later adopted at large.
- Record of generating new customer business.
- Lived and worked in many countries. Proficient in a number of languages.
- Strong turnaround and people-management skills.

AMBANK, N.A.   1979-Present

Individual Bank   2009-Present
Vice President/Regional Treasurer
Middle East/Africa & Greece - Dubai
Established and controlled Treasury Units for the Individual Bank in Greece, Saudi Arabia, Oman, Bahrain, and the U.A.E. to manage the risks of a portfolio totaling $3,200 billion.

- Set up Treasury function in 3 countries. Earned $2 million in 2009 ($1 million above budget).
- Developed a unique funding strategy that overcame local regulatory restrictions and reduced Ambank (Greece) borrowing costs by 5%.
- Developed a hedging strategy in highly restricted market. Avoided losses in excess of $1 million.
- Analyzed and identified the liquidity and interest-rate risks inherent in the business and developed and implemented a strategic plan to manage the risk.
- More than doubled foreign-exchange business in one year.

Investment Bank   2008-2009
Vice President/Treasurer - Panama
Created and managed a team of 7 professionals to control funding and liquidity of $350 million, managed foreign exchange, and observed regulatory constraints.

- Reorganized the treasury to address foreign-exchange needs. Expanded the marketing function.
- Increased corporate FX business tenfold in 14 months. Expanded FX into Central American currencies (Ambank became a "Market Maker" in Central American currencies).
- Installed an independent system to record Ambank's liquidity position in order to implement effective funding and reduce risk.
- Structured and implemented one of the first third-party debt deals in Central America. Reduced El Salvador's debt at substantial savings. Ambank's first-year fee exceeded $100 million.

DAVID WALTERS - Page 2

Institutional Bank   2004-2008
Vice President/Training Center Administration Manager, Puerto Rico

Brought in to design and teach courses to develop Treasury in Latin America. Managed a team who coordinated all training-center courses.

- Developed treasury courses for all management levels. Consistently received high ratings.
- Managed a team of 4 administrators. Quickly turned a department in disarray with no budget controls into a smooth-running operation.
- Negotiated to reduce hotel costs 50%. Negotiated the construction of a classroom to Ambank specifications (which the hotel named the "Ambankgarden Room").
- Consulted with local management in Honduras and the Dominican Republic on new products and treasury services.
-

Vice President/Division Treasurer, Venezuela   2003-2004

Controlled the Treasury function in 4 countries (Venezuela, Aruba, Ecuador, and Colombia). Assisted local management in developing and implementing a treasury strategy.

- To grow customer business, obtained permission from government authorities to engage in fiduciary business. This represents at least $2 million annual earnings and is a major source of income.

Vice President/Cash and Currency Consultant, Hong Kong   2000-2001

Created and managed the cash- and currency-consulting function in Asia, which was used by multinational customers as well as within Ambank.

- Consulted with approximately 50 multinational companies.
- **Created 4 major new products which were successfully used in 8 countries**.

International Money Market, New York   prior to 2000
Corporate Systems Advisory Unit Head

Managed a team of 5 consultants and 2 administrators to design Foreign Exchange Exposure reports and perform international cash-management studies for multinational companies.

- Created AMBANKDATA/AMBANKRATE, a currency database which 15 years later is being actively used by corporate clients as well as in-house.
- Completed 10 Cash Management Studies.

HOECHST ETECO, S.A., Ecuador   1987-1989
Managed the Chemical and Dyestuff Department, supervising 2 salesmen. Tripled sales in 15 months.

LANGUAGES
Fluent in Spanish and German. Familiar with Portuguese and Dutch.

OTHER ACTIVITIES
Regularly lecture on currency management and cash management issues,
including two appearances at Sloan School/MIT.

Martin: Is a One-Page Résumé Better?

The Five O'Clock Club®

Who would not say that it is the essence of folly to do
lazily and rebelliously what has to be done...?

SENECA

Many people think a one-page résumé is better because they think it is more likely to get read. But the average résumé is looked at for only 10 seconds—*regardless of length*. The question is: What does the reader see in those 10 seconds?

Martin's résumé proves that a short résumé is not necessarily better. His résumé was not presenting him the way he wanted to be presented. A lot of information forced into one unreadable page does not advance his cause. Besides, it is the typical historical résumé—focusing on the past. It states each job and describes what he did in each.

Martin had been searching for six months by the time I met him, but he had not managed to get any meetings with people at a level higher than his. He earned in excess of $200,000 and would be on payroll for another full year (lucky him), but he was very discouraged.

Take a look at Martin's old résumé. It is written in dense paragraphs with narrow margins and a small font. No one will read it! Yet he had taken such pains to get it all onto one page—because conventional wisdom has held that one-page résumés get *read*.

Not only is it unreadable, the eye cannot scan it. Remember: The reader has to get your message in only 10 seconds. At the very least, the accomplishments should be bulleted to make them readable, and that alone will generally make the résumé longer than one page.

The old résumé has a summary, but it, too, is historical. For example, the second bullet brags that Martin moved a data-processing facility from New York to New Jersey. The reader will probably think: "We don't need to have a data processing center moved." It's not a selling point to the majority of his readers—so let's not mention it.

What is Martin's *real* message here? It's that he saved the company $1 million—so that's what we mention on the new résumé. We highlight those things the reader might be interested in, which Martin would like to do again. For example, he wanted to be positioned as a key member of the senior management team. This kind of thinking resulted in a strategic résumé.

Carefully study Martin's résumé—before and after. Compare the old summary to the new one and the write-up of each old job to the new write-up. It should give you a better feel for how you want to position yourself on *your* new résumé.

"Before" Résumé

MARTIN G. BUDIANSKY

6 Cucumber Lane	Dorrisville, NJ 07000	(201) 555-6878

PROFILE

Senior Information Systems executive with significant record of accomplishments and experience in multiple industries, both domestic and international. An unbroken record of increasing responsibilities marked by measurable achievements in support of business growth and profitability objectives. Unique ability to successfully integrate and consolidate business functions into the mainstream organization. A successful leader and motivator of people who possesses the practical judgment to function successfully in centralized and decentralized business cultures. A consistent contributor to the attainment of business goals and maximizing operating efficiencies.

- Consolidated into a single order-processing, customer-service operation 4 distinct businesses totaling $270 million in sales; this yielded a net annual savings of $1.4 million and enabled the business units to achieve additional synergies.
- Saved $1 million annually by relocating an entire data-processing organization from New York to New Jersey. Additional savings followed by the relocation of all support operations. This was accomplished without sacrifice to operating efficiency.
- Created and implemented international financial reporting system for 72 worldwide locations. Provided real-time delivery of financial data; continuous cash-flow monitoring, ongoing assessment of profitability, and consolidation of all data to generate financial statements.

CAREER SUMMARY

Senior Vice President, MIS   HARCOURT & SIMON, INC.   2009-Present
Organize and direct a Management Information Systems group with a $16.5 million operating budget; responsible for 135 employees. Establish policies and strategic direction; manage development of application systems, operation of the corporate center and all telecommunications. Responsible for data processing activities at 23 remote locations; consolidated 11 of these into the central location. Personally developed strategic and tactical plans for integration and consolidation of all newly acquired businesses. Consolidated all systems for payroll, general ledger, accounts payable, inventory accounting, and accounts receivable into centralized applications. Reduced the number of Central Processing Units at the corporate center from four to one.

Group Director, MIS   ESTÉE LAUDER INC   2003-2009
Developed MIS strategies and budgets for seven domestic and seven international companies in the Health Care Division, while overseeing the fulfillment of those plans at 29 domestic and international data-processing centers. Initiated and developed worldwide financial reporting system. Represented division on corporate steering committee.

Director, Information Systems and Services   ROHRER INC.   1996-2003
Directed all systems development, computer operations and telecommunications at the corporate center and three division data-processing centers. Promoted to Director in 1990 after managing the activities of a six-day 24-hour computer operation. Established procedures for introduction of new application and system software. Reorganized departments to improve service and reduce the required number of personnel.

Systems Manager/Analyst NJ   BELL TELEPHONE COMPANY   1982-1996
Various interdepartmental assignments with heavy exposure to data processing and business systems development. Progressed from sales trainee to Manager, Business Systems.

EDUCATION

B.S. in Economics	Villanova University	1982
Advanced Studies (Executive Programs)	Duke University	1989
	Dartmouth College	2001

Martin G. Budiansky

6 Cucumber Lane
Dorrisville, N.J. 07000

201-555-6878
mgbud76@aol.com

Senior Information Systems Executive

- Manufacturing
- Health Services
- Telecommunications
- Pharmaceuticals
- Consumer Goods
- Publishing

Key member of management team. Report directly to the COO or CEO.
Managed technological needs <u>for companies ranging from $250 million to over $1 billion</u>.

Rapidly Integrate/Consolidate Acquisitions/Businesses

- Consolidated the technologies and systems of <u>**over $1 billion in acquisitions**</u>.
- Consolidated **4 distinct businesses** totaling **$270 million** in sales into a single operation.
  - Net annual **savings of $1.4 million**.
  - Completely integrated within 8 months.
    - Enabled the business units to achieve significant additional savings.
- <u>**Saved $1 million annually on $5 million**</u> data processing budget—with no sacrifice to operating efficiency.
- Developed **composite information base**.
  - Helped management see company as a logical, manageable organization and find other market opportunities that fit in.
  - Company avoided the problems so often associated with multiple acquisitions.
- Created **international financial reporting** system for **73 locations worldwide**.
  - Real-time delivery of financial data.
  - Ongoing assessment of profitability.
  - Continuous cash-flow monitoring.
  - Consolidation of financial statements.

Key Member of Senior Management Team

- Use technology to **support and implement the strategic plans of the company**.
- Developed 3-year strategic plan. Presented to corporate Board of Directors.
- Sensitive to profitability and enhancement of investment.

Develop Systems That Support Today's Business Environment

- Telecommunications network for **32 locations; 1,400 terminals** online to mainframe.
- Quickly develop/introduce new systems: use the latest methodologies and techniques.
- Developed security and contingency back-up plans that **assure continuous operation**.

A business manager and key member of the management team.
Use technology to achieve the strategic and profit plan of the organization
to allow companies to achieve a greater participation in their marketplace.

Strong hands-on, project-oriented business manager, strategic planner, and leader.
Successful in centralized and decentralized business cultures.
Manage and control major development projects.

SENIOR VICE PRESIDENT, MIS
HARCOURT & SIMON, INC.   2009-Present

<u>Staff of 135</u>. $16.5 million operating budget.

- As key member of senior management team
    - set policies and direction to **implement overall strategic goals of company**.
    - personally developed strategic and tactical plans for integration and **consolidation of all 39 newly acquired businesses.**
- **Developed methodology to quickly consolidate all companies** for payroll, general ledger, accounts payable, inventory accounting & accounts receivable into centralized applications.
    - **All went smoothly. No adverse impact** on any of the companies involved.
    - **Company saved $35 million.**
- Manage application development, computer operations, and all telecommunications.
- Also responsible for data processing at 23 remote locations. Consolidated 11 centrally.
    - For **quick development and introduction of new systems.**
    - **Helps company stay competitive and on top of a dynamically growing organization.**
- Closed 3 data-processing centers with no adverse impact.
    - **Saved company $1 million annually on $5 million** data-processing budget.
- **Developed management personnel** so they operated effectively and independently.

GROUP DIRECTOR
ESTÉE LAUDER, INC.   2003-2009

- Managed MIS plans, budgets & activities at **22 domestic and 7 international centers** (230 people).
- **Managed 7 domestic and 7 international companies.**
- Initiated and developed **worldwide financial reporting system**.

DIRECTOR, INFORMATION SYSTEMS AND SERVICES
ROHRER, INC.   1996-2003

Directed all systems development, computer operations and telecommunications at the **corporate center and 3 division data-processing centers.**

- Established procedures for "problem-free" introduction of new application and system software.
- Improved service and reduced the required number of personnel.

SYSTEMS MANAGER/ANALYST
NJ BELL TELEPHONE COMPANY   1987-1996

Regularly promoted. Progressed from sales trainee to Manager, Business Systems.

EDUCATION
B.S., Economics, Villanova University, 1982
Executive Program, Duke University, 1999
Executive Program, Dartmouth College, 2001

Norman: *Hiding* His Most Recent Job

*How long must I wrestle with my thoughts and every
day have sorrow in my heart?
How long will my enemy triumph over me?
. . . But I trust in your unfailing love; my heart rejoices
in your salvation.
I will sing to the Lord, for he has been good to me.*

PSALM 13, *Old Testament*

---

*Life has got to be lived—that's all there is to it. At 70
I would say the advantage is that you take life more
calmly. You know that "This too shall pass!"*

ELEANOR ROOSEVELT

Yes, Virginia, there is a Santa Claus.

New York Sun EDITORIAL, 1897

Norman called me in distress from California.
He was not proud of his performance in the last
three years and felt that he had failed. He wanted
a résumé that would exclude that time.

We did the entire project over the phone. It
took about six hours total to talk about his situation and background and complete the résumé—
which did *not* hide what he had done during the
past three years.

Most of the people we work with have had
great careers—until just a little while before we
meet them. That's why they are calling us. Things
are negative. They want to move on and are not
sure how to position their present situation.

In Norman's case, my business background
came in handy. He told me what had happened
during the past three years. The way he described
it, it seemed terrible. After taking many notes, I
noticed the positives. Often, ambitious people do
not fulfill the goals they had in mind and thus
consider themselves failures. They discount everything that they have done—even the positives.
Yet, a person has often done something worthwhile, has learned much from a failing situation,
and can market that experience. It simply requires
a different spin.

I said to him, "Norman, here's what it sounds
like to me: You did a great job growing the company, but it ran a bit ahead of your working capital. When you realized this, you hustled around
to find someone to conduct a friendly takeover of
the firm. These people liked and respected you so
well that they wanted to keep you on to run that
company and another company of theirs as well. Is
that right?"

Norman couldn't believe his ears. "Everything
you said is true! But I haven't been looking at it
that way." Later, he said, "For three years, I've been
very depressed. Now I feel like a new person."

Many of you may be in a similar situation. You
are glum. Perhaps it looks as if you have done a
bad job. Maybe you have. But chances are, there is
a good explanation for what happened. If you can
get some distance and look at it with new eyes,
you may be on the road to resolving the predica-
ment you are now in.

Norman's résumé is a good example of many
of the things we preach. First of all, he did the
Seven Stories Exercise so it would become clear

which parts we should highlight. The stories gave a good overview of his career—what he was good at and what he was proud of.

Norman originally wanted two résumés: one he could use in the fashion industry, where he had spent his working life, and another in case he had to look outside the industry, given its present condition. Actually, as so often happens, one résumé served both purposes.

Now let's take a look at Norman's résumé in detail.

Norman's summary positions him as a person who grows profitable businesses. This is in stark contrast to his old résumé, which made him look like a manufacturing expert.

In real life, Norman's résumé is on one piece of paper (17" across X 11" down) folded—so it comes out 8.5" X 11". It's four pages long, but it looks like a booklet. The summary appears on the front. Page 2 appears on the inside left, page 3 on the inside right, and page 4 on the back.

Hiding Three Years

Page 2 contains the years he wanted to hide. If we had had a shorter summary on page 1, part of this time frame would have appeared on page 1, and that would not have been good. Another strategy would have been to cut this part very short.

But I felt Norman had a lot to brag about during those years, and I didn't want to shortchange him. The most important story in his résumé is on page 3. Therefore, page 2 contains a lot of information. It contains so much that the reader's eye tends to skip right across to page 3. The second page was made crowded intentionally.

Highlighting the Main Story

On page 2, the word PRESIDENT is meant to stand out before the reader's eye goes on to page 3. On page 3, the story is that Norman started this company. The main message runs down the center of the page: Took the Company from 0 to $13 million...from Business Start-up...and

Financing...to Business Development...and the running of Day-to-Day Operations. That's the main message.

There are subordinate messages too. For example, under Business Start-up, the subordinate message is "Hired all key sales." This message is underlined because it is so important, yet it does not detract from the main message. There are other subordinate messages. For example, under Financing, "creative financing techniques" is highlighted—but not enough to detract from the main message. Under Business Development, the subordinate message is "7,500 women at the Republican National Convention." And under the last section, the subordinate message is "skilled negotiator."

Full of Inconsistencies

Now take a look at all the job titles and company names. On page 2, the first job has no title at all. That's because the job title there would have detracted from the main message, which is that Norman runs entire companies. The word *president* in the middle of that page is highlighted. At the top of page 2, the company name is underlined and bolded. The company name at the middle of the page, however, is neither underlined nor bolded, to de-emphasize it.

On page 3, the company name is in caps because this company name is prestigious (the real one, that is—this one is fictitious). On the back page, the job title that sticks out most is "president." The other company names or job titles are highlighted as appropriate.

I can assure you that no one asks why a certain title or company name is highlighted. It's obvious why. And it isn't offensive, is it?

Various but Appropriate Formats

There is a further inconsistency in this résumé. It has four pages, and each one is in a *completely different format*. Each page is formatted in a way that is appropriate for the message we are trying to convey on that page. The summary is very different from page 2, which is different from page 3. The back page approaches a more normal résumé format, but there are still inconsistencies in the titles and company names.

We are trying to tell a story. And we use the format that does this best. No one looks at this résumé and notices that there are four different formats.

Our Main Goal: Get the Message Across

Decide what message you are trying to tell. Does your story pop out? Or do you simply record your history and leave it up to the reader to figure out its significance? That's not good enough! It is your job to decide how you want to position yourself and then go to the trouble of doing it.

The result is a résumé that speaks for you and interviews where people tend to ask you about the parts you want to emphasize.

There's no reason to have your present negative situation color the entire rest of your background. The résumé proudly presents your experience so that the reader recognizes your accomplishments and your potential within the marketplace.

Norman S. Neumann

5341 Churchcross Road
Los Angeles, California 90074
213-555-7220
213-555-0876 (cell)
normneumann@yahoo.com

Summary of Qualifications

Senior General Management Executive with over 20 years of P&L and functional management experience. Consistently **grow profitable businesses from 0 to millions in a short time frame**.

Areas of Expertise include:

- Overall Business Management
- Start-up Operations
- Financing
- New Business Development
- Negotiations with Landlords, Labor Unions, and Vendors
- Sales and Marketing Management
- Manufacturing and Operations Management
- Merchandising and Cost Control
- Management/Planning/Restructuring

- A strong **start-up manager**. A troubleshooter and problem solver. Successfully open up new companies. Expert in situations requiring high growth.
- **Attract top-level sales and management teams on a national level**.
- Well-known, respected, and trusted in the industry as a top-of-the-table negotiator.
- **Strong working relationships at all levels in national chain and specialty stores** such as Neiman Marcus, Saks Fifth Avenue, Bergdorf Goodman, Lord & Taylor, I. Magnin & Company, Bullocks Wilshire, Robinsons, and Martha.
- Motivate executives as well as store personnel to back products and **ensure success**.
- **Strong public image**. Inspire a high level of confidence.
- Strong presentation skills: to 7,500 women at the Republican National Convention, formal fashion shows for Saks and Neiman Marcus, and TV talk-show appearances.
- Highly experienced and successful in putting together National Co-op Advertising Programs in publications such as *Harper's, Vogue,,W, Town and Country, and Connoisseur*.
- Senior-level experience in working with **Japanese-owned companies**.

**A business-builder: able to produce high-quality merchandise,
motivate a sales force, and develop long-term relationships
with national chains and specialty stores of the highest quality.**

Outgoing, friendly, intense, ambitious, well-traveled, straightforward "people-person."

Wearmagic, Inc.   2013-present

Manage two divisions: one start-up division and one turnaround of a problem division.

- **Reorganized and redirected a problem business** (R. L. Meyer Division).
  - Restored balance and revenue growth.
  - Now a $4 million business. Projected revenues of $6 million for 2004.

- In November, 2011, **developed and introduced the Koki Selman label**, a high-priced designer line of ladies' suits, costumes, and dresses.
  - Project growth **from 0 to $3 million within first 12 months**.
  - Achieved **national product exposure** for Koki Selman **at a very low cost**. In catalogs such as Bergdorf's, Montaldo's, Talbot's, I. Magnin, and Neiman Marcus.
  - Implemented cooperative advertising programs.
  - **One of the top five showrooms in America.**

PRESIDENT   2011-2013

R. L. Meyer, Inc. (Later acquired by Wearmagic, Inc.)

Joined company in mid-2011, after it had loss for fiscal year just ended of $1.3 million sales. Company had antiquated plant and equipment, no equity, and a work force of 42—primarily workers on Social Security. **Immediately developed and implemented plan to turn around performance**:

- Strengthened financial and operating controls;
- **Negotiated favorable terms with a national factor and a substantially larger banking line of credit**;
- Revamped product line; to control costs, reorganized production operations;
- Increased prices by 30 to 40% to reflect actual costs that had never been analyzed;
- Started a sales force where none previously existed. Established sales organizations in New York, Chicago, and Los Angeles;
- Broadened distribution and **increased sales to $6 million within one year**;
- **Negotiated major labor contract concessions**;
- Attracted large national catalogs and retail operations such as Talbot's, I. Magnin, Neiman Marcus, Saks Fifth Avenue, Bergdorf Goodman, Nordstrom.

As a consequence, sales increased dramatically. To attract the necessary long-term capital to support increased business, took the following actions:

- Initiated discussions with prospective equity partners.
- Took advantage of legal reorganization provisions.
- Developed a workable plan for reorganization and found purchasers for a friendly takeover.

Company became and is now a division of Wearmagic, Inc. Became responsible for:

- the continued growth of R. L. Meyer, and
- the start-up of another, now highly successful, division.

Stockholder/Vice President/Secretary   2003-2011

JORDAN HANES, INC.

<u>**Founded company**</u> with Jordan Hanes, designer. Established an exclusive manufacturing business of fine women's apparel. Collection of day and evening wear retailing from $250 to $1,600.

<u>**Took the Company from 0 to $13 million, giving it**</u>
<u>**a national reputation for quality and leadership.**</u>

<u>**Managed the entire business side of the company from:**</u>

<u>**Business Start-up ...**</u>

- Established company from its inception: Procured leases, all necessary business licenses, Dun's number, and listing with Dun & Bradstreet.
- Organized, contracted, and executed construction of facilities including all project management, and negotiation of budgeting and costing with all manufacturing contractors.
- <u>**Hired all key sales and management personnel. All are still in place today**</u>.

<u>**and Financing ...**</u>

- Built a solid financial reputation on a national and international level.
- Used <u>**creative financing techniques**</u> to obtain favorable financing during start-up as well as during extraordinary growth. Received backing of national commercial factors.
- Secured lease in prime area of L.A. for only one-third of market rate.
- Through financing, increased capitalization by 40%; this increased profits by 10%.

<u>**to Business Development ...**</u>

- Established and maintained a customer base of 803 active accounts including: Neiman Marcus, Saks Fifth Avenue, Bergdorf Goodman, Lord & Taylor, I. Magnin, Bullocks Wilshire, Robinsons.
- Staged 150-200 fashion shows, seminars, and charity events including shows for the finest stores in America, and for <u>**7,500 women at the Republican National Convention**</u>.
- Ran national clinics, fashion shows, and trunk shows.
- Handled all advertising and promotional functions; negotiated and contracted with media/publications.

<u>**and the running of all Day-to-Day Operations.**</u>

- Created, planned, and implemented company fringe-benefit plan. Worked with corporate attorneys and accountants. Obtained government approval of pension and profit-sharing plans and tax-effective benefits for employees as well as executives.
- <u>**A skilled negotiator**</u> with vendors, suppliers, and leasing companies. Obtained the lowest available cost while maintaining quality.
- Installed efficient administrative systems and controls that are still being used today.
- Set up and oversaw an efficient manufacturing production system that ensured quality-control inspection and scheduling.
- Developed all procedure manuals and administrative responsibilities, shipping/receiving, importing, and inventory control.

Key Account Sales Consultant   2000-2003
Young Stuff, Incorporated

- **Starting with a territory of 0, developed sales into $6 million**, which accounted for 1/3 of total company billing.

La Milagros Cordero, **a national sales organization**   1999-2000

- A start-up operation.
- With partner, grew company **from 0 to $20 million**, sales offices in New York and Los Angeles, and 11 salesmen.
- Negotiated exclusive rights to market in the U.S. and Mexico. Upscale, high-quality Spanish merchandise which included the finest-quality leather and suedes.

PRESIDENT   1993-1999
Mr. Chris for Men (high-quality men's clothing and furnishings)

- Company had been heavily in debt. **Within one year:**
  - removed all debt,
  - increased volume 120%
  - and square footage by 100%.

- **Made company highly profitable** with a volume of $4 million and 3 locations.
  - Made company cash-heavy and financially secure.
  - Received backing of national and local factors.
  - Through bank, negotiated substantial and favorable SBA loan for capital improvements.

- **Negotiated lease(s)**:
  - that are still in place today and are producing substantial revenues.
  - with largest shopping center in America.
  - with major motion picture studio's real estate division.

Direct Sales Agent   1989-1993
John Rose California

- Assigned the company's smallest territory.
- **Starting from virtually 0, increased sales to over $3 million**.
- This accounted for **50% of the company's total sales**.

EDUCATION

B.S., Business Administration, The University of Southern California
Graduate, General Studies, The Mercersburg Academy

The
Five
O'Clock
Club®

Janet: Changing Her Job Title; Downplaying Too Many Jobs

We act as though comfort and luxury were the chief requirements of life, when all we need to make us happy is something to be enthusiastic about.

CHARLES KINGSLEY

Janet was tired of telling people that she was more than a lawyer. Her title was Corporate Counsel, but her other responsibilities were more important.

After much probing, we discovered that the ideal next job for Janet would be Chief Financial and Administrative Officer in a medium-sized firm—exactly what she was currently doing. With clients, I sometimes feel like Perry Mason in court. Here is a shortened version of our discussion:

Kate: "Janet, you are having trouble with your job search because you list corporate counsel as your job title, and that is how people see you. You keep trying to convince people that you were actually doing something else. But if you call yourself corporate counsel on your résumé, you are creating a handicap for yourself."

Janet: "That was my title, but if people read my résumé very closely, they will see that I also handled all financial and administrative matters for the company."

Kate: "People won't read your résumé very closely. Your résumé is a marketing piece, not a legal document. Could we truthfully say that you were the chief financial officer for the company?"

Janet: "That wasn't my title."

Kate: "Was there anyone else in the company who could have been called the chief financial officer?"

Janet: "No. I was it."

Kate: "If I had called your company and asked for the chief financial officer, who would I have gotten?"

Janet: "You would have gotten me."

Kate: "Then, in fact, you were the company's chief financial officer?"

Janet: "Yes. But that wasn't my title."

Kate: "Can you see that you are misleading the reader when you call yourself Corporate Counsel when you were in fact the company's Chief Financial Officer? And can you see that **we want to put on your résumé a job title that honestly reflects the actual job you were doing**—rather than some title they happened to give you? And can you also see that you will not get a job as a Chief Financial Officer if you insist on describing your function as Corporate Counsel?"

Janet: "I can see that."

Kate: "Is it true that you were responsible for all administrative matters in the company, such as personnel, computers, and so on?"

Janet: "Yes. That's true."

Kate: "Is it also true that you were the chief financial as well as the chief administrative officer for the firm, in addition to being counsel?"

Janet: "That's true."

Kate: "Would it be inaccurate if we listed your job title as chief financial and administrative officer?"

Janet: "No."

Kate: "**<u>Listing that as your job title would not only be more accurate, but it would also increase your chances of being viewed that way by the reader</u>**. And that would increase your chances of getting another job doing that same thing. So, let's write it up this way and see how you do in your search with this changed positioning."

Janet: "Okay! Let's go for it."

When you do your résumé, think about the kind of job you want next, and then search your background to find things that support the direction you want to take. In Janet's résumé, we played down her legal background, and played up the financial and administrative experiences.

Janet had another problem: she had had a lot of different jobs. You'll notice, at the bottom of page 3, how we list four jobs in such a way that the number is de-emphasized.

By the way, Janet's résumé is on a 17" X 11" sheet folded so page 1 is on the front, pages 2 and 3 are inside, and page 4 is on the back.

> Her accomplishments are one long list (instead of bullets and sub-bullets).
> There seems to be no order. If she has a *message*, it's difficult to find.

JANET H. FUDYMA

2 Grove Street
Philadelphia, PA 19109

jfudyma@att.net

Office: (215) 554-2345
Home: (215) 556-1234

SUMMARY

Senior-level executive with broad-based management background. Experienced in corporate, legal, and financial matters, human resources, strategic planning, and regulatory affairs. Strong emphasis on analyzing and exploiting business opportunities and resolving business problems.

EXPERIENCE

CHICO-LAY U.S.A. INC.   2010-PRESENT

Vice President/Corporate Counsel

Vice President/Corporate Counsel for $80 million affiliate of leading multinational food and beverage products company. Corporate officer with primary responsibility for corporate, legal, financial, treasury, human resources, and quality control/quality assurance matters.

- Member of senior management team responsible for establishing brand cost, pricing, and promotional strategies.
- Innovated promotion authorization structure resulting in more accurate forecasting and customer profitability analysis while reducing improper deductions.
- Restructured benefits program to tailor coverage to specific needs of work force, thereby increasing employee morale while decreasing overall benefits costs.
- Restructured credit and accounts payable departments, dramatically increasing operating efficiencies and resulting in significant cash-flow benefits.
- Established quality control departments and directed implementation of Q.C. processes within production, warehousing, and distribution functions, resulted in decreased scrap and costs associated with improper product handling and rotation.
- Successfully defended numerous advertising claims and challenged those of competitors, allowing company to continue aggressive thrust of products comparisons, while forcing competitors to retreat from focal issues of their campaign.
- Significantly curtailed rapidly growing trend toward illegal imports of company products by instituting landmark lawsuit against gray importers.
- Developed comprehensive emergency product recall procedures designed to ensure rapid and coordinated actions to minimize company losses and maintain consumer brand loyalty.
- Instituted consumer communication program which drastically reduced response time in addressing consumer inquiries, resulting in increased consumer satisfaction and improved relations with customers and brokers.

DAVIS & ASSOCIATES INC.   2008-2010

Vice President and Head of Midwest office of Financial and Management Consulting firm. Engagements included client firms in construction, manufacturing, service, communication, and retail sectors.

- Opened new office in highly competitive environment and successfully established company reputation for quality and professionalism.

JANET FUDYMA

2 Grove Street
Philadelphia, PA 19109

Residence: 215-556-1234
Business: 215-554-2345

SUMMARY OF QUALIFICATIONS

Chief Financial and Chief Administrative Officer
Corporate Counsel

Manage all areas of corporate, financial, and legal matters, strategic planning, regulatory affairs, human resources, and quality control.

Areas of Expertise include:

- **Overall Business Management**
- **Financing**
- **Financial, Business & Production Controls**
- **Management/Planning/Restructuring**

- **Developing Management Personnel**
- **Strategic Planning**
- **Negotiating Skills**
- **New Business Development**

- Served as CFO for **entrepreneurially driven $80 million company**.
- Actively involved in all aspects of running company.
- Provide financial and administrative support to high-growth situations:
  - Expert trouble-shooter and problem solver.
  - Generate operating efficiencies and productivity improvements.
- A **skilled negotiator**: from dealings with vendors and suppliers to complex contracts and legal matters.
- Develop and motivate staff and management team.
- Strong **support to the sales and marketing functions**:
  - With CEO and VP of Operations, established all cost, pricing, and promotional strategies.
  - Set all marketing, advertising, and promotional budgets.
  - Approved all brand and product communication, labeling, copy, and packaging.

A business manager who focuses on profits in growth situations.
Strong strategic vision coupled with overall business sense.
Able to translate strategic vision into workable organizational game plan.

Personable, pragmatic, and analytical.
A straightforward people person conversant in many disciplines.
Brings order out of chaos.

CHIEF FINANCIAL AND ADMINISTRATIVE OFFICER   2010-Present
        CORPORATE COUNSEL
        Chico-Lay USA, Incorporated

Member of Senior management team running this $80 million company.

Corporate officer with primary responsibility for all corporate, financial, and legal matters,
strategic planning, regulatory affairs, human resources, and quality control.
Actively involved in all aspects of running the company.

- Designed and implemented **system for structuring deals**:
  - Analyzed account profitability.
  - Improved sales forecasting.
  - Reduced improper customer deductions.

- Managed **all financial and administrative areas**:
  - Took credit and A/R departments that were in disarray and turned them around.
    - **Dramatically improved cashflow.**
    - Significantly **increased operating efficiencies**.

- Completely **restructured benefits program.**
    - Decreased overall benefit costs.
    - Increased employee morale.

- Established **Quality Control/Quality Assurance** department:
  - **Decreased** manufacturing **costs**.
  - Developed comprehensive **emergency product recall procedures**:
    - To minimize company losses.
    - To maintain consumer brand loyalty.
  - **Managed Consumer Affairs** function:
    - Drastically reduced response time.
    - Improved relations with customers and brokers.

- As **Corporate Counsel**:
  - **Initiated a landmark lawsuit to curtail illegal gray market imports**.
  - **Forced major competitor to retreat** ...
                    ...from overly aggressive trade advertising.

VICE PRESIDENT and HEAD OF CHICAGO OFFICE   2008-2010
Davis & Associates Incorporated (**Financial and Management Consulting Firm**)

Engagements included client firms in construction, manufacturing, service, retail, and communications sectors.

- Opened new office in highly competitive environment.
- Successfully established company reputation for quality and professionalism.
- Arranged and brokered **$40 million in financing and contracts** on behalf of clients.
- Developed **innovative compensation system**.
  - Yielded increased productivity and employee morale.
- Served as **chief spokesperson** for company.
  - Appeared on panels, TV, and radio.
  - Increased company visibility.
- Designed **programs to win new clients**.
  - Developed and delivered series of seminars.
- Resulted in **10% increase in client base**.

KODAK/MGM PICTURES   2006-2008

Manager of Financial Analysis—
for nation's largest videotape duplicator.

- **Troubleshooter for cost overruns and program delays**.
- **Headed** finance department **group responsible for** financial analysis of **special project**.
- Responsible for **capital appropriation studies** and **customer/product profitability analysis**.
- Directed corporate treasury activities.

> Janet had four jobs in a short time, but see how formatting made these four jobs appear as one on her résumé.

Dobbs, Johnson, McLaughlin & Petersen   2004-2005
- **Associate attorney** with law firm specializing in tax-related matters.

Bucks County Health Department   2002-2004
- **Fiscal Officer** with primary responsibility for all financial and budgetary matters.

Burke Enterprises Incorporated   1998-2002
- **Controller** for chain of restaurants and night clubs.

EDUCATION

Kellogg Graduate School of Management, Northwestern University, 2009-2010
J.D., Thomas M. Cooley Law School, 2003
M.B.A. (Management), Central Michigan University, 2000
B.S. (Accounting), Penn State University, 1997

PROFESSIONAL LICENSES

Admitted to Bar:
State of Pennsylvania - February 2004
State of Illinois - December 2004

PROFESSIONAL AFFILIATIONS

Planning Forum
American Bar Association
Pennsylvania State Bar Association
American Corporate Counsel Association

The
Five
O'Clock
Club

Shana: Even Attorneys Use
The Five O'Clock Club Approach

Understanding is a wellspring of life to him that hath it.
PROVERBS 16:22

Shana's résumé has been passed around from attorney to attorney as an example of how to make yourself stand out. Most attorneys think they should use an old-fashioned, standard, boring format—so all attorney résumés tend to look alike. But in today's competitive market, it's important to stand out and differentiate yourself from your competitors. A hiring manager's response should be, "Oh my gosh. Call this person in!"

In this case study, you can see how Shana's cover letter and résumé work together. Although hers is a narrow field, when Shana wrote to 20 executives who had not advertised positions, six of them contacted *her* immediately for an exploratory meeting.

Shana L. Kingsley

883 Ledger Lane, Minneapolis, MN 88888
(555) 555-2268
skingsley@msn.com
July 19, 201x

Mr. Theobold J. Yegerlehner
Vice President, Tax
United Telecom Corporation
United Telecom Building
Minneapolis, MN 88801

Dear Mr. Yegerlehner,

Could United Telecom benefit from a hands-on tax director and counsel with international expertise and the ability to drive strategic initiatives?

I have designed and implemented tax strategies for businesses in the U.S. and more than 35 other countries.

I know how to work with operations, finance, and legal people to deliver tailored solutions that get results. I have managed cross-functional teams in North America, Europe, Latin America, and Asia-Pacific in complex projects, including:

- Executing a **$4 billion U.S. recapitalization**.
- Refinancing global operations to **extract cash from overseas** without crippling operations or paying significant taxes.
- Implementing a global trading company to streamline production, increase sales, and
- **reduce the global effective tax rate by 50%**.
- Reconfiguring a global sales organization to isolate and manage an estimated **$100 million foreign tax exposure**.

I am very interested in meeting with you. I believe you will find even a brief meeting beneficial. I will call your office in the next few days to see when I can get on your calendar.

Sincerely,

Shana E. Kingsley

883 Ledger Lane, Minneapolis, MN 88888
(555) 555-2268
skingsley@msn.com

SENIOR TAX DIRECTOR AND COUNSEL

Specializing in delivery of value-driven global tax strategies.

Tax expertise includes

- Business Tax Planning
- Joint Ventures/Strategic Alliances
- Legislative Action/Negotiation
- Transfer Pricing
- Reorganizations/Restructurings
- Acquisitions/Dispositions
- Financing/Capital Structuring
- Audit Defense

<u>Tax planning executive</u> with proven success in reducing cash taxes and effective tax rates, assessing and managing risk. Industry experience includes consumer and household products, food and beverage, heavy equipment, and financial services.

<u>International tax expert</u>, experienced in both U.S. and foreign country tax strategies.

- Tax planning and transactional experience in 35 countries, including U.S., Canada, Mexico, Brazil, Western Europe, China, India, Japan, Korea, and Australia.
- Cross-border financings, repatriations, and restructurings.
- Chair of International Tax Committee, Tax Executives Institute, Minneapolis Chapter.

<u>Strategic team leader</u>, adept at managing cross-functional projects, including:

- Tax and treasury execution of $1.5 billion business disposition.
- Tax, treasury, and legal delivery of $4 billion U.S. recapitalization.
- Finance, legal, and operations implementation of global trading company.
- Tax and legal design of pan-European financial services organization.

<u>Experienced in building and managing new organizations</u>:

- Built Tax Legal function to structure transactions for newly public company.
- Served on Management Team charged with growing financial services unit.
- Co-founded new office of top-tier international law firm.

Personable, energetic, pragmatic, and analytical.
Driven achiever with exceptional communication and presentation skills.
A straightforward people person and "can-do" problem solver.

VICE-PRESIDENT, INTERNATIONAL TAXES, AND SENIOR TAX COUNSEL   2011-2013

- FERNGIST, World's largest premium drinks business; $16 billion in sales. U.K.-based; publicly traded on NYSE and London Stock Exchange.

Member of Global Strategic Tax Team charged with optimizing capital structure.

- Executed **$4 billion U.S. recapitalization to eliminate $275 million cash tax liability**.
  - Led tax and legal team through development of strategy and transaction structure.
  - Guided implementation and documentation by global transaction team in U.K., Ireland, Netherlands, and U.S.
- Led global tax and treasury in **$1.5 billion disposition of Wendy's Corporation**.
  - Overcame suspicion and distrust between Seller and Target to create collaborative and reliable deal team.
  - Unwound and replaced financing and foreign exchange positions, repatriated offshore earnings, monitored cash management and funding plans, recapitalized legal entities and reconstituted global structure of 35 legal entities with operations in 55 countries.
  - Delivered over **$20 million cash tax reduction** in final week of transaction.
- Pursued U.S. tax legislative initiatives with government affairs group; served as Board Member of Organization for International Investment, a Washington-based trade group.

SAFIRE CORPORATION/LGD GLOBAL NV   2006-2010

$12 billion agricultural and construction equipment manufacturer; global financial services unit with $11 billion managed portfolio. LGD Global was formed in 2009 business merger of Safire Corporation and Mullane NV. Listed on NYSE; 84% owned by Italian Fiat group.

VICE PRESIDENT, TAXES, FINANCIAL SERVICES GROUP, 2009-2010

Created post-merger structure and financing facility for global business unit.

- Designed post-merger **restructuring plan for 35 legal entities** in 20 countries.
  - Recruited combined tax and legal team to develop prioritized global plan.
  - Delivered detailed plans for merging operating companies, eliminating unnecessary legal entities, utilizing tax assets, and minimizing tax cost of business combination.
- Established new state tax structure to issue **$1.1 billion asset-backed securitization** that assured uninterrupted financing for newly merged business.
- Led European-based tax and legal team through development of unique Pan-European Irish bank structure resulting in **25% reduction of European effective tax rate**.

Shana E. Kingsley - Page 3

SAFIRE CORPORATION (continued)

<u>DIRECTOR, TAX LEGAL</u>, 2006-2009

Managed new tax unit in structuring transactions and implementing global tax strategies.

- Recruited three senior tax attorneys; managed external advisors with annual billings exceeding $2.5 million.
- Identified more than **<u>$200 million in tax enhancements</u>** for proposed and completed **<u>acquisitions, joint ventures, strategic alliances, and financings</u>** in over 30 countries.
    - Transaction values ranged from $1 million to more than $3 billion.
    - Managed tax function for deal team that received CEO commendation for speed.
- Implemented transfer pricing enhancements with annual benefit exceeding $20 million.
- Established internal hedging center to process $500 million in foreign exchange exposure.
- Created structure to manage $100 million risk of foreign permanent establishments.
- Served on COO's 6-person **<u>Global Excavator Strategy Team</u>**
    - Structured global manufacturing and marketing alliance with Japanese partner.
    - Developed and utilized shared objectives approach to tax negotiations; persuaded Japanese partner to accept U.S.-favored tax principles and structure.
    - Team received CEO commendation for effective partnering with business.

STILLMARK INTERNATIONAL, INC.   1997-2006

Newly public $3 billion multinational conglomerate, including Tupperware, Hobart commercial kitchen equipment, West Bend appliances, Wilsonart, Florida Tile and Precor fitness equipment. Publicly traded on NYSE; subsequently acquired by Illinois Tool Works.

<u>TAX COUNSEL</u>

Delivered $50 million annual cash tax benefit/50% effective tax rate reduction.

- Co-managed 11 local country teams in implementation of Swiss-based **<u>global trading company</u>** to utilize excess foreign tax credits.
    - Customized legal, tax, I.T., and business structure to satisfy business and regulatory requirements in 12 European countries; assessed feasibility in 8 Asia-Pacific countries.
    - Negotiated business changes with local management, advisors, and boards.
    - Negotiated **<u>$10 million headquarters tax incentives</u>** with European tax authorities.
- Provided tax planning advice for multiple operating units; advised corporate treasury on structured financing proposals.

PRIVATE LAW PRACTICE, 1975-1987

FOX ROTHCHILD

Philadelphia Office: Counsel, 1996-1997

- Provided tax advice, structuring, and opinions for **Eurodollar and equity offerings, private offshore hedging fund and captive insurance company** for consortium of charitable hospitals.

BAKER & MCKENZIE

Philadelphia Office: Associate, 1985-1992; Partner, 1992-1994

Cleveland Office: Founding Partner, 1994-1996

- Practice concentrated in **U.S. and international business tax planning**, transactions, transfer pricing, IRS rulings, audit protests, and appellate briefs. Clients included major U.S.-based multinational manufacturers, pharmaceuticals, and leasing companies.
- **Cofounder of Cleveland Office**
  - Developed business plan and opened new office in highly competitive environment.
  - Designed and implemented promotional campaign to successfully establish firm presence and reputation; represented firm in local professional and business organizations.
  - Co-managed operations and staff; supervised office build-out.
  - Reported to Global Executive Committee; liaison to U.S. and European offices.

EDUCATION AND BAR ADMISSIONS

- Columbia University School of Law, L.L.M. (in Taxation).
- University of Chicago, The Law School, J.D.
- Pepperdine University Graziadio School of Business, Graduate Business Study.
- Kalamazoo College, B.A.
- Admitted to practice in Pennsylvania and U.S. Tax Court.

PROFESSIONAL ACTIVITIES

- Member: Tax Executives Institute (TEI), Association of Corporate Counsel, American Bar Association, Minnesota State Bar Association.
- Committee Leadership: Chair of International Tax Committee, Minneapolis Chapter of TEI, 2014-15; Chair of U.S. Federal Tax and International Tax Committees, Chicago Bar Association, 1992, 1996, 1997.
- Former editor: "Tax Notes" column for **American Bar Association Journal**.
- Frequent speaker and seminar leader for local and national continuing education programs.

The
Five
O'Clock
Club®

Helen: Résumé Looked Like Every Other Executive's

Helen was one more "results-oriented leader with diverse experience." She, like every other executive, had "strong leadership and problem-solving skills." These are common clichés. They don't provide details or information and they *don't* help make your case.

Helen had been unemployed for a year, and her résumé with clichés wasn't helping. With her new résumé, she landed a terrific job in three weeks and got serious calls from two other employers. Of course, building an accomplishment-based résumé (one that doesn't rely on clichés!) starts with the Seven Stories Exercise and deciding what to brag about. With the help of a coach, get it down on paper.

Helen's résumé is actually a 4-page foldout. That is, it's printed on 11" X 17" paper and folded (Kinko's or another print shop can do it for you.). The 4-page foldout is very handsome, appropriate for senior executives, and separates you from the competition.

The next page contains the beginning of Helen's "before" résumé. The "after" résumé is on the following four pages.

Of course, all of the company names and so on have been changed.

Helen's "Before" Résumé

PROFESSIONAL PROFILE

- Results-oriented leader with diverse experience at Stuart Brothers, JoS. A. Bank Clothiers, JPMorgan Chase, and Bergdorf Goodman.
- Strong leadership, conceptualization, organizational, planning, and problem-solving skills
- Expertise in merchandising and store operations in men's, women's, and hard lines
- Extensive experience in private label development, licensing, real estate, and construction in both Domestic and International markets
- Appraised asset recovery values for under-performing inventory, real estate, and FF&E
- Excels in motivation and team building through mentoring and coaching of development skills
- Established track record in volume, gross margin, expense control, and bottom-line performance
- Expertise in developing strategies for bidding and winning retail bankruptcy projects in court

STUART BROTHERS   **2013-PRESENT**

Managing Director/Team Leader

Lead projects involved monetizing under-performing assets for various retailers. Projects have included healthy retailers such as Sears Canada and Saks, Inc., as well as bankruptcies, i.e.: Casual Male, Regal Lighting, People's Pottery, and Rodier. Each process includes:

- Due Diligence: Reviewing clients' inventory levels and mix, sales trends, expenses, payroll, brand equity, and systems to determine achievable recovery value
- Expense Management: Putting controls in place to minimize costs of labor, inventory shrinkage, on-site management, regulations, taxes, and advertising
- Merchandising: Improving store appearance and displays to maximize sales and approving plans for signing, radio, direct mail, and newspapers
- Landlord Relations: Maintaining communications with landlord to ensure compliance with lease parameters. Developing strategy with landlord to manage disposition of retail sites as needed
- Bidding: Developing strategy and executing an action plan at bankruptcy court

JoS. A. Bank Clothiers   **2007-2013**

President, Factory Stores, 2011-2013

- Full P&L accountability of $180 million division of JoS. A. Bank
- Established new merchandising strategies, implemented new company standards, and rebuilt team
- Restructured entire store organization
- Gross margin from 47.2% to 48.1%

HELEN G. KLEIN

17 Sterling Circle
Saw Creek, NY 55543
IrwinKlein1845@aol.com

555-4444-7777
648-555-8888 cell

Retail C.O.O.
specializing in strategic brand development and turnaround management
JoS. A. Bank   JPMorgan Chase   Bergdorf Goodman

- **Shaped the future of JoS. A. Bank by changing its image, people, and stores**
  - After eight years of losses, company became profitable
  - Developed and executed comprehensive real estate strategy to include remodeling existing sites and expanding to new locations
  - Located, designed, and built Fifth Avenue Flagship Branch
  - Expanded outlet division from 35 to 75 stores
  - Put District Manager structure in place
  - **Full P&L responsibility for $180m** Outlet Division
  - Served on Executive Committee

- **Introduced retailing concepts to traditional banking culture at JPMorgan Chase.**
  - Re-allocated resources to focus on revenue-producing opportunities
  - **Created flagship branch of the future**: The largest ATM center in Manhattan
  - Brought retail sales culture to New York Consumer Bank
  - Grand Central Branch became centerpiece for expansion into Connecticut
  - Organized off-site retail seminar for entire management team in NY Retail Bank
  - **Managed largest region** in New York Consumer Bank: 53 branches; $11.9b in footings

- **Developed and executed merchandising and store strategy consistent with Bergdorf Goodman brand**
  - Built Private Label program to serve as centerpiece of merchandising strategy for Men's Furnishings Division
  - Grew sales volume from $43m to $73m in three years
  - Awarded Chairman's Award for Highest Gross Margin Division
  - Built Bala-Cynwyd store into fastest-growing store in region
  - Led total renovation of Michigan Avenue store
  - As Vice-President, Northeast Region, full profit responsibility for 7 stores; $150m in sales

Create a store culture consistent with the future of the brand.
Identify opportunity and maximize return: people, bricks & mortar, capital.
A controlled risk taker.

STUART BROTHERS   2013-Present
Managing Director/Team Leader

Lead projects involved monetizing under-performing assets for various retailers. Projects have included healthy retailers such as Sears Canada and Saks, Inc., as well as bankruptcies, i.e.: Casual Male, Regal Lighting, People's Pottery, and Rodier.

- **For Sears Canada**: Took over two outlet stores, and within four months, gross profit dollar increase was better than the other 13 stores combined
- **For Saks, Inc**: Managed closing of several department stores and significantly overachieved projected recovery values for each

JoS. A. Bank Clothiers   1995-2001
<u>President</u>, Factory Stores Division, 2009-2011

Shaped the image of JoS. A. Bank (founded in 1905)
by changing its image, its people, and its stores

- Full P&L responsibility for <u>**$180m**</u> division; Increased gross margin from 47.2% to 48.1%
- <u>**Increased four-wall profit from 19.9% to 21%**</u>

Changed Its Image:

- <u>**Took old, stodgy image and rebuilt the brand to be relevant**</u>
  - Participated with senior management in focus groups
  - Analyzed results and helped to develop strategic vision
  - Recruited and trained staff to reflect brand image
  - Renovated and expanded fleet of stores to reflect brand image
  - Participated as part of Executive Committee in major decisions across all functions

Changed Its People:

- <u>**Changed attitude of sales staff**</u> from standoffish and snobby to warm and friendly
- Assessed talent and <u>**changed 75% of store management within first 18 months without disruption**</u>
- Developed strategy to train, recognize, and recruit as necessary
- Created an atmosphere that encouraged friendly, welcoming service

Changed Its Stores:

- Reviewed and developed strategy for real estate
- Recruited and developed in-house real estate and construction team
- <u>**Built retail store fleet into 80 stores**</u>, modern looking, in line with new merchandise and revitalized staff
- <u>**Expanded outlet division from 35 to 75 stores**</u>
- Developed and executed strategy to locate and <u>**build Flagship on Fifth Avenue**</u>

HELEN G. KLEIN - page 3

JoS. A. Bank Clothiers, contd.
Executive Vice President, 2007-2011
International & New Business Development, Licenses, Legal Efforts, Real Estate, and Construction
- Managed design and development of $30 million Fifth Avenue store
- Managed process for negotiating golf license
- Implemented strategy for expansion into Southeast
- Responsible for 70 shop-in-shops in Japan
- Successfully opened 39 outlet stores and 32 retail stores

JPMORGAN CHASE 1999-2005
Vice President, Retail Bank Director, Citibank
Eastern Region, North Manhattan, Bronx, and Connecticut, 2001-2005

Introduced retailing concepts to traditional banking culture at JPMorgan Chase

- **During major downsizing, redirected resources** to focus on revenue opportunities
- Developed and executed concept for Grand Central Branch
- Used as model for Connecticut expansion
- Created and implemented strategy for 16-branch expansion into Connecticut marketplace
- Identified site, negotiated leases, helped develop organizational structure for staffing branches
- Conceived/executed **week-long training program in retailing for entire senior management staff in Eastern Region**

*Increased revenue and decreased expense base of 53-branch network
in mature market while strategizing 16-branch expansion*

- **$11.9 billion in footings** and 1,016 full-time employees
- Enhanced profitability by decreasing FTE from 1,300 to 1,016 while shifting focus to sale of traditional and nontraditional banking products
- Increased consumer net revenue by 13.9%

Senior Vice President, Chase Florida, 2003-2005
- Developed and executed strategy:
  changed emphasis from mass market to affluent customer base
- Repositioned franchise in Florida marketplace
- **Changed organizational structure of branches**: maximized profitability of target market opportunity
- Implemented sales process to **change from transactional to revenue-based culture**
- Created self-funding five-year distribution plan to reposition branch network
- Developed micro-marketing approach to lead generation capitalizing on affluent market
- Managed 19 branches and served on Executive Committee for Florida.

HELEN G. KLEIN - page 4

BERGDORF GOODMAN 1989-2001

Vice President, Northeast Region, New York, NY, 2000-2001

Developed and executed merchandising and store strategy consistent with the Bergdorf Goodman brand

- Profit responsibility for seven stores in Northeast region, as well as visual presentation, coordination of branch merchandising strategies, sales management, and communication of branch merchandising opportunities to corporate buying organization.
- Annual sales were **$150 million with 1,200 full-time employees**
- **Increased profitability** by maximizing emphasis on most profitable merchandising areas in each location
- Planned and executed **$20 million in renovations throughout region**
- Leveraged synergy between branch store opportunities and central merchandising function
- Developed quarterly strategies based on **micro-market opportunities**
- **Increased sales by 6% in very difficult economic environment**
- Maximized employee potential by mentoring **high-potential executives**

Vice President, Merchandise Manager—Men's Furnishings, 1996-2000

- Profit responsibility for men's furnishing area, development and execution of merchandising strategies, and communication with branch organization
- **Developed focused approach toward improving quality of private label assortment across all areas in men's furnishings**
- Executed specific point of view toward growing better merchandise categories throughout division by upgrading quality
- **Increased sales by 18.7%, 9.4% better than planned**
- **Increased gross margin two full percentage points to 52.2%, second highest in company**
- Sourced product in Europe, Asia and United States
- Stressed private label along with exclusives within branded lines

General Manager, Michigan Avenue Store, Chicago, 1993-1996
General Manager, Bala Cynwyd, Pennsylvania, 1981-1983
Assistant Manager, Troy, Michigan, 1989-1991

MAY COMPANY (Famous Barr Company) 1981-1989

EDUCATION

B.S., Business Administration, University of Missouri, St. Louis, 1981
MILITARY HISTORY: **United States Army Reserves, 1980 to 1986**

The
Five
O'Clock
Club®

PART SIX

Résumés for Managers and High-Level Professionals

The Five O'Clock Club

Jessie: Pulling Together Her Background to Move Up

Jessie's background is in marketing, customer service, and training. She had also done a lot of work in database administration, but she didn't want to do *that* again.

When Jessie had done her Forty-Year Vision (see our book *Targeting a Great Career*), she discovered that **she wanted to have her own training company someday**. She also thought she'd like to have four or five people working for her.

To head in that direction, it would be best if Jessie could work for a training consulting company (rather than in a corporate training department) and learn how the consulting firm ran its business. For example, she could learn how the firm marketed itself, priced services, administered programs, and so on. Jessie thought it would be best if she not only did stand-up training for the firm but also managed a few projects.

Jessie needed to decide what to write at the top of her résumé to position herself for the job she wanted next. **You are most strongly positioned when you can say that you already _are_ exactly what you want to do next**. Since Jessie had already done training and project management, she highlighted those two skills at the top of her résumé. This increased the chance that hiring managers would want her to do exactly that for them. Since Jessie was also willing to market training programs, she highlighted her marketing skills as well.

When Jessie made up her list of target companies to contact in her search, she focused exclusively on training firms. She listed all of the companies she could find in the training industry and called each one to find out the names of the people she should contact at each firm. (Often, this information can be gathered by visiting websites.) She sent this résumé to each person with a cover letter, and followed up with phone calls (see our book *Shortcut Your Job Search*).

Jessie got lots of meetings and landed long-term assignments with three consulting firms. **She got to see how three different firms operated**! The pay was excellent, by the way, and far exceeded what she had made in her corporate job. And she was learning how to run her own business when she was ready.

JESSIE WOODWARD

3010 Norwood Lane   jessie.woodward@prodigy.net   (555) 826-3555 (Home)
Mansfield, Texas 55222   (555) 622-5800 (Office)

Training Manager / Project Manager
• Administration   • Product Marketing

- **Coordinated 36 consultants and 200 executive seminars per year.**
  - — In the course of four years, a class was never canceled due to mis-scheduling.
- Key player in design and implementation of a "Self-Directed Team," five-day training program.
- **Delivered a three-month training program. Designed curriculum.**
- Key player in $1 million dollar renovation of a four-story training facility.
- **Marketed training programs and materials.**
- Regularly taught a thirteen-day training program.
  - — **Trained 25 students on bank procedures and computer systems.**
  - — **Managed computer setup, testing, and troubleshooting.**
- Created a training guide for instructors to utilize during a thirteen-day program.
- Content knowledge includes: Organization Vision & Values, Professional Image, Management Essentials, Customer Service / Sales Techniques, Retail/Wholesale Product Knowledge.

Dynamic, goal-oriented, enthusiastic manager
with "outstanding interpersonal skills."

InterFirst Bank, N.A.   2008-present
Operations / Customer Service Manager

Administration / Negotiation / Information Systems

Marketing / Customer Service
- Managed a customer-service team of **four direct reports.**
  - — Conducted coaching sessions and performance reviews.
- Established goals and objectives.
- **Opened an average of 15 new accounts per quarter.**
- Maintained a standard of exceptional service for 200 middle market business customers.
  - — Praised by customers for anticipating their needs and communicating effectively.

Information Systems / Administration
- Maintained a database of credit facilities over $80 million dollars.
  - — **Provided ongoing training to the staff on system upgrades.**
- Maintained a tracking system for account activity.
- **Successfully negotiated past due loan payments in excess of $125,000.**
- Generated monthly document exception reports.
- Approved/processed money transfers, bankers' acceptances, and letters of credit.

Training Officer / Project Manager
- Performed needs analyses and actions plans as the organization moved forward.
  - — Met with division executives to determine training goals and objectives.
  - — Developed training curriculum and calendar.
- Provided training and coaching in the area of branch operations and sales techniques.
  - — **Recognized as a seasoned trainer by top management.**

JESSIE WOODWARD - page 2

InterFirst Bank, N.A., contd.   2008-present
<u>**Training Officer / Project Manager**</u>, contd.
- Researched vendor services and negotiated contracts.
    — Managed a $250,000 expense budget.
- Facilitated "train-the-trainer" sessions.
- Interviewed and recruited retail bank staff.
- Managed the production of a training video.
- Maintained inventory of training material.

<u>**Training Manager / Administrator / Project Manager**</u>
- Managed an annual expense budget of $1 million dollars.
- Coordinated multiple executive-level seminars. Consistently praised for quality.
- Negotiated contracts with vendors and outside training facilities.
- Interfaced with domestic and international consultants on program design.
- Purchased office equipment. Organized training sessions.
- Managed the reorganization of a training library.

<u>**Sales Assistant**</u>, Dean Witter Reynolds   2003-2008
- Communicated products to high-profile customers.
- Assisted a senior vice president with daily sales. Opened new accounts.
- Researched companies, annual reports, Standard & Poor's ratings, etc.

<u>**Trainer**</u>, Cashier Training Institute   2002-2003
- Delivered multiple programs on a daily basis to a typical group size of 25 participants.
- Provided training on retail bank procedures, computer systems, and secretarial techniques.
- Monitored participants' performance over a three-month time span.

<u>**Trainer / Operations Supervisor**</u>, Manufacturers Hanover Trust Company   1998-2001
- Supervised branch staff.
- Cross-sold products and opened accounts.
- Provided training in the areas of:
    - Customer Service
    - Sales Techniques
    - Computer Systems
    - Branch Procedures

EDUCATION
University of Dallas—B.S., 1996, School of Industrial and Labor Relations
University of Texas, Arlington—Business Administration degree expected June 2017

AFFILIATIONS
Texas State Mentoring Program

The Five O'Clock Club®

Sara: Overcoming Her Background

You gain strength, courage and confidence by every experience in which you really stop to look fear in the face. You are able to say to yourself," I lived through this horror. I can take the next thing that comes along."
...You must do the thing you think you cannot do.

ELEANOR ROOSEVELT, *You Learn by Living*

There is one characteristic that appears in every peak performer I have studied: a sense of mission. Mission is the source of peak performance. Mission—an image of a desired state of affairs that inspires action—determines behavior and fuels motivation. When you pay attention to someone who is clearly going somewhere, you can soon see at least an approximate statement of that person's mission. My own is: to discover the principles of high achievement and communicate them to top performers and would-be top performers.

DR. CHARLES GARFIELD, *Peak Performers*
(WILLIAM MORROW PAPERBACKS)

We often injure our cause by calling in that which is weak to support that which is strong.

CHARLES CALEB COLTON

Sometimes, when I'm in the shower, I see flashes of the past. I ask myself 'What if this terrible thing hadn't happened? What if I hadn't done that?' But you know, then I wouldn't be where I am right now.

ROMAN POLANSKI

Sara had spent some time as an actor. When corporate hiring managers saw this on the résumé, they didn't want to see her. It overshadowed the solid corporate experience she already had. What's more, if she did get in for an interview, managers probed to find out why she had chosen acting as a career. It made her business experience look less substantial.

On her revised résumé, of which we have included only the first page, a summary statement puts a corporate spin on her theater experience (which included more than acting) and highlights her education more.

In addition, she dropped the name of the second company on her résumé (Golden Bo Tree East Co.), since it is irrelevant and distracting.

When testing your résumé in the market, notice if anything about your background is operating as a handicap for you. Think of how you can reposition this part to downplay it and how you can highlight those parts you want the reader to focus on.

SARA G. HARRIS

355 South York Avenue   sara.harris@hotmail.com   Home: (212) 555-2351
New York, New York 10483   Office: (212) 555-3320

EXPERIENCE

Amrock, New York   2011-Present

Management Development Associate. In-house Corporate Human Resources consultant.

Developed, designed, and implemented vehicles to enhance Human Resource professionalism within Amrock worldwide. Accomplishments include:

- Executive Development—Created and implemented nomination process whereby top performers are selected to attend Executive Education programs. Coordinated the entire process, serving as a liaison between the university and participants to ensure appropriate developmental match.
- High Potential Development—Initiated database to: identify and source candidates for potential job assignments, track institutional progress, and follow up on development plans.
- Focus Groups—Assessment of Development Needs—Managed all aspects of project design and implementation: met with senior management, prepared protocol, conducted sessions with over 120 HR professionals both in the U.S. and Europe, and analyzed and integrated data.
- Questionnaire Development—Designed feedback instrument for HR professionals worldwide to elicit recommendations on key HR development needs.
- Program Development—Researched and designed seminars for senior human resources offsite. Included compensation seminars on Incentive Plan Design, Long Term Incentive and Tax Effective Comp. Coached presenters through feedback sessions.

Golden Bo Tree East Co., Ltd., Bangkok, Thailand   2010

Organization Development Consultant. Process consultant to senior management on cross-cultural issues around goal clarification, decision making, and team building. Resulted in improved organizational effectiveness in adapting to Thailand business demands.

Actor   2002-2008

EDUCATION

Columbia University, New York; **Master of Arts**, Organizational Psychology   2010-2011
Awarded Academic Scholarship—3.7 G.P.A.

New York University, New York; **Master of Arts**, Counseling Psychology   2008-2010
Awarded Academic Scholarship—**3.6 G.P.A.**

Utah State University, Bachelor of Fine Arts—Acting   1998-2002
Awarded Full Tuition Scholarship

PUBLICATIONS

A Case Study: Organization Development in a Health Care System
New York University Psychology Quarterly—September, 2005

Additional Information

Languages: Thai
Affiliations: American Psychological Association; NY Organization Development Network
Computer Skills: Mac OS, Software—Microsoft Office 08; SPSSX

SARA G. HARRIS

355 South York Avenue
New York, New York 10483

Home: (212) 555-2351
Office: (212) 555-3320

Management/Organization Development Specialist

Over 8 years of development and stand-up experience.
Financial, Entertainment, and Exporting Industries.

- **Proven consulting expertise in:**

- Executive and High Potential Development • Needs Assessment • Organizational Research
- Two masters' degrees in Organizational and Counseling Psychology.
- Extensive exposure in Southeast Asia; fluent in Thai.

Professional Experience

Amrock, New York   2011-Present
Manager of Management Development

In-house Corporate Human Resources consultant. Developed, designed, and implemented vehicles to enhance the professionalism of over 2,000 officers worldwide.

Accomplishments include:

- **High-Potential Development**
  Assess and identify top performers to: meet specific business talent needs, attend Executive University programs, and facilitate succession planning.

- **Executive Development**
  Created and implemented nomination process whereby top performers are selected to attend executive education programs. Coordinated the entire process, serving as a liaison between the university and participants to ensure appropriate developmental match.

- **Focus Groups—Assessment of Development Needs**
  Managed all aspects of project design and implementation: met with senior management, prepared protocol, conducted sessions with over 500 officers throughout the U.S. and Europe, and analyzed and integrated data.

- **Organizational Research**
  Use of statistical and research design (SPSSX) to conduct surveys, climate studies, turnover studies. Designed feedback instrument for HR professionals worldwide to elicit recommendations on key training needs.

- **Program Development**
  Researched and designed seminars for senior offsite. Included compensation seminars on Incentive Plan Design, Long Term Incentive and Tax Effective Compensation. Coached presenters through feedback sessions.

The Five O'Clock Club®

Richard: His Experience Was Hidden

The psychic task which a person can and must set for himself, is not to feel secure, but to be able to tolerate insecurity, without panic and undue fear.

ERICH FROMM, *The Sane Society*

To endure is greater than to dare; to tire out hostile fortune, to be daunted by no difficulty; to keep heart when all have lost it; to go through intrigue spotless; to forgo even ambition when the end is gained— who can say this is not greatness?

WILLIAM THACKERAY, *The Virginians*

Richard had been unemployed for a year and was desperate. He finally met with a Five O'Clock Club career coach, re-did his résumé, joined the small group, and found the job of his dreams within six weeks.

Some problems with Richard's résumé were obvious: He seemed to be a job hopper, and there was no theme—no key message. Although he specialized in competitive intelligence and research, his most recent temporary job was not related directly to his target. However, since he highlighted it (by CAPITALIZING the company name on his résumé), interviewers always asked him about it, and that got the interview off on the wrong foot.

Remember to highlight (that is caps, bold, underline) the job titles and organization names

that you want them to notice! Don't aim for consistency. This is a marketing piece.

One further problem was that Richard had lost sight of his dream. He had not worked in health-care research for over 10 years and felt doomed to take whatever job came along. Prospective employers had to wade through three jobs before they got to one that was in health care. And they couldn't tell from his résumé that Richard was even especially interested in health care. Still, Richard needed to hedge his bets in his new résumé, and he highlighted health care first and financial services second by putting both into his summary, with an emphasis on health care.

To make the résumé more aesthetically pleasing, you may notice that there is a 4-point space below the words *Research Director* as well as after the third line of his summary. That way, those four lines are close to each other but not bunched up. We dropped his most recent consulting assignment, which he had done for only a month.

Finally, the points he wants to highlight are both <u>**underlined and bolded**</u>. It is not enough to do <u>one</u> or the **other**. If you want to highlight something, do both. Just trust me on this.

On the following page, we present only page one of Richard's "before" résumé, followed by only the first page of Richard's revised three-page résumé. You'll get the idea. The summary is what matters most.

Richard L. Thomas

1402 Bayberry Street
Fair Hills, Michigan 55590

Telephone: 555-555-0669
Email: rlt468@ix.netcom.com

Skill Highlights

- 15+ years' experience managing knowledge management personnel including internal staffs, outside contractors, and personnel in widely dispersed locations.
- Experienced buyer and evaluator of consulting firm products for multinational corporations.
- **15+** years' experience in **competitor intelligence, technology, and market development research**.
- Recognized for **successes in partnering with business development and acquisition teams**.
- Very experienced information product contract negotiator.
- **Highly experienced developer of customized information** delivery services.
- Excellent communicator across business units and management levels for stakeholder management and product promotion in worldwide organizations.

Professional Experience

TRILOG® Adult Issues North Group

Ann Arbor, Michigan

Consultant

April 2012 to date

- Currently coordinating efforts of local business executives, community leaders, a regional mental healthcare agency, and state government to offer career and related support services to adults with Asperger Syndrome.
- Developed customized job process, from career counseling to on-the-job mentoring, for highly educated, talented adults with Asperger Syndrome, a nonverbal learning disability.

efinanceworks Management Corporation

Dudley, Michigan

($300 million incubator/accelerator in the e-finance sector created by General Atlantic Partners and Capital Z)

Director, Research

August 2011-April 2012

- **Developed knowledge management solutions** for capital investment decisions. This included:
  - Creating knowledge base on corporations, industries, people, trends, and technologies.
  - Information tools evaluation, testing, and end-user training.
  - Developing customized critical news alerting services.
  - Tailoring research delivery for both local and distant user needs.
  - Creating end-user training programs for effective resource use.
- **Created highly successful internal consulting function for investment decision research**.

GE Capital—Financial Guaranty Insurance Company

Detroit, Michigan

Manager, Information Services

September 1991-July 2011

- Led team of internal and outsourced information specialists specializing in asset and mortgage-backed securities, and municipal bond and specialty insurance services.
- **Contributions while partnering with new business development and acquisition teams recognized with** FGIC~Corporate Leadership Team Award
- Team leader with overall responsibility for developing all company end-user software training programs.
- Developed company-wide Internet and Intranet training programs.

Richard L. Thomas

1402 Bayberry Street
Fair Hills, Michigan 55590

Telephone: 555-555-0669
Email: rlt468@ix.netcom.com

Research Director

*Experienced project manager with strong customer orientation
And extensive health-care & financial services experience*

• Wyeth   • GE Capital

- Managed **staff of 6** plus outside firms.
- **Expert in competitive intelligence and knowledge management**.
  - Marshaled internal and external knowledge to support business development.
  - Collaborated with new business development teams: Developed leads; qualified targets; verified market sizes; monitored competitor activities.
- Health-care experience: **8+ years monitoring health-care markets for Lederle**.
  - Deep research background in pharmaceutical marketing and trends research.
  - Developed competitive intelligence alerts for Lederle Marketing.
  - Member, Pharmaceutical & Health Technology Division, SLA.
  - Attended seminars such as the Dialog Biomedical in Philadelphia in April 2010.
- Expert in **negotiating contracts** for online data and electronic information products.
  - Trained employees and clients in use of Internet and data tools.
  - Served as the interface for **electronic data** between technologists and end users.
- Regularly address groups of 10 to 200 internally.
  - Address professional associations (groups of up to 500) semiannually.
- Regularly write for internal newsletters and outside journals.

*Dedicated to customer service:
Provides what the customer needs to be effective in his/her job.
Develops and implements <u>all</u> phases of finding strategic information.*

Director, Research   August 2011-April 2012
efinanceworks Management Corporation
($300 million incubator/accelerator in the **e-finance** sector created by General Atlantic Partners and Capital Z)

- **Developed knowledge management solutions** for capital investment decisions. This included:
  - Creating knowledge base on corporations, industries, people, trends, and technologies.
  - Information tools evaluation, testing, and end-user training.
  - Developing customized critical news alerting services.
  - Tailoring research delivery for both local and distant user needs.
  - Creating end-user training programs for effective resource use.
- **Created highly successful internal consulting function** for investment decision research.

Manager, Information Services   2001-July 2011
GE Capital—Financial Guaranty Insurance Company (FGIC)
- **Team Leader: Competitive intelligence and knowledge management**.
  - Led team of internal and outsourced information specialists specializing in asset and mortgage-backed securities, and municipal bond and specialty insurance services.
  - Designed and managed company-wide initiative to manage internal knowledge.

The Five O'Clock Club®

Philippe: Needed Two Résumés for Two Very Different Targets

We do not succeed in changing things according to our desire, but gradually our desire changes. The situation that we hoped to change because it was intolerable becomes unimportant. We have not managed to surmount the obstacle, as we were absolutely determined to do, but life has taken us round it, led us past it, and then if we turn round to gaze at the remote past, we can barely catch sight of it, so imperceptible has it become.

MARCEL PROUST

I'm very lucky. If it wasn't for golf, I don't know what I'd be doing. If my IQ had been two points lower, I'd have been a plant somewhere.

LEE TREVINO, AS QUOTED IN *Golfweek*

Since he was looking for a job anyway, Philippe thought he might as well explore two targets: one in his current field (purchasing) and one having to do with his passion (sports).

He would need two résumés, since these were such different targets. Many job hunters think they need different résumés for every target they are going after. But usually the fields that interest you are not as different as they may seem. For instance, Norman Neumann, whose résumé we saw earlier, had wanted one for the fashion industry and one for a job search outside that industry. In fact, one résumé served both purposes.

Philippe ended up with an excellent position in the purchasing field—one very close to home and with an increase in salary.

But his exploration of the sports field helped him understand just how important it was in his life. As it happens, managing cycling events was central to his family life. His entire family participated in running an annual event, and he was unwilling to give it up. After Philippe negotiated the salary for the new job, he told the hiring manager that he had been an Olympic cyclist and that he was committed to running the annual cycling event in his town, a project that took two weeks of his and his family's time. Philippe asked if "there was any way" he could get an extra two weeks off every year to run the event.

The company agreed to the extra time off—with pay—and offered to sponsor the event!

Philippe Mardig

47 Courbet Plaza   Home: (555) 555-7844
Bernini Square, MS 55700   mardig888@hotmail.com   Business: (222) 555-5564

Innovative Purchasing Department Head
($55 million annually) with a high level of integrity and over 15 years at Amdahl.

- Experience in automation, equipment evaluation, forms management, and data processing.
- Created a divisional Purchasing Department resulting in $4 million in savings.
- Served as Corporate Fleet Administrator (a fleet of 1,300) and
- Contracts Negotiator resulting in savings of $2.4 million.

AMDAHL   1997-Present

<u>PURCHASING MANAGER</u>   2012-Present
Amdahl Properties

Supervise staff of 8 in Purchasing and 6 in Payables, $55 million annual volume, 3,600 purchase orders processed annually.

- Selected to **create divisional purchasing department where none previously existed**.

  - <u>Served as the standard for other Amdahl purchasing departments.</u>
  - Trained managers to set up other purchasing departments.
  - A professionally run model operation set up as a profit center, charging for our services.
  - Set up automated purchasing system.
  - Produced a total package of controls to inform management regarding spending.
  - Developed an MIS interface with fixed asset, financial control, and the corporate technology areas.
  - Consistently exceeded goals set by minority/women's vendor program.

- Consistently developed innovative cost-saving methods.

  - <u>**Saved $4 million**</u> through creation of computer and copier lease analysis program.
  - Renegotiated corporate discount on personal computers from 15% to 35%, resulting in a **savings of $1 million**.
  - Created a surplus and trade-in program resulting in a **<u>savings of $200,000</u>**.

- Wrote the *Purchasing Policy Manual*

  - Served as a prototype for other divisions in Amdahl.
  - Evaluated personal computers, desktop publishing, facsimile, microfilm, office, and other equipment.

- Preparation of all budget and financial reports.

- <u>**Published purchasing newsletter**</u> for distribution to other purchasing departments, financial controllers, and end users.

Phillippe Mardig - Page 2

SENIOR BUYER   2010-2012
AMDAHL Corporate Purchasing Department

- Rated #1 buyer.
- Assisted in the purchase of $50 million annually of computers and related equipment.
- Negotiated national and short-term contracts for corporate and specific needs.
- Served as Corporate Fleet Administrator
    - Fleet of 1,330 vehicles.
    - <u>**Saved $2.4 million**</u> through renegotiation of lease.
    - Supervised fleet administrators throughout United States.
    - Developed recommended vehicle list with emphasis on reduced operating costs.
    - Set up mailroom operation for AMDAHL Delaware.

CITIBANK Corporate Payables Department   2007-2009
<u>Senior Operator/Assistant Systems Analyst</u>
- Involved in selection, testing, and installation of new equipment.
- Project coordinator for implementation of online purchasing system.
- Served as telecommunications intermediary for in-house and external clients.
- Handled leasing requirements of users.

CITIBANK Corporate Machine Repair   2000-2006
<u>Senior Service Technician</u>
- Service full range of microfilm equipment and automated filing systems.
- Supervise equipment warehouse facility for storage and distribution of surplus.
- Renegotiated replacement parts purchase discount, resulting in a savings of $300,000.

SPERRY RAND CORPORATION   1995-2000
Territorial responsibility for service of complete line of microfilm and automated filing systems.

EDUCATION
A.A.S., Business, City University of New York

Sports Résumé

Philippe Mardig

47 Courbet Plaza
Bernini Square, MS 55700

mardig888@hotmail.com

Home: (555) 555-7844
Business: (222) 555-5564

A lifetime involvement in competitive sports:
participation, administration, and promotion

- Ongoing relationships with corporate sponsors and local governments.
- Personal connections with TV, radio, and newspapers to bring events to the public.
- Work closely with The U.S. Cycling Federation. Manage cycling championships.
- Won over 100 races including 3rd place in 2002 Olympic Trials.
- **Former President of MSSC. Annually promote the largest race in the state.**
- Persuasive detail-oriented manager who overcomes obstacles to successfully complete projects.

PARTICIPATION

Extensive athletic background including scholastic involvement in gymnastics, track, karate, amateur-level weight lifting and cycling.
- National Cycling Champion, 1987
- 3rd Place, 2002 Olympic Trials—kilometer
- Won over 100 races.

ASSOCIATION POSITIONS HELD

Utilized expertise and personal contacts to successfully organize, develop, and present cycling events exhibitions to showcase cycling to business, and potential sponsoring organizations.

President, GBSC
- Secured sponsorship of Windsor bicycles.
- Put together a national-level team including 6 state, national, and Olympic winners.
- Oversaw or directed:
  - awards banquet,
  - annual racing program, and
  - 5 races.
- Served as media contact.

President and Founder, Mississippi Bicycle Club
Formed to promote development of Olympic cyclists in the state.
- Organized the 7-Eleven Mississippi Cycling Classics.
  - Worked with sponsors, government, Chamber of Commerce.
  - Directed it for 5 years.
- Brought Olympic-level cycling (featuring Eric Heyden) to Mississippi.
- Served as media contact.

Race Chairman, Mississippi Wheelman
- Conducted weight lifting and training clinics.
- Directed the Mississippi County Cycling Classic.
- Secured sponsorship from bicycle companies.
- Served as media contact.

GOVERNMENT-RELATED EVENTS RUN

Successfully work with governments and government agencies to secure necessary service (police and ambulance), highway sanitation. Coordinate mailings and promotions with government PR people, sports units, Chambers of Commerce. Examples include:

- U.S.C.F.
    - Meet regularly with The District Representative.
    - Meet weekly with The Assistant Executive Director to organize National championships.
    - Arrange housing, food, and welcoming reception.
- Eliot County, Department of Recreation and Parks
    - Handle every detail. Close contact covering every detail from sign making and banners to securing showmobile platform, hiring the announcer and phototimer.
    - Coordinate publicity and distribute information with Sports Unit.
    - Work with Commissioner to handle logistics.
    - Work with Sponsorship Coordinator to attract sponsors.
    - Missouri Tourism Bureau
- For major events, secure the cooperation of all the governments and agencies involved.

PROMOTE MAJOR EVENTS

- Served as cycling spokesperson for Mississippi.
- 7-Eleven Cycling Classic
    - Initiated and developed this national event.
    - Recruited Eric Heyden and other members of the Olympic Team.
    - Handled all details for 5 years.
    - Served as the media contact.
    - Secured the sponsorship of 7-Eleven.
- Put together programs for events (coordinate typesetters, printers, etc.)
- Interface with all major media: radio, TV, and print. Personally know all the reporters and editors.
- Outstanding Citizen Award from Eliot County, 2003.

Other Events Promoted:

Mississippi Cycling Classic	Giacometti Dave Cycling Classic
Eliot Country Cycling Classic	2011 Masters National Criterion Championships
Byron Lake	Halloween Cycling Classic

SECURED CORPORATE SPONSORS

7-Eleven	Hewlett-Packard	Nynex	
Manchester	Epson	NEC	Saven

ALSO HAVE EXTENSIVE CORPORATE EXPERIENCE

The Five O'Clock Club®

George: Positioned for a New Field after *Retirement*

Why not go out on a limb? That's where the fruit is.

WILL ROGERS

The earth is a place to live in, where we must put up with sights, with sounds, with smells, too, by Jove!— breathe dead hippo, so to speak, and not be contaminated. And there, don't you see? Your strength comes in, the faith in your ability for the digging of unostentatious holes to bury the stuff in—your power of devotion, not to yourself, but to an obscure, backbreaking business.

JOSEPH CONRAD, *Heart of Darkness*

George had spent his career life on Wall Street. At the young age of 50, he decided to take early retirement. He knew he could easily work for another 20 years and felt that it was better to make his move now rather than wait until he was older. Luckily, George already knew that he wanted to teach in a private high school. (If *you* are not clear about what you could do next, start with our book *Targeting a Great Career).*

George made one slight error: Given his excellent background, he thought that the not-for-profit world would jump at the chance to hire him. After all, he had been a successful executive and had worked in academia earlier in his career. But being accomplished is not enough. Every industry wants people who *fit in* well: People don't want their organization disrupted by outsiders. The world of Wall Street (competitive, brusque) is very different from the world of academia (collegial, slower paced). After a few meetings, George realized he was going to have problems getting in—unless he changed.

George needed to look, act, and dress the part for his new role: a less starchy appearance, a slightly longer haircut than he was used to (though still well-groomed), and a lot less aggressive in his speech and manner. Wall Street had left its mark on George, and his current persona would likely be off-putting in academia.

Rather than rush out and meet more people in academia right away, George needed to settle into a new mind-set. His demeanor slowly changed as he developed his list of schools to contact and then sent for and studied school bulletins. George became more relaxed, started to speak more slowly, and actually started to look more appropriate for the industry he had targeted. There had been another George hidden under the Wall Street veneer.

Now he needed an appropriate résumé. When making a career change, the strategy is to put at the top of your résumé the things that would be of most interest to your target market. Because George had been sincerely interested in education for quite some time, even when he was on Wall Street, he had taken on a few education-related assignments. For example, he had recruited graduates from major universities to work at his Wall Street firm.

George highlighted those experiences and his earlier experiences in education at the top of his résumé. In the body of his résumé, he went into some depth about his most recent position, which was impressive. However, the bulk of his résumé highlighted only the experiences that he thought would be of interest to those in academia. He simply listed with no supporting detail those jobs that would be of no interest to those in academia.

Now, rather than thinking he would just walk into a job in academia, George humbled himself a little and asked for meetings to gather information about how he could get in. He was very well received and was given a lot of good advice.

Within a few short months, George had landed two part-time assignments at excellent secondary schools. George was paying his dues, learning the system, and would soon become settled in his new field. He could see that it was only a matter of time before he would be working the number of hours he wanted in the field he had dreamed about for so long.

GEORGE THOMAS

78 Silver Ridge Road   Stamford, CT 99999   (555) 555-2475   gthomas7825@aol.com

---

SENIOR EXECUTIVE
• **Program Director**   • **Top Recruiter**   • **Educator**

- Started, organized, and managed nontraditional MBA training program; <u>**taught for 16 years**</u>.
- For 10 years, <u>**headed recruiting at major universities**</u>: University of Chicago, University of Pennsylvania (Wharton School), University of Virginia (Darden), Dartmouth University (Amos Tuck).
  - Recruited at both the MBA and BA levels.
- Ran Citibank's highest-profile college recruiting program.
- Managing Director/Trading Manager, Citibank Securities, Inc.
  - $30 billion under management, amounting to 10% of the bank's assets.
  - Revenue of over $160 million in 11 years.
- <u>**Private-school educator and department head**</u>.
- PhD candidate (ABD), MA, BA, The Catholic University of America.
- <u>**Edited series of 15 books**</u>, The European Religious Experience.

A leader with substantial hands-on experience.
An individual whose personal philosophy and values
have enabled him to succeed and to inspire and lead others.

CITIBANK SECURITIES, INC. — 1995-Present

Managing Director; Trading Manager   (2000-Present)

As a senior officer, started, organized, and managed a highly profitable business.
- Built a highly visible business responsible for financing the bank's U.S. Treasury positions.
- Achieved $30 billion under management, which amounted to 10% of Citibank's balance sheet.
- Managed a team of 6 senior traders.
- Earned revenue over $160 million in 11 years.
- Managed significant profit and loss with senior risk authority.
- Oversaw all compliance, legal, systems, and operational issues

Citibank MBA Program   (1997-Present)

In keeping with corporate philosophy that line managers should be actively involved in recruiting and training: started, organized, and managed the first nontraditional MBA training program at Citibank.

<u>**Training:**</u>
- Developed new programs involving 20-30 line managers as trainers.
- Built on MBA classroom knowledge with presentations of a practical nature.
- The three-month program trained 50 individuals from top universities.
- Personally taught in the program for 16 years, including technical modules on the financing businesses, selling skills, and the government securities markets. Also presented a special series on elements of a successful career in the financial services industry.

<u>**Recruiting:**</u>
- For 10 years a leading recruiter at major universities, including University of Chicago, University of Pennsylvania (Wharton), University of Virginia (Darden) and Dartmouth (Amos Tuck).
- Recruited at both the MBA and BA levels.
- Extensive on-campus and in-house interviewing experience. Presented to groups of 40 to 300.
- Served as relationship manager for the Amos Tuck School at Dartmouth University.

GEORGE THOMAS - page 2

Manager, College Recruiting (1999)
- Hired 50 people from top 10 universities.
- Organized and delivered presentations, managed MBA recruiting schedules, follow-up, and closure process for all candidates.
- For the first time, involved senior management in the recruiting process by inviting prospects to the firm.

Vice President and Assistant Sales Manager, Government Bond Department (1993) Sales Person, Government Bond Department (1990)

GOLDMAN SACHS AND CO., New York, NY 1994-1995

Sales Person. Responsible for individual Accounts in Commodities Division.

DATONA BROTHERS, INC., San Juan, Puerto Rico 1990-1994

Vice President of family-owned wholesale hardware firm.

- As member of management team introduced 5 new product lines into local market.
- Succeeded in becoming fluent in Spanish, while mastering Latin business culture.

SCHOOL OF THE HOLY CROSS, Potomac, MD 1988-1990

Head of Religion Department

- Developed curriculum, taught upper-level courses in Western Religious Thought and Greek.

ST. LUKE SCHOOL, Robertson, MD 1981-1988

- Developed, managed, and taught in the Parish Adult Education program, which resulted in expanded educational opportunities for entire neighborhood.

EDUCATION

THE CATHOLIC UNIVERSITY OF AMERICA, Washington, DC
PhD Candidate (ABD), Department of Religious Studies, 1990
Area of Concentration: Philosophical Theology
MA, Department of Religious Studies, 1988; Minor, Philosophy
BA, Department of Religious Studies, 1986; Minor, Anthropology

ARTICLES
"Dialectical Panentheism: Rahner and Hegel"
The Irish Theological Quarterly, Vol. XLII, No. 2, April 1985

PERSONAL

Married, Three children
Fluent in Spanish
Reading knowledge in French and German
Registrations, Series 7, 63, 24
Special Olympics, Spring 2013

Member, CAEL and The Alliance
Interests: American History, The Civil War
Classical Music, Poetry Securities
Boy Scouts of America, Council Member
Troop 70, New Canaan, CT, 2002-2009

The
Five
O'Clock
Club

Various Résumés for
Managers and Professionals

They can have anything they want, but they <u>can't</u> have everything they want. There is more to life than Kansas. The key is choosing what we want most (our heart's desire), letting go of everything else we want (for now), and moving (mentally, emotionally and physically) toward our goal.

JOHN-ROGER AND PETER MCWILLIAMS,
Do It! Let's Get Off Our Buts

". . . sir, I would like to become a psychologist, but it requires so much training that I'm afraid I would be too old when I finish."
The wise man sat in silence for a few moments, smiled, and then asked ,"Young lady, how long would it take you to become a psychologist?"
"About seven years," she replied.
"How old would you be then?" was the next question.
"I will be twenty-five."
Then the man asked, "How old will you be in seven years if you don't become a psychologist?"
Of course, her answer was the same."Well, I guess I would be about twenty-five."
Time waits for no one.... Remember, your future is exactly what you make it.

DENNIS KIMBRO,
Think and Grow Rich: A Black Choice

On the following pages are additional résumés for people of various levels. In each case, the person thought about his or her target area and positioned his or her background to fit the target.

Now, take a crack at your own résumé. Then test it with friends. Ask them, "When you look at this résumé, how do I come across?"

That's a very specific question, and you're looking for a very specific answer.

The danger here is that, when you ask people for comments, you may get a host of suggestions about things *that don't matter*. Don't get derailed, for example, by amateurish advice about résumé length. Pay attention to criticisms that have to do with the way you are *positioned*. If you intend to come across as someone who manages people, but the reader sees you as a person who has written press releases, that's a problem worth paying attention to. If your friends don't get the point, chances are hiring managers won't either. Some people think they're being helpful by suggesting word or punctuation changes: Some of these may be different but not necessarily better.

Incorporate all valuable suggestions, of course, but use friends and associates to help fine-tune the *positioning of the résumé*—then hit your target areas.

He wants a job as a manager of <u>all</u> employee benefits. In the past, he has managed various parts of it. This résumé presents him as a person who could run the whole thing.

Archibald Alexander

25 Campanas Street
Santa Fe, NM 87555
505-555-6281
aalexander@aft.net

SUMMARY OF QUALIFICATIONS

14 years' experience in design and administration in **all areas of employee benefit plans**, including 5 years with **Briar Consultants**. Advised some of the largest and most prestigious companies in the country. Excellent training and communications skills. MBA in Finance. **An effective manager who delivers consistent results**.

NYNAX CORPORATION   2008-Present

Manager, Stock Plans Administration

Manage an 8-person unit administering Employee Stock Purchase and Executive Stock Option plans.

- Personal contact with the **4,000 most senior executives**.
- Accounting and record keeping for **$178 million** in plan assets.
- **Reduced expenses 25%** through automation and productivity enhancements.
- Successfully conducted major stock purchase plan offering on tight schedule; the largest the company had ever undertaken: **90 countries**; data from 16 payroll systems; distribution of personalized packages to 60,000 employees.
- Implemented state-of-the-art transaction confirmations system.

BANKERS FIRST COMPANY   2007-2008

Defined Contribution Plans

- Manager Managed unit of six; **$750 million in plan assets**; 25 client plans.
- Managed all record keeping, trust, and administrative services for very large corporate clients' savings, 401(K), and stock ownership plans.
- Handled all regulatory and ERISA compliance, cash and securities management, consulting, trust administration, and accounting.
- **Reduced overtime 50%; computer usage 25%; expenses 33%.**

BRIAR CONSULTANTS   2002-2007

Defined Contributions Plans Consultant

Managed a unit of 10 consulting on all phases of design, implementation, and administration of Fortune 500 company plans.

- **Increased profits 170%.**
- Handled 25 accounts worth $3.2 million in annual revenue.
- Managed plan, systems, and database design.
- Supervised system conversions and daily production.
- Performed market analysis.
- Delivered sales presentations.
- Negotiated contracts and fees.
- Designed reports, statements, and administrative forms.

Archibald Alexander - Page 2

BRIAR CONSULTANTS, INC. (Cont'd)

Defined Benefit Plans Manager
- Consulted on pension plan design and interpretation, governmental reporting and compliance, record keeping, administrative practices and procedures, and the development and use of compliance manuals.
- Introduced standardized administration manuals and paperwork reduction techniques which **generated more than $1.2 million in consulting revenue**.

ROYAL INSURANCE COMPANY   2001-2002
Assistant Manager, Employee Benefits

- Compliance officer.
- Administered the company's pension, health and other employee benefit plans.
- Performed medical plan cost containment study and implemented changes resulting in a leveling of insurance premiums.
- Offered and implemented HMOs.
- Negotiated insurance contracts with carriers.
- Performed statistical compensation analysis.

NATIONAL BULK CARRIERS   2001
Employee Benefits Manager
- Administered domestic and overseas pension and group medical, life, disability and workers' compensation insurance plans. **Secretary Pension and Employee Benefits Committees**.

STANDARD BRANDS INCORPORATED (now RJR Nabisco)   1998-2001
Assistant Pension Supervisor

Administered 12 domestic pension plans covering 23,000 bargaining and non-bargaining employees.

EDUCATION
MBA, Economics and Finance, June 2005
BA, Psychology, June 1996
ST. JOHN'S UNIVERSITY

Helen Louise Albelo

44 Cliff Lake Town
Clarksville, New York 10001
Business: 914-555-2550
Residence: 914-555-4557
hlalbelo@rr.com

8 years' executive experience managing facilities and support services.

Managed and developed **9 service departments** with a **staff of 120**. Reorganized and set quality standards to reduce costs and lower turnover. Implemented training programs, improved morale and the respect of workers for each other. Strong negotiation skills. Work with high technology applications. In a building of 50,000 sq. ft., responsible for **office planning, telecommunications, maintenance, record retention**, and company promotion.

Professional Experience

VICE PRESIDENT, OPERATIONS & SUPPORT SERVICES   2004-present
THE KELLOGG GROUP (A subsidiary of Time, Inc.)

Manage a **staff of 120 in 9 service departments**.
Responsible for all **facilities management** for a **50,000 sq. ft. office**.
Manage a budget of **$7-10 million**.
Report directly to the Chairman.

Budgeting, Management and Cost Control
- Manage internal costs. Regularly renegotiate and monitor contracts to **keep costs down**.
- Conduct special analyses and cost comparisons, and purchase research.
- Regularly develop innovative solutions that cut costs in both the short and long term.
- Control work overflow resulting in a **smooth-running operation** with few complaints.
- Set up **system to handle bottlenecks and crisis deadlines**.

Telephones
- Select and maintain a system of **300 phones: central to this telemarketing business**.
- Establish special relationships with MCI, WATS, FAX, TELEX.
  - Allows for **special testing**, such as the 96 local lines that were installed for a 3-week test period and removed.
- Developed **a system that never goes down**.

Construction and Maintenance
- Regularly manage demolition and construction of space ranging from 3,000 to 7,000 sq. ft.
- Handle all city filings, HVAC regulations, and fire alarm systems.
- Handle all design and decoration including carpets, furniture, lighting and wall coverings.
- Maintain 50,000 sq. ft.: floors, walls, and so on.
- Negotiate/maintain cleaning contracts and maintenance contracts for business machines.

Records Retention
Manage the storage of **30,000 sq. ft. of records**.
- Established a successful **system for quick recall and timely destruction**.
- **Cut storage costs by two-thirds**.

Helen Louise Albelo - Page 2

VICE PRESIDENT, OPERATIONS & SUPPORT SERVICES, contd.

Printing and Mailings
- Coordinate writing, approval process, and actual printing:
  - company brochures,
  - redesign of company logo, and
  - annual Christmas card (designed by kids at Ronald McDonald House).
- Maintain company mailing list. Produce mailings, brochures, and self-promotional materials.
- Monitor **high volume, complex, on-deadline outside printing**.

Research Production Department
- **Handle 56 million copies/year.**
- Set up staff to monitor work flow and productivity of research projects as they pass through various areas of the company.
- Monitor project from proposal letter, questionnaire development, word processing, production, distribution and return, validation checking, coding, keypunching, data processing, and final report.

Data Processing
- Staff of 10.
- Develop programs for customized research studies.
- UNIX system.
- Maintain 13 remote PCs that are tied in to the UNIX.

N.Y. State Society of CPS's   2002-2004
Office Manager
- Staff of 10.
- Supervised equipment and production requirements to ensure progressive departmental growth.
- Supported three organizational divisions.

NU Financial Aid Department   1997-2002
Assistant to Loan Officer

Advanced Education
Various technical and managerial courses.

Dr. Carol Jackson

1336 Union Street
Miami, FL 99213
999-555-5803
jacksonedd@iec.net

Summary of Qualifications

20 years' experience in Program Development for universities and agencies.
Managed **projects ranging from $500,000 to $10 million.**
Directed small art museum. Determined cultural policy for a small country.
Ed.D. in International Education, University of Massachusetts, Amherst, MA

Areas of Expertise

- **International Education** in developing countries
- **Arts and Museum Administration**
- Securing **grants of $1 to $5 million each**
- Writing, researching, and **publishing**
- Teaching English, African and Caribbean Studies, etc.
- Fluent in English and French

Program Development Experience

Institute of Social and Economic Research   2013-2014

University of Trinidad Research Fellow
- Managed budget of **$1 million** for special project.
- Conducted an analysis of the effects of senior comprehensive schooling on the labor market performance of a sample of vocational graduates.
- **Edited 300-page book.**

Director, The National Museum, West Indies   2012-2013
- Designed and managed efforts to secure and maintain **$5 million** in government assistance to support museum's efforts.
- **Ran day-to-day operation of the museum**.
- **Trained 50 volunteers**.
- **Arranged exhibitions, lectures, panel discussions, etc**.

Senior Professional   2002-2012
Ministry of Sport, Culture and Youth Affairs, West Indies
- **Wrote national policies** on culture and youth.
- Identified and evaluated socioeconomic trends.
- Advised Minister on strategies for disbursement of **$60 million budget**.

University of Miami Graduate School   2006-2008

and the Puerto Rican Traveling Theater
Coordinator, Performance Education Program for the U.S. Office of Education
- **Administered after-school program** for minority children.
- Annual budget of $500,000 and a client population of 1,000.

Dr. Carol Jackson - Page 2

University of Michigan   2003-2006
Program Specialist
  • Coordinator, The Ghana Project.
  • Part of a **$10 million** five-year institutional development project funded by the U.S. Agency for
    International Development.

Assistant Director   1997-2003
Central Detroit Model Cities
  • Administered the Early Childhood Resource Center, catering to inner-city children.

Teaching Experience

Adjunct Lecturer, Ann Arbor College; Africana and Puerto Rican Studies Dept.	1999-2002
Educational Opportunity Center, Detroit; English, GED program	2001-2003
Adjunct Lecturer	
University of Michigan, School of Education	2003-2006
College of Boca Raton, School of New Resources	2007-2009
University of the West Indies, Department of Language and Linguistics	2010-2014

Consultancies
Dept. of Indian and Eskimo Affairs, Gov't of Canada
Caribbean/American Community Services Council Inc., NYC.
Oxum International, Miami, Florida
Creative Arts Center, University of the West Indies
Organization of American States, Washington, DC
U.S. Agency for International Development/Caricom Secretariat

Professional Affiliations
Phi Delta Kappa
Comparative and International Education Society
Caribbean Studies Association
Anti-Apartheid Organisation of Trinidad and Tobago

Publications
  • Carol Jackson (2011, **300 pp.**)
The Independence Experience of The West Indies,
I.S.E.R., Trinidad & Tobago
  • **The Vision of Black Artists**:
Carol Jackson (2010)
The Center for African American Art

In Progress:
  • Caribbean Contemporary Art
  • Focus on Southern Africa

Wilma Albrecht

806 Riverside Estates Road
Altus, N.C. 99712
999-555-9873
wilma.albrecht@flossb.com

Summary of Qualifications
Ten years' freelance experience in writing, editing, and proofreading.

Have **edited the writing of at least 45 people**. Backed by 4 years'experience teaching English. Keep balance between respect for the writer's art and the standards set by the organization. Accomplish tasks/goals in an organized, efficient manner with an attitude of pride, sensitivity, and self-discipline. Adhere to stylistic standards. B.A. in English.

Professional Experience

Mail Order Manager, Still Pond, Inc.   Jan.-Nov. 2014
Received/processed orders; set up/maintained filing system; corresponded with customers.

Internationally Recognized Not-for-Profit Organization   1999-2012
Organization focuses on improving communication techniques, especially in the areas of marriage and family living.

- **Managed a program of 14 presentations a week.**
  - Wrote and delivered 6 different presentations each weekend to groups of 45 people.
  - Edited 8 other presentations each week for 9 years.
  - Critiqued, proofread, and edited the writings of at least 45 other presenters.
  - Regularly met countless deadlines in both writing and critiquing/editing.
- **Edited bi-monthly newsletter.**
  - Wrote articles for every issue.
- **Co-Director of Operations**, Western North Carolina (1999-2001)
  - Coordinated and gave final approval of all writing assignments.
  - Responsible for hiring and firing, budgets and finances.
  - Maintained a balance:
    - sensitivity/respect toward writers and their work,
    - a focus on final "product" and **meeting standards set by the organizations,** and
    - the needs of seminar attendants.
  - **Edited** the organization's new brochure (2005).

Altus Elementary School, Parent Volunteer   1999-2008
- Assisted teachers with **proofreading/grading students' creative writing assignments**.
- **Coordinated/edited newspapers** for two class groups.

Teacher, English and Reading   1991-1995
Altus School System, primarily 7th and 8th grades
Focused on grammar/punctuation rules and an appreciation for creative writing and literature.

Education
B.A., English, Altus College, Altus, N.C., 1991
- 3.6 G.P.A. in the 16 English courses taken
- Nominated for Woodrow Wilson Fellowship (1991)
- **Literary Editor** for college yearbook (1990-1991)

The
Five
O'Clock
Club®

PART SEVEN

CVs for those in Education, Government, and Other Fields That Require a CV

The Five O'Clock Club®

Harold: In a Government Job; Aiming for a Promotion

You work that you may keep pace with the earth and the soul of the earth. For to be idle is to become a stranger unto the seasons, and to step out of life's procession, that marches in majesty and proud submission towards the infinite.

KAHLIL GIBRAN

I never did anything worth doing by accident, nor did any of my inventions come by accident; they came by work.

THOMAS A. EDISON

A person working for the government who wants another government job has to be low-key in stating his accomplishments. He can't brag, for example, about the famous criminals he has captured.

However, the following résumé lists Harold's extensive certifications and commendations, which take all of page 3, followed by all of his specialized training and courses, which take another page, followed by his education and then outside activities that show he was a good citizen (Cubmaster, etc.). It is easy to see that he has

always been an outstanding performer. In addition, Harold thought it was important to include the personal information at the end of his résumé. Since he had not yet met some of the people who would decide about the promotion, he wanted them to know about his stable family situation, as well as his physical size—given the kind of work he did.

You can see how Harold understated his accomplishments. Do not worry about the résumé length. It was necessary to take this many pages to present the information in a readable way. For example, if he had squeezed his basic career history onto one page, it would have been unreadable. The material was presented on high-quality ivory stock, stapled in the upper left-hand corner. Harold came across as someone who cared—someone who did more, tried to learn more, and was recognized throughout his career.

By the way, Harold's résumé helped him get the major promotion he wanted. There were many competitors for the job, but none had Harold's credentials—and it is safe to assume that no one presented his or her credentials as well as Harold did.

Harold R. Greenberg

15 Haverbrook Drive
Cash-in-Hand, NV 14555

Summary of Qualifications

Career State Investigator having 19 years experience;
over 14 years with the Division of Criminal Justice.

Extended diversified exposure both conducting and supervising investigation into the areas of economic crime, organized crime, and official corruption.

Since 1997, was a Division Instructor and representative to groups interested in the subject of various types of finance-related crime, its detection, investigation, and prosecution.

Professional Experience

Nevada Division of Criminal Justice, 1993-present
Office of the Attorney General

SUPERVISING STATE INVESTIGATOR OF THE ORGANIZED CRIME AND RACKETEERING BUREAU

2002-present

Conduct both financial and nonfinancial investigations of allegations concerning organized crime and official corruption.

Special Prosecutions Section

2007-2012

- Assigned to this section to investigate allegations of organized crime and official corruption.
- Specialized in financial implications.
- Investigations conducted for most part with Nevada State Police and allied agencies.

Major Fraud Unit

2000-2007_

Senior State Investigator
State Investigator

- Conducted primarily finance-related investigations.
- Investigations involved areas such as:
  - bank fraud and embezzlements,
  - securities fraud (stocks, bonds, commodities, and other investment schemes),
  - insurance fraud (including reinsurance fraud),

Major Fraud Unit, contd.
- Areas involved, contd.:
  - taxation frauds (including income taxation),
  - sales and use tax,
  - excise taxes (such as, motor fuels and employment taxes),
  - unemployment fraud conspiracies, and
  - other various schemes and offenses.
- Conducted investigation on individual and supervisory basis with Division personnel, and with allied governmental agencies as necessary.

Nevada State Law Enforcement Planning Agency   1997-2000
Executive Office of the Governor
   Audit Supervisor
   Auditor
- Established audit procedures and audit programs.
- Conducted audits.
- Supervised 5 staff auditors on statewide basis.

Internal Revenue Service, Reno District   1996-1997
   Internal Revenue Agent—Field Audit
Conducted audits of individuals, partnerships, and corporations as to Federal income taxes.

Nevada State Treasury, Division of Taxation   1995-1996
   Auditor-Accountant: Field
- After college graduation, began as auditor-accountant trainee in corporate tax bureau.
- Then assigned as Field Auditor responsible for individual audits of corporations as to state taxes.

CERTIFICATIONS AND COMMENDATIONS
Certified Police Instructor
Since 2002, Division Lecturer on various types of
White-Collar Crime, Organized Crime, and Official Corruption.
Specialized presentations on:
- Arson for Profit,
- Money Laundering, and
- Counterfeiting.

Certificate of Commendation
Upperville County Prosecutor's Office

Letter of Commendation
United States Congressman Martin Shulman

Letter of Commendation
Donald O'Connor
1st Assistant Attorney General and Director of Criminal Justice

Letter of Commendation
Dr. Saul Valvanis, Commissioner
Nevada Department of Education

Letter of Commendation
Commissioner Mary Purcello
Nevada Department of Banking

Letters of Commendation from
Various Societies and Organizations
American Bankers Association
Northern and Southern Districts of Nevada
American Society for Industrial Security Officers
Petroleum Security Officers Association
Nevada State University
Accounting Society
Nevada Commission of Investigation (S.C.I.)
Others as to state employment

Citation: Nevada State Assembly
as to community work with Scouts as Cubmaster

SPECIALIZED TRAINING AND COURSES

2014-present

Certified Public Manager Program

Continuing program sponsored by
Nevada Department of Personnel and Reno University.

2014

Roundtable: Money Laundering

Two-day seminar held at Main Treasury Building, Washington, D.C.,
sponsored by U.S. Assistant Secretary of Treasury.

2012

Supervising Undercover Investigations

Four-day course sponsored by the **University of Delaware** concentrating on
covert narcotics and organized-crime investigations.

2007

Racketeer Influenced Corrupt Organization (R.I.C.O.)

Sponsored by Nevada Division of Criminal Justice. 1 week course.
Also participated as Instructor for "Interpreting Financial Statements."

2006

Seminar: White Collar Crime-Investigation and Prosecution

1 week, Battelle Institute, Seattle, Washington
Also participated as Instructor as to utilizing the "Net Worth" approach as an investigative technique.

2000

Special Agent Training: Intelligence Division, U.S. Treasury

As State Investigator, completed 8-week course at National Training Center in Washington, D.C., by
enrollment in class of Federal Agents. Final two weeks was Inter-Agency training with Secret Service,
Securities & Exchange Commission, F.B.I., and Bureau of Alcohol, Tobacco & Firearms.

Firearms Training and Personal Defense

Police Academy, Upperville County, 2 weeks.

Investigation of White-Collar Crime and Official Corruption

Sponsored by **Seton Hall University** in conjunction with Peat, Marwick & Mitchell, 2-week course.

1999

Advanced Training for State Auditors

Held at Federal Inter-Agency Training Center, San Diego, CA, 3 weeks.

1997

Basic Training for State Auditors

Held at the Federal Inter-Agency Training Center, San Diego, CA, 3 weeks.

<u>SPECIALIZED TRAINING AND COURSES</u>, contd.

1996
<u>Internal Revenue Agent Training</u>

Held in Philadelphia, PA. This 7-week course included education and application of Taxation Code, Regs, Cases and Rulings, and audit procedures.

On other various dates received specialized training held
at Division of Criminal Justice such as related to:

- Wiretap and Electronic Surveillance,
- Grand Jury Training,
- Search and Seizure, etc.

<u>EDUCATION</u>

1995	B.S., Commerce, Reno College Major: Business Administration/Accounting Post-degree coursework in: Taxation, Investments, and Computers
2002	Passed Nevada State examination for Investment Securities Brokers and Dealers Received principal rating.
current	Certified Public Manager program, in conjunction with Nevada State University Completed two of three sessions.

<u>OUTSIDE ACTIVITIES</u>

Cubmaster—Pack 60

Cub Scouts, Cash-in-Hand, Nevada

Trustee and Treasurer

Robert Jordan Memorial Scholarship Fund

<u>PERSONAL</u>

Married, 3 children

Age—43

Height—6'3"

Weight—218 lbs.

The
Five
O'Clock
Club

Heba: Her "CV" for a Job in Education

By Anita Attridge, Certified Five O'Clock Club Career Coach

In the previous case study, Harold needed a CV (Curriculum Vitae) to look for another job in government. A person may be asked for a CV if he or she is seeking a position in education, research, or in a nonprofit advocacy, justice or health organization.

Still, the CV does not have to be a bland recitation of a person's history. It is in your best interests to have a summary, as Heba did.

Heba had been in one public school system for most of her career. Her progression during her 30 years there was impressive. However, her CV failed to demonstrate this.

In her old CV (not shown), the first page focused on her contact information, education, certificates and employment history, which was listed by title and focused on her duties instead of her accomplishments. Since she listed the titles, followed by the institution, it was not easy to see that she had progressed from being the Science Instructor to the Chief Academic Officer in the same school system.

A section titled Achievements and Awards listed awards interspersed with accomplishments so the impressive awards she had received were lost in the list. The publication list did not differentiate the book she had written from the articles she wrote. It was difficult to quickly comprehend her impressive accomplishments, awards, and publications.

With all of her accomplishments in creatively educating K-12 students in science and technology, and her innovative programs that increased student retention and learning, she did not understand why her CV did not stand out from her competition.

Her revised CV focused on what she had accomplished instead of her duties, listed her key awards so that they could be easily recognized, and differentiated her books from her publications. Heba found that she was much more effectively positioned for the positions that interested her.

Here, we are showing only the summary page of her 7-page resume. That is followed by:

- Pages 2 through 4: three pages of employment history with accomplishments directly related to the kind of job she wants to have next
- Page 5 contains:
  - **Related Employment**, such as her work as a Government Affairs Liaison, an Adjunct Faculty Member. This takes five lines since no accomplishments are stated.
  - **Education**: listing her four degrees
  - **Professional Certifications** (3 lines)
  - **Training** (5 lines)
  - **Awards** (11 lines)
- Page 6 contains:
  - **Service Appointments**, such as her various Board of Directors positions. (12 lines)
  - **Professional Memberships** (4 memberships)
  - **Publications**, starting with books.
- Page 7 contains:
  - **Presentations**, 9 of them, starting with the most important.

Heba Mosalem, Ed.S

1224 Chesterfield Road
Point Pleasant, MO 63156

hmosalem@sbcglobal.net

Home: (555) 555-6375
Cell: (555) 555-8745

EDUCATIONAL ADMINISTRATOR AND LEADER

Large districts   *Small districts*   *Charter schools*

*Progressed from being the Science Instructor to the Chief Academic Officer
in the same school system*

- Increased student performance by quantifying student achievement data
- Conducted needs assessments to achieve district goals
- Collaboratively developed strategic plans to optimize operations
- Significantly improved school and academic performance
- Designed professional development programs to enhance the skills of teachers and leaders
- Developed the infrastructure for Charter schools

EXPERT IN:

Analysis of achievement data   Keynote presentations

Academic and program evaluations   Leadership development

Whole-school reform planning   Curriculum-Instruction-Assessment

RESULTS

- **Revamped the teaching and learning of science, mathematics and technology in 74 schools**. Increased proficiency from 9% to more than state average of 51% in three years
- **Principal**: Developed diverse after-school programs with 70% participation rate that ultimately reversed declining student achievement and created positive cultural change
- **Chief Academic Officer**: Introduced an academic model to evaluate all departments. Increased consistency and performance of services to students, teachers and parents
- Introduced the direction and operation of all major district-wide programs by creating and implementing **sustainable "Academic Model"**
- **Chief of Staff**: Developed plans including comprehensive school improvement plan, professional development plan; performance based evaluation and accountability plan
- Created and organized project-based **competition for 110 schools** and high level robotics competition for high schools
- **A polished speaker**: Represented my districts by presenting to several **local and national audiences** on pertinent issues in education and served on numerous panel discussions

The
Five
O'Clock
Club®

PART EIGHT

Résumés for Lower-Level Professionals

For Junior-Level Employees:
A Summary Makes the Difference

*The greatest discovery of my generation
is that a human being can alter his life by
altering his attitudes of mind.*

WILLIAM JAMES

---

*Opportunity is missed by most people because it is
dressed in overalls and looks like work.*

THOMAS EDISON

---

*In the last analysis, the only freedom is the
freedom to discipline ourselves.*

BERNARD BARUCH

Cecilia is four years out of school; Lillian is a young administrative assistant. In both cases, a summary statement differentiates them from their competitors. Even recent graduates should have a summary—to separate them from all of the other job hunters just out of school.

All résumés—no matter what a person's level is—can include personality traits. It's not enough to know that you have done certain things; it is also relevant to know *how* you did them. Are you especially organized, discreet, or innovative? Let the reader know, because your personality is one of the most important things you have to offer.

You will notice that the résumés in this book—even that of the most senior executives—mention personality traits. That way readers will get a feeling for the way people accomplish their tasks.

Cecilia Dobbs

499 East Lancaster Avenue
Wayne, PA 19063

cdobbs462@hotmail.com

(215) 555-1765 (residence)
(215) 555-8024 (office)

Summary of Qualifications

An honors degree in Marketing (**magna cum laude**) is coupled with **four years of professional marketing experience** and a solid history of **successful projects, promotions, and awards**. Ability to coordinate the efforts of many to meet organizational goals. High in energy with strong interpersonal skills.

Professional Skills

Hands-on experience within Marketing includes: market research, marketing support, project management, public speaking, training, computers, and vendor relations.

Staris Information Services Company   2013 to Present

Marketing Analyst

Supported Product Managers by designing and implementing a variety of projects. Results achieved in this position include:

- Developed contracts, visited branch offices, gave presentations to sales staff/management.
- Prepared **special reports such as "Analysis of Commercial Revenue**," "Guide to Writing a Proposal."
- Awarded Marketing's "**Outstanding Performer**" of the Month," July 2009. Received for creatively organizing over 300 pages of material for sales manuals at significant cost savings, ahead of schedule and within one month's time.
- **Developed and implemented the contracting system** for our division. Made presentations **instructing the field** on the system's processes. Project in line with goal to reopen channel between marketing and sales force.
- **Designed** Product Blue Book, a handy marketing guide to our products for sales personnel.
- **Restructured the** Marketing Guide to be marketing oriented; previously a marketing policy and procedure manual.
- **Created profile questionnaire for a** Competitive Information System.
- **Managed computerized distribution** of marketing manuals; controlled the content of each.

Bringhan Advertising, Inc.   2012 to 2013

Project Director

Responsible for directing research project of agency clients in the consumer package goods field. Results achieved in this position include:

- **Employed various quantitative and qualitative methods** for concept tests, taste tests and pre- and post-advertising tests.
- Met critical deadline three weeks after hire, one week ahead of schedule.
- Involved in all phases of studies from **basic design to client presentation**.
- Researched and prepared special report on Solar Energy Marketplace.
- Developed strong relations with several research suppliers.

Cecilia Dobbs - Page 2

Hilton Research Services   2010-2012
Study Director
- <u>**Coordinated**</u> all production for various **<u>market research studies</u>**: questionnaire construction, pretesting, sampling, interviewing, editing, coding, tabulation, assisting in report writing
- <u>**Supervised the work of 50 people**</u> in a research project for a large data-processing client. Consisted of **<u>20,000 interviews</u>** conducted via CRTs. **<u>Resulted in significant change</u>** to client's market strategy.
- <u>**Advised study directors**</u> on design of online research studies.

<u>Survey Programmer II</u>
- Assisted programmers in developing electronic questionnaires for the CRT. Maintained survey data and verified tabulated research results.
- <u>**Received three promotions**</u> within 11 months of hire.

B. M. Smith & Associates   Summer Practicum 2002
<u>Study Coordinator</u>
Conducted research project to determine most effective renovation of client's shopping center. Sample/questionnaire design, collection of primary/secondary data, tabulation, interpretive analysis of data.

Marymount College of Virginia   September 2000 to May 2010
<u>Study Skills Instructor</u>
Taught study, presentation, and interpersonal skills in 15-week courses to students with academic and personal problems.

<u>**Chilton Research Services, Interviewer**</u>   November 2010 to August 2011
Conducted telephone interviews for both consumer and industrial studies. Exceeded quota 100% of the time.

EDUCATION
BA, **<u>magna cum laude</u>**, Business Administration, Marymount College of Virginia, 2010
AA, Business Administration/General Merchandising, Marymount College of Virginia, 2009
<u>Honors and Awards:</u>
- Selected twice for "Who's Who in American Universities."
- Vice President of Student Faculty Council for two successive years.
- Member of four honor societies

CONTINUING EDUCATION
Attended various American Marketing Association seminars on market research techniques, as well as courses on written communication.

OUTSIDE ACTIVITIES
<u>Television, Radio and Advertising Club</u> (TRAC)
Designed and conducted 2013 membership study.
<u>Network of Women in Computer Technology</u> (NWCT)
Designed and conducted 2014 membership study.

LILLIAN LOWANS

43 Marlborough Lane
North Orange, New Jersey 07999
(908) 555-1111
llowans46@aol.com

Four years of executive assistant / analytical experience
coupled with continuing college education.

A solid history of **excellent work relationships**, both with the public and with internal personnel at all organizational levels. High in **initiative and energy** with strong ability to exercise **independent judgment**. Excellent writing skills. Trustworthy and discreet.

Professional Skills
Proficient in the use of computers: Database software, Word, Windows, Excel, Lotus, Powerpoint.
But more importantly, can take on **major projects** and handle
from initiation and planning through to implementation and follow-up.

DataPro   2011 to Present

Senior Administrative Assistant to Manager of Department
Performed general secretarial duties with minimum supervision.

- **Represent manager** in collecting activity reports from departmental professional staff; compile and draft final report for signature.
- Compose letters independently or from general direction as required.
- **Administer the entire** Competitive Information System from receipt of information through acknowledgment, analysis flow, publicity, and final entry into the computer system.
- Maintain and monitor correspondence/communication follow-up system.
- **Monitor status** of departmental projects.
- Supervise temporary typists.

Intercounty Savings Association   2009 to 2011

Executive Assistant to President
Performed general administrative/analytical duties and **coordinated all personal and business affairs of the President**.

- Acted as **liaison between president and branch offices**, as well as service corporations, the **general public**, insurance companies, government agencies and members of the U.S. Senate and House of Representatives.
- Calculated **daily subsidiary figures** to allow determination of funds flow. Based on the outcome, **wired and borrowed funds**.
- Prepared **minutes for Board of Directors** and Committee meetings.
- **Solicited bids** and handled insurance for Association and personnel to comply with Federal guidelines. Maintained approximately 100 personnel records.
- Distributed and administered travelers checks and U.S. Government savings bonds for all branches.

LILLIAN LOWANS - Page 2

Yarway Corporation Administrative   2006- 2009
Assistant to Manager of Manufacturing/Plant Engineering   2007-2009
Performed a variety of duties with little supervision.

- **Directed the work flow** through the department and **supervised a full-time clerk**.
- **Collected, analyzed, and assembled data** from reports and print-outs into meaningful logs and charts for manager's use.
- **Coordinated the flow** of blueprint adaptations to obtain bids for the manufacturing of special tooling.
- Handled a **variety of projects** at the request of manager.

Assistant to Administrative Assistant of **Vice President of Manufacturing**   June 2006 to May 2007
and **President of Yarway North American Division**

Typed **large volumes** of correspondence and reports in a timely fashion; distributed reports; **updated manuals, including the Quality Assurance Manual for the ASME**; performed general clerical duties.

Cost Accounting Clerk (part-time, work/study program)   September 2005 to June 2006

Analyzed routings to determine individual costs of labor and material; posted figures; and assisted other members of the Accounting Department in routing accounting functions.

EDUCATION
Plymouth Whitemarsh Senior High School, Whitemarsh, PA
Graduated Class of 2006. Business Major, Work/Study Program

SUPPLEMENTAL EDUCATION (Most recent)
Basic Principles of Supervisory Management, Work Organization, Time Management,
Improving Management Skills of Secretaries, and
Various Computer Courses

Résumés for People with *Nothing to Offer*

One's prime is elusive....You must be on the alert to recognize your prime at whatever time of life it may occur.

MURIEL SPARK, *The Prime of Miss Jean Brodie*

Recent college graduates, homemakers, or those with very little or very low-level work experience often feel as though they have nothing to offer. They say: "Kate, if I had the experience the people in your examples had, I'd have no trouble writing a résumé."

These people are wrong in a number of ways.

1. Even the highest-level executives have a great deal of difficulty figuring out what their accomplishments have been and preparing their own résumés. Résumé preparation is a skill, just as marketing or finance is a skill, and it is not something executives need to do every day on their jobs.

2. You are not competing with high-powered executives. Therefore, it doesn't matter that you haven't run a division of 600 people. If you had run that division, you'd have other problems in preparing your résumé.

3. It's better for each of us, no matter what our experiences, to cultivate a positive outlook: to assure ourselves that we have done okay, despite mistakes and wrong turns. Our experiences have made us what we are today, and that's not so bad. We should be proud of whoever we are and make the most of it. We should each strive—executive, young person, homemaker—to uncover our special gifts and contributions and let the world know.

On a national TV program, I was once asked to work with an "ordinary housewife" and develop a résumé for her. It was promoted as something akin to magic. Can Kate make this nothing into a something? The producers picked someone who had been at home for 20 years. That would be a good one! Without even seeing her (which increased the illusion of magic), I interviewed the woman and developed a great résumé for her.

Afterward, the people who worked in the studio said it wasn't fair: We should have picked someone who *really* had nothing to offer. They were convinced that a typical "ordinary homemaker" could not possibly have an interesting résumé. These studio executives were voicing a prejudice that reinforces the way many people feel about themselves.

I was successful with the "ordinary homemaker" because, in real life, most homemakers are not sitting home doing nothing for 20 years. A career coach can help find the things anyone has to offer. Every homemaker and every young person has *done things*. With an open mind and the right help, these can be presented well in a résumé.

The Process

Prior to showtime, I spent one hour on the phone with Maria, with no preparation on her part. You, however, would be wise to prepare by doing some of the exercises listed below. If you have trouble doing them, don't worry. You can do them with your coach.

1. **List the fields you think you would like to go into**. If you have a clear idea about what you want to do in the future, that's great. Even if you don't, you can still have a fine résumé.

2. **List all the work you have ever done** before your marriage (or school) or during it. It does not matter whether you earned money doing this work. For example, Maria "helped out" in her daughter's store. She didn't get paid for it, but it added a lot to her résumé.

3. **List all the volunteer work you have ever done** for your place of worship, school, neighbors, and friends. What are the things you find yourself doing again and again? For example, do you find you are always baking cakes for parties, babysitting, or volunteering to tutor? List these things.

4. **List any organizations you have belonged to and any courses you have taken**.

5. **List your most important personality traits**. Are your detail-oriented? Are you able to motivate others? Do you follow through on everything you tackle?

6. **List your favorite hobbies, pastimes, or interests**. Perhaps, for example, you enjoy needlepoint. I had one client whose passion was bowling—she not only bowled but she also scheduled tournaments. We were able to make a résumé out of it, and she got a job with a bowling association!

Try to list everything, no matter how silly it seems. Then **set up an appointment with your coach**.

These are essentially the same exercises top executives do. Again, the Seven Stories Exercise is the key to uncovering those things you enjoyed doing and also did well—and would like to do again. And the exercise is helpful in uncovering other things as well. Through the exercise, you will find out:

- what you have done that you are proud of. In the sample résumés that follow, each person has found something to be proud of, whether it's earning money to go through school or helping a daughter in her shop.

- personality traits that will separate you from the competition, such as the ones noted in the summary statement of Larry's résumé, which follows: productive, self-motivated, and so on.

- how to look at your work, school, and volunteer experience objectively. In Larry's example, he spent a great deal of time analyzing the job he had. This analysis gave his résumé a lot of substance.

Even young people with no "real" work experience, or housewives who have been out of the workforce a long while can develop strong résumés—if they can think about their experiences objectively.

And, as with executives, the experiences have to be "repositioned" to fit the target market. For example, Maria said she had helped her daughter in the store. The fact is, Maria was alone in the store a lot of the time. Therefore, she was "managing the store." And when she went shopping with her daughter for things to sell in the store, they were not "shopping" but "buying."

Give it a try. With a little help and an open mind, you too can develop a résumé that truly reflects you.

There's always a struggle, a striving for something bigger than yourself in all forms of art. And even if you don't achieve greatness—even if you fail, which we all must—everything you do in your work is somehow connected with your attitude toward life, your deepest secret feelings.

REX HARRISON, AS QUOTED IN *The New York Times*

Do not be too timid and squeamish about your actions. All life is an experiment.

RALPH WALDO EMERSON

Young Person's Résumé

LAWRENCE A. DiCAPPA
1112 Vermont Lane, Downingtown, PA
(215) 555-1111; dicappajr@lowmail.net

Salesperson
with a solid history of success

Extensive product knowledge is coupled with creative ideas for product applications. A proven ability to **develop sales potential in new market areas**. Strong analytical and planning skills, combined with the ability to coordinate the efforts of many to meet organizational goals. **Productive and efficient** work habits without supervision. Self-motivator and high energy.

A solid background in sales and product experience.
Additional supervisory as well as training experience.

Telephone Sales Representative, AMP Special Industries   June 1999-Present
- **Achieved 140% growth** in assigned account responsibility: from $90,000 to $230,000 in the year 2000. Accounts were previously declining at 35% annually.
- **Developed a complete marketing program where none previously existed**. Program now serves as a guide for new hires and future departmental growth.
- **Set up and established new territory** by:
    - Devising a technique for introducing the sales concept and then the product to customers.
    - Designing an introductory call script, which is now a standard for the department.
    - Developing a strategy for attacking and penetrating a customer master list.
    - Serving as product specialist and trainer for six new hires.
    - Developing complete managerial outline for continued growth and success of the department.
- Finished in top three in both advanced and basic sales training classes.

Office Manager, American Excelsior Company   1995-1999
(approximately two years full-time while attending college)
- **Responsible for internal sales service**.
- **Purchased 70% of company's raw materials**.
- **Managed work flow** for an office of five personnel.
- **Coordinated the workload** of warehouse and trucking personnel in arranging shipments of customer orders via company-owned fleet and common carriers.

EDUCATION
BS, Business Administration, Drexel University, Philadelphia, PA, 1999
Major: Marketing, **4.0 average in field of concentration**.
65% of total college expenses were earned through full-time and part-time employment.

Homemaker

1234 'XYZ' Street
City, State 11999
515-555-3456
e-mail

Summary of Qualifications

The most important highlight of your experience is placed first. This is followed by your other experiences and skills. Perhaps you are an excellent administrator or organizer, work well with all kinds of people, or have some other special experience. The coach will help determine the best way to express your strengths.

Professional Experience

Job Title or function you performed   dates or years

Company or organization name or project you worked on
- Here are listed some of the things you did there.
- **Think about what you _really_ did, whether or not it was your job to do it**.
- It is **_very_** difficult to think about these things yourself. A career coach is able to develop a résumé that reflects your experience. Your résumé will look like this one.

Another Job Title or function you performed   dates or years

Company or organization name or project you worked on
- A list of the things you did, **whether or not you were paid for them**.
- If the work you did was not for an organization but was for family or friends, that's okay. We can make a résumé out of those experiences also.

PTA   1986 to present
- Maria thought her PTA experience was useless. But we expressed what she had done in a way that reflected her efforts. We can do the same for you. Do not compare your experiences to Maria's. Comparing yourself to someone else will prevent you from thinking about those things you truly did well, enjoyed doing, and are proud of.
- Instead, **think only about yourself**: What do you enjoy doing? What are you good at? What do you find yourself doing again and again? Do you find yourself "catering" parties for friends? Then, let's talk about it. Do you stage raffles for your church or synagogue? Let's talk about it. Have you held posts in an organization? What do others say about your work? What do you _think_ about your work? Let's talk about it, and put it down on paper.
- I know you are proud of your spouse and children. But instead of telling me about their accomplishments, tell me about yours. This may be difficult for you because you may be used to building them up instead of yourself. But we are not trying to get **_them_** a job. We're trying to get **_you_** a job, and so we have to talk about you and how good you are. Let's give it a try. Believe it or not, **_everyone_** comes out with a good résumé.

Coursework
We'll list here any courses you have taken if they are appropriate.

Maria Salerno

4756 Cashew Lane
Sweet Briar, Missouri 99000
999-555-3456
mariasalerno@google.net

Summary of Qualifications

9 years' experience in office management and the fashion industry. 10 years as an officer or committee member for a not-for-profit organization. A thorough, conscientious, and hard worker who meets deadlines and gets the job done. Works well with others, including management, peers, and the public.

Professional Experience

Salesperson/Store Manager (Part-time)   1-1/2 years

Propaganda Boutique **(top-of-the-line women's clothing)**
- As Assistant Buyer, went to showrooms, selected clothing and accessories.
- Managed the store. Dealt with the public. Handled complaints.

Office Manager   3 years

Micro-Ohm Corporation, a 30-person company.
- Kept books, did the payroll, answered the phones.
- Regular contact with clients and employees. Worked closely with the President.

Bookkeeping Department

Lansing Knitwear (Also modeled clothing)   2 years

Chase Manhattan Bank   3 years

PTA   1991 to present

Over the course of 13 years, served as Vice President and on every Committee.
- Received **Certificate of Appreciation** for outstanding service and dedication.
- As **Vice President** (2 years),
  - Substituted for the President. Attended the Board meetings of all Committees.
- With members of the **International Committee**,
- **Researched foreign countries**. Visited consulates. Recruited speakers.
  - **Held special events** to represent each country to the students. Served foreign foods, handed out flags, had dancers, or did whatever else was appropriate for that country.
- As a member of other committees,
  - **Recruited various speakers** to address the students.
  - These included a nutritionist, a computer expert, a Chinese cook, experts on drug and alcohol abuse, and so on. Also had **State senators and representatives** come in to address parents' concerns.
- As PTA Liaison, regularly meet with the Principal, Department Heads, and faculty members. Meetings are held to update the PTA, and to ask questions of the faculty.
- Serve as a delegate to other schools as a representative of the PTA.

Fluent in Italian; Familiar with Spanish.

The Five O'Clock Club®

Before and After Résumés For Someone in College

Julie, a college sophomore majoring in architecture, wanted summer employment. Although she had some relevant job experience, her résumé was a cookie-cutter version: it looked like everyone else's, and started out with her education.

Most of the 24,000 undergraduates attending the University of Michigan will have résumés that start out exactly the same: BA, History, University of Michigan, 201X.

If she wants a job with an architectural firm, Julie must make sure the reader would see her as quite a find for summer help at an architectural firm. The average résumé is looked at for only 10 seconds. Julie needed to make it easier for the employer to see what she had to offer—and to distinguish herself from her competition: all of the undergrads in her geographic area. The way to do that, most often, is to highlight your work experience, not your education.

Under "Work Experience," highlight the jobs that would be of most interest to your target market. Julie had listed first her work as a library aid—certainly not something that would make architectural firms sit up and take notice. Julie's relevant experience was buried in the middle of her résumé.

The Start of a Good Résumé

So Julie did what every Five O'Clock Clubber does: She didn't skip the assessment. She took time to do her Seven Stories Exercise as well as her Forty-Year Vision. Through the Seven Stories, she uncovered those things she "enjoyed doing and also did well." The results would help confirm whether architecture was the right path, and give her accomplishments to talk about on her résumé and cover letter, as well as in the interviewing process.

Here are the results of Julie's Seven Stories Exercise:
1. editor of yearbook
2. soloist in 7th and 8th grades
3. played Gwendolyn in 11th grade play
4. built chair for design class this year
5. built igloo with family
6. trained my dog
7. built stand for cinderblock; it held
8. learned autoCADD--fast & accurately
9. organized binders at work
10. wrote poems that got published
11. helped establish a cappella group
12. won "best science and math student" in my high school (of 40 students)
13. created dance with friends for talent show and won!

Here's Julie's ranked list:
1. editor of yearbook
2. built stand for cinderblock; it held
3. built chair for design class this year
4. wrote poems that got published
5. helped establish a cappella group
6. built igloo with family
7. learned autoCADD- fast & accurately

Julie's Seven Stories results contain elements that support her interest in architecture. At age 11, she was interested in building the igloo. She enjoyed her architecture courses and did well in them. She worked in a civil engineering firm using AutoCADD, a tool that architects use. She enjoyed doing it and did it well. She even enjoyed editing her high school yearbook, which included extensive design work, albeit of another kind.

Julie's Forty-Year Vision

At age 29:

Since Julie had not worked on her Forty-Year Vision before we met, we did a quick version together. Julie imagined herself 10 years from now—at age 29—working for a small architecture firm with about 20 employees. Although Julie was interested in building museums, very few museums get built— as compared with other structures. So she imagined herself in a firm that built family houses, schools and new business owners' offices.

By age 29, Julie did not want to be working on the nitty-gritty everyday work, but wanted to be more involved in planning and have client contact.

At age 39:

"I'll have my architect's license, and would be able to start my own firm if I wanted to. However, 39 may be young to start my own firm, but I would be the person others go to in my present firm."

So, Julie's Forty-Year Vision fits in nicely with the results of her Seven Stories Exercise.

What kind of summer job should Julie aim for now at age 19?

Julie wanted hands-on experience as much as possible, and she was more likely to get that at a smaller firm. She was afraid of getting assigned to doing Auto-CADD all day long, and actually preferred administrative work, perhaps as an assistant to a busy architect, lining up meetings, putting proposals together, and so on. She could see herself doing a variety of computer work.

Her Résumé

So Julie's new résumé emphasized her administrative expertise over her AutoCADD experience. Most often, a student will have a brief summary and list accomplishments under each job. But in Julie's case, we wanted to keep all of her Auto-CADD experience together, so we had to put all of it in her summary.

In addition, Julie was hoping to have some client contact. She had no related experience (unless you count talking to customers in a grocery store!), so at the end of her summary, we have listed some personality traits. Perhaps the hiring team will consider Julie for client contact work.

Wherever possible, we quantified Julie's accomplishments. Details can show substance and attract attention!

On the following pages are Julie's "before" and "after" résumés.

Julie Angelo

julieangelo@umich.edu
angelo555@yahoo.com
76 North Churchill Rd.
Brewster MI 99945

Education

University of Michigan	2009-2013
BA, Architecture	Current GPA: 3.42

The Curtis School	2005-2009
Graduated Salutatorian, with Highest Honors	

Work Experience

Library Aid   2009-2011
University of Michigan Blain Library
- Answer customer questions
- Shelved and checked out books

Assistant Office Manager   2009-2011
Engineering Firm: J. Robert Folchetti and Associates, L.L.C.
- Ran office when needed
- Typed and formatted Correspondence
- Answered 8 line phone

Assistant Cadd Operator   Summer 2010
Engineering Firm: J. Robert Folchetti and Associates, L.L.C.
- Corrected and Revised Details
- Convert drawings to CADD 2000 format

Produce Manager, Assistant   Summer 2008
Kobakers Grocery Store
- Organize and Layout Produce
- Answer customer questions

Skills

<u>Computer</u>: Auto CADD 2010, Adobe InDesign, Power Point, Word,
Word Perfect, Excel, Adobe Photoshop, QuarkExpress
<u>Languages</u>: proficient in German, knowledgeable in Spanish

Julie Angelo

julieangelo@umich.edu
angelo555@yahoo.com
76 North Churchill Rd.
Brewster MI 99945

University of Michigan Box #3124
863 Erie Avenue
Ann Arbor, MI 99999
555-666-4693

Assistant Office Manager / Assistant AutoCADD Operator
With Civil Engineering Firm

- A strong administrator
  - Organized 90-page client proposals.
  - Organized all forms used in office. Put together 7 binders of forms.
  - Reshelved 400 catalogs.
  - Ran office when needed; answered 8 phone lines; typed and formatted correspondence.

- AutoCADD experience
  - Took intensive 40-hour AutoCADD course.
  - Routinely handled small AutoCADD assignments for engineers, saving them hours.

- Converted drawings to CADD 2000 format.
  - Put together 70-page AutoCADD Manual with drawings.
  - Offered full-time AutoCADD job.
- In Architecture class, won contests: "most structurally sound design," "most pleasing to eye."
- Computer experience: AutoCADD 2010, Adobe InDesign, Quark Express, Adobe Photoshop, PowerPoint, Excel, Word, Word Perfect
- Languages: proficient in German, knowledgeable in Spanish

Strong working relationships at all levels.
Known for getting the job done efficiently and correctly, and putting in the hours needed.

Work History

Assistant Office Manager / Assistant AutoCADD Operator   Summer, 2010 & 2009 to present
Engineering Firm: J. Robert Folchetti and Associates, L.L.C.

Library Aid   2009 to present
University of Michigan Blain Library
- Answer customer questions; shelve and check out books

Produce Manager, Assistant   Summer 2008
Kobakers Grocery Store
- Organized and laid out produce; answered customer questions

Education

BA, Architecture, University of Michigan pending (Current GPA: 3.42)   2009-2013
- Helped to develop and create a new a cappella group.

The Curtis School   2005-2009
- Graduated Salutatorian, with Highest Honors
- Yearbook Editor: Developed 250-page book celebrating school's 150th anniversary
- Wrote poem for national publication; selected as one of ten for audio cassette

The Five O'Clock Club®

PART NINE

Résumé Checklist: How Good Is Your Résumé?

The
Five
O'Clock
Club®

Quotes to Inspire You

This is the true joy in life, the being used for a purpose recognized by yourself as a mighty one, the being thoroughly worn out before you are thrown on the scrap heap; the being a force of nature instead of a feverish selfish little clod of ailments and grievances complaining that the world will not devote itself to making you happy.

GEORGE BERNARD SHAW IN RICHARD WARREN'S *The Purpose Driven Life* (ZONDERVAN PUBLISHERS)

Dear sir, Be patient toward all that is unsolved in your heart and try to love the <u>questions themselves</u> like locked rooms and like books that are written in a very foreign tongue. Do not now seek the answers, which cannot be given you because you would not be able to live them. And the point is, to live everything. <u>Live</u> the questions now. Perhaps you will then gradually, without noticing it, live along some distant day into the answer. Perhaps you do carry within yourself the possibility of shaping and forming as a particularly happy and pure way of living; train yourself to it—but take whatever comes with trust, and if only it comes out of your own will, out of some need of your inmost being, take it upon yourself and hate nothing.

RAINER MARIA RILKE, *Letters to a Young Poet*

The Five O'Clock Club®

Résumé Checklist: How Good Is Your Résumé?

1. Positioning:
- If I spend just **10 seconds** glancing at my résumé, what are the ideas/words that pop out? (specific job titles, my degrees, specific company names): _____
  _____
  _____
- This is how I am positioned by my résumé. Is this how I want to be positioned for this target area? Or is this positioning a handicap for the area I am targeting?

2. Level:
- What level do I appear to be at? Is it easy for the reader to guess in 10 seconds what my level is? (For example, if I say I "install computer systems," I could be making anywhere from $15,000 a year to $200,000 a year.)

3. Summary Statement:
- If I have no summary statement, I am being positioned by the most recent job on my résumé. Is that how I want to be positioned?
  — If I have a summary, does the very first line position me for the kind of job I want next?
  — Is this followed by a statement that elaborates on the first statement?
  — Is this followed by statements that prove how good I am or differentiate me from my likely competitors?
  — Have I included a statement or two that give the reader an indication of my personality or my approach to my job?

4. Accomplishments:
- Within each job, did I merely list historically what I had done, or did I state my accomplishments with an eye to what would interest the reader in my target area?
- Are the accomplishments easy to read?
  — Bulleted rather than long paragraphs.
  — No extraneous words.
  — Action oriented.
  — Measurable and specific.
  — Relevant. Would be of interest to the readers in my target area. Either the accomplishment is something they would want me to do for them, or it shows the breadth of my experience.

5. Overall Appearance:
- Is there plenty of white space? Or is the information squeezed so I can get it on one or two pages?
- Is it laid out nicely so it can serve as my marketing brochure?

6. Miscellaneous:
- Length: Is the résumé as short as it can be while still being readable?
- Writing style: Can the reader understand the point I am trying to make in each statement?
- Clarity: Am I just hoping the reader will draw the right conclusion from what I've said? Or do I take the trouble to state things so clearly that there is no doubt that the reader will come away with the right message?
- Completeness: Is all important information included? Have all dates been accounted for?
- Typos: Is my résumé error free?

The Five O'Clock Club

There's No Reason to Lie on Your Résumé:
Just Reposition Yourself Honestly and Punch-Up Your Achievements

Yahoo CEO Scott Thompson lied on his résumé, claiming he had a degree in computer science when he didn't. Dan Lyons, a blogger, wrote this:

> "The ultimate irony is that the lie you told was so needless. Yahoo didn't hire you because it thought you had a computer-science degree from Stonehill College. Good grief!
>
> "By the time you got recruited into Yahoo you'd been CEO of PayPal, and before that held top jobs at Inovant, a subsidiary of Visa, and at Barclay's Global Investors. Even if you had studied computer science at Stonehill College in the 1970s, whatever you learned there would have been obsolete by about, um, the moment you left school."

Lying on résumés has reached an all-time peak from little fibs about job titles to exaggerations regarding responsibilities to fictitious claims of advanced degrees. With reports of résumé padding proliferating in the press, employers are becoming more vigilant about background checking and are stepping up efforts to weed out fakers.

There's no reason to lie. The slightest inaccuracy on your résumé can come back to bite you in the face and disqualify you for a position you have the skills and experience to win honestly. To distinguish yourself from the competition and make your résumé stand out from the crowd, you need to highlight and reposition your accomplishments

so they accurately reflect what you are capable of doing. Remember, your résumé has two purposes: it's a sales tool designed to get you the interview, and it's a roadmap to guide the interviewer.

Here are some research-based suggestions for writing a truthful résumé that stands out:

- Brainstorm and rank your accomplishments. Think about and rank the tasks you've enjoyed doing and have also done well in your career. Be sure appropriate accomplishments are clearly visible on your resume. List them as bullets in the summary section at the top of your résumé. Leave off the responsibilities that are not important, even if they took up a disproportionate amount of your time (such as answering phones) if it's something you don't want the reader to focus on.

- Don't lie about a degree. If you attended college, but did not graduate, list the name of the school, the years you attended and your major area of concentration. If your résumé is well written, people might overlook the fact that you don't have a degree.

- Use a descriptive job title. Often the title a company assigns to a job is not a true indicator of the responsibilities the position includes. An administrative assistant, for example, can do secretarial work, account research or sophisticated power point presentations. Make sure your title accurately reflects the scope of your duties.

- Don't give each job equal prominence. Highlight or underline the jobs you want the hiring manager to notice. The position or experience you want to emphasize should stand-out visually on the page.
- Position yourself at the right level. You won't need to lie about salary if you position yourself at the right level. Is it easy for the reader to guess in 10 seconds what your level is? Don't say you "install computer systems" because you could be making anywhere from $15,000 a year to $200,000 a year. Use specific language to signal your experience and the level you are seeking.
- Use a Summary at the Top. What are the first words at the top of your résumé? Without a summary statement you are positioned by your most recent job. Is that what you want? Use a summary to make sure the very first line positions you for the kind of job you want next. For example, if you are looking for a job as an accounting manager and you have that kind of experience, the first words on your resume should be, "Accounting Manager." This should be followed by statements that prove how good you are or that differentiate you from your likely competitors.
- Reason for Leaving. Don't lie about your reason for leaving a job if it was not voluntary. In today's economy -- with plant closings, outsourcing, downsizing, mergers and acquisitions -- it's not unusual to lose a job through no fault of your own. Human resource managers understand this and should not judge you unfairly for it. You simply got caught in a downsizing just like everyone else.

PART TEN

What Is
The Five O'Clock Club?

"Where Professional Success Gets Personal Attention"

How to Join the Club

The Five O'Clock Club:

Find your personal path in job search and career success

"One organization with a long record of success in helping people find jobs is The Five O'Clock Club."

Fortune

- Weekly Job-Search Strategy Groups
- Private Coaching
- Books, Audio CDs and audio downloads
- Membership Information
- When Your Employer Pays

THERE *IS* A FIVE O'CLOCK CLUB NEAR YOU!
For more information on becoming a member, please fill out the Membership Application Form in this book, sign up on the web at: www.fiveoclockclub.com, or call: 1-800-538-6645 (or 212-286-4500 in New York)

The Five O'Clock Club Search Process

The Five O'Clock Club process, as outlined in *The Five O'Clock Club* books, is a targeted, strategic approach to career development and job search.

Five O'Clock Club members become proficient at skills that prove invaluable during their entire working lives.

Career Management

We train our members to manage their careers and always look ahead to their next job search. Research shows that an average worker spends only four years in a job—and will have 12 jobs in as many as 5 career fields—during his or her working life.

Getting Jobs . . . Faster

Five O'Clock Club members find more satisfying jobs, faster. The average professional, manager, or executive Five O'Clock Club member who regularly attends weekly sessions finds a job by his or her 10th session. Even the discouraged, long-term job searcher can find immediate help.

The keystone to The Five O'Clock Club process is teaching our members an understanding of the entire *hiring* process. A first interview is primarily a time for exchanging critical information. The real work starts *after the interview*. We teach our members how to *turn job interviews into offers* and to negotiate the best possible employment package.

Setting Targets

The Five O'Clock Club is action oriented. *We'll help you decide what you should do this very next week to move your search along.* By their third session, our members have set definite job targets by industry or company size, position, and geographic area, and are out in the field gathering information and making contacts that will lead to interviews with hiring managers.

Our approach evolves with the changing job market. We're able to synthesize information from hundreds of Five O'Clock Club members and come up with new approaches for our members. For example, we discuss temporary placement for executives, how to use voice mail and the Internet, the use of LinkedIn and other social media, and how to network when doors are slamming shut all over town.

The Five O'Clock Club's Weekly Small Group Strategy Sessions

The Five O'Clock Club weekly meeting includes you, 6 to 8 peers (people at your same salary level) and a senior Five O'Clock Club career coach who has been certified by us. The meeting is a carefully planned *job-search strategy program where participants go away with an assignment to help them get more interviews in their target markets or turn those interviews into offers.* We provide members with the tools and tricks necessary to get a good job fast—even in a tight market. Networking and emotional support are also included in the meeting.

Participate in 10 *consecutive* small-group strategy sessions to enable your group and career coach to get to know you and to develop momentum in your search.

Weekly Presentations via Audio CDs or audio Downloads

Prior to each week's teleconference, listen to the assigned audio presentation covering part of The Five O'Clock Club methodology. These are

scheduled on a rotating basis so you may join the Club at any time.

Small-Group Strategy Sessions

During the first few minutes of the teleconference, your small group discusses the topic of the week and hears from people who have landed jobs. Then you have the chance to get feedback and advice on your own search strategy, listen to and learn from others, and build your network. All groups are led by trained career coaches with years of experience. The small group is generally no more than six to eight people, so everyone gets the chance to speak up.

Let us consider how we may spur one another on toward love and good deeds. Let us not give up meeting together, as some are in the habit of doing, but let us encourage one another.

HEBREWS 10:24-25

Private Coaching

You may meet with your small-group coach—or another coach—for private coaching by phone or in person. A coach helps you develop a career path, solve current job problems, prepare your résumé, or guide your search.

Many members develop long-term relationships with their coaches to get advice throughout their careers. If you are paying for the coaching yourself (as opposed to having your employer pay), please pay the coach directly (charges vary from $100 to $175 per hour). Private coaching is not included in The Five O'Clock Club seminar or membership fee and the Club gets no portion of whatever you pay the coach. For coach matching, see our website or call 1-800-538-6645 (or 212-286-4500 in New York).

From the Club History, Written in the 1890s

At The Five O'Clock Club, [people] of all shades of political belief—as might be said of all trades and creeds—have met together.... The variety continues almost to a monotony.... [The Club's] good fellowship and geniality—not to say hospitality—has reached them all.

It has been remarked of clubs that they serve to level rank. If that were possible in this country, it would probably be true, if leveling rank means the appreciation of people of equal abilities as equals; but in The Five O'Clock Club it has been a most gratifying and noteworthy fact that no lines have ever been drawn save those which are essential to the honor and good name of any association. Strangers are invited by the club or by any members, [as gentlepeople], irrespective of aristocracy, plutocracy or occupation, and are so treated always. Nor does the thought of a [person's] social position ever enter into the meetings. People of wealth and people of moderate means sit side by side, finding in each other much to praise and admire and little to justify snarlishness or adverse criticism. People meet as people—not as the representatives of a set—and having so met, dwell not in worlds of envy or distrust, but in union and collegiality, forming kindly thoughts of each other in their heart of hearts.

In its methods, The Five O'Clock Club is plain, easy-going and unconventional. It has its "isms" and some peculiarities of procedure, but simplicity characterizes them all. The sense of propriety, rather than rules of order, governs its meetings, and that informality which carries with it sincerity of motive and spontaneity of effort, prevails within it. Its very name indicates informality, and, indeed, one of the reasons said to have induced its adoption was the fact that members or guests need not don their dress suits to attend the meetings, if they so desired. This informality, however, must be distinguished from the informality of Bohemianism. For The Five O'Clock Club, informality, above convenience, means sobriety, refinement of thought and speech, good breeding and good order. To this sort of informality much of its success is due.

Fortune, The New York Times, Black Enterprise, Business Week, **The TODAY Show, NPR, CNBC and ABC-TV are some of the places you've seen, heard, or read about us.**

The Schedule

See our website for the specific dates for each topic. All groups use a similar schedule in each time zone.

Fee: $49 for LIFETIME membership (includes Beginners Kit, a LIFETIME subscription to *The Five O'Clock News*, and LIFETIME access to the Members Only section of our website), **plus** session fees based on member's income (the price for the Insider Program includes audio-CD lectures, which retail for as much as $150).

Reservations are required for your first session. Unused sessions that you paid for (as opposed to employer-paid programs) are transferable to anyone you choose or will be donated to members attending more than 16 sessions who are having financial difficulty.

The Five O'Clock Club's programs are geared to professionals, managers, and executives from a wide variety of industries and professions, and also recent graduates. Most earn from $30,000 to $500,000 per year. Half of the members are employed; half are unemployed. You will be in a group of your peers.

To register, please fill out form on the web (at www.fiveoclockclub.com) or call 1-800-538-6645 (or 212-286-4500 in New York).

Lecture Presentation Schedule

- History of the Five O'Clock Club
- The Five O'Clock Club Approach to Job Search
- Developing New Targets for Your Search
- Two-Minute Pitch: Keystone of Your Search
- Using Research and Internet for Your Search
- The Keys to Effective Networking
- Getting the Most Out of Your Contacts
- Getting Interviews: Direct/Targeted Mail
- Beat the Odds when Using Search Firms and Ads
- Developing New Momentum in Your Search
- The Five O'Clock Club Approach to Interviewing
- Advanced Interviewing Techniques
- How to Handle Difficult Interview Questions
- How to Turn Job Interviews into Offers
- Successful Job Hunter's Report
- Four-Step Salary-Negotiation Method

Audio excerpts from many of these presentations can be found on our website in the "How to Get a Job" section.

All groups run continuously. Dates are posted on our website. The textbooks used by all members of The Five O'Clock Club may be ordered on our website or purchased at major bookstores.

The original Five O'Clock Club was formed in Philadelphia in 1883. It was made up of the leaders of the day who shared their experiences "in a spirit of fellowship and good humor."

The
Five
O'Clock
Club®

Questions You May Have about the Weekly Job-Search Strategy Group

Job hunters are not always the best judges of what they need during a search. For example, most are interested in lectures on answering ads on the Internet or working with search firms. We cover those topics, but strategically they are relatively unimportant in an effective job search.

At The Five O'Clock Club, you get the information you really need in your search—*such as how to target more effectively, how to get more interviews, and how to turn job interviews into offers.*

What's more, you will work in a small group with the best coaches in the business. In these strategy sessions, your group will help you decide what to do, this week and every week, to move your search along. You will learn by being coached and by coaching others in your group.

We find ourselves not independently of other people and institutions but through them. We never get to the bottom of our selves on our own. We discover who we are face to face and side by side with others in work, love, and learning.

Robert N. Bellah, et al., *Habits of the Heart*

Here are a few other points:

- For best results, attend on a regular basis. Your group gets to know you and will coach you to eliminate whatever you may be doing wrong—or refine what you are doing right. Our research shows that if

you attend only once a month, the group will have little or no impact on your search results.
- The Five O'Clock Club is a members-only organization. To get started in the small-group teleconference sessions, you must purchase a minimum of 10 sessions.
- The teleconference sessions include the set of 16 audio-CD presentations on Five O'Clock Club methodology. In-person groups do not include CDs.
- After that, you may purchase blocks of 5 or 10 sessions.
- We sell multiple sessions to make administration easier.
- If you miss a session, you may make it up any time. You may even transfer unused time to a friend.
- Although many people find jobs quickly (even people who have been unemployed a long time), others have more difficult searches. Plan to be in it for the long haul and you'll do better.

Carefully read all of the material in this section. It will help you decide whether or not to attend.

- The first week, pay attention to the strategies used by the others in your group. Soak up all the information you can.
- Read the books before you come in the second week. They will help you move your search along.

To register:

1. Read this section and fill out the application.
2. After you become a member and get your Beginners Kit, call to reserve a space for the first time you attend.

To assign you to a career coach, we need to know:

- your current (or last) field or industry
- the kind of job you would like next (if you know)
- your desired salary range in general terms

For private coaching, we suggest you attend the small group and ask to see your group leader, to give you continuity.

The Five O'Clock Club is plain, easy-going and unconventional.... Members or guests need not don their dress suits to attend the meetings.

(FROM THE CLUB HISTORY, WRITTEN IN THE 1890s)

What Happens at the Meetings?

Each week, job searchers from various industries and professions meet in small groups. The groups specialize in professionals, managers, executives, or recent college graduates. Usually, half are employed and half are unemployed.

The weekly program is in two parts. First, listen to a lecture on some aspect of The Five O'Clock Club methodology. Then, job hunters meet in small groups headed by senior full-time professional career coaches.

The first week, get the textbooks, listen to the lecture, and meet with your small group and the senior coach who is leading the group. During your first session, listen to the others in your group. You learn a lot by listening to how your peers are strategizing their searches.

By the second week, you will have read the materials. Now we can start to work on your search strategy and help *you* decide what to do next to move your search along. For example, we'll help you figure out how to get more interviews in your target area or how to turn interviews into job offers.

In the third week, you will see major progress made by other members of your group and you may notice major progress in your own search as well.

By the third or fourth week, most members are conducting full and effective searches. Over the remaining weeks, you will tend to keep up a full search rather than go after only one or two leads. You will regularly aim to have 6 to 10 things *in the works at all times*. These will generally be in specific target areas you have identified, will keep your search on target, and will increase your chances of getting multiple job offers from which to choose.

Those who stick with the process find it works.

Some people prefer to just listen for a few weeks before they start their job search and that's okay, too.

How Much Does It Cost?

It is against the policy of The Five O'Clock Club to charge individuals heavy up-front fees. Our competitors charge $4,000 to $6,000 or more, up front. Our average fee is $360 for 10 sessions (which includes audio CDs (or downloads) of 16 presentations for those in the teleconference program). Those in the $100,000+ range pay an average of $540 for 10 sessions. For administrative reasons, we charge for 5 or 10 additional sessions at a time.

You must have the books so you can begin studying them before the second session. (You can purchase them on our website, at Amazon.com, or ask for them at your local library.) If you don't do the homework, you will tend to waste the time of others in the group by asking questions covered in the texts.

Is the Small Group Right for Me?

The Five O'Clock Club process is for you if:
- You are truly interested in job hunting.
- You have some idea of the kind of job you want.
- You are a professional, manager, or executive— or want to be.
- You want to participate in a group process on a regular basis.
- You realize that finding or changing jobs and careers is hard work, but you are absolutely willing and able to do it.

If you have no idea about the kind of job you want next, you may attend one or two group sessions to start. *Then see a coach privately for one or two sessions*, develop tentative job targets, and return to the group. You may work with your small-group coach or **contact us through our website or by calling 1-800-538-6645** (or 212-286-4500 in New York) for referral to a private coach.

How Long Will It Take Me to Get a Job?

Although our members tend to be from fields or industries where they expect to have difficult searches, the average person who attends regularly finds a new position within 10 sessions. Some take less time and others take more. During the worst recessions, our average professional, manager and executive still found employment in an average of 16.4 weeks (as opposed to the 35 weeks that the population as a whole was taking—assuming they didn't give up on searching).

One thing we know for sure: **Research shows that those who** regularly **attend the small-group strategy sessions get more satisfying jobs faster and at higher rates of pay than those who search on their own,** only **work privately with a career coach, or simply take a course**. This makes sense. If a person comes only when they think they have a problem, they are usually wrong. They probably had a problem a few weeks ago but didn't realize it. Or the problem may be different from the one they thought they

had. Those who come regularly benefit from the observations others make about their searches. Problems are solved before they become severe or are prevented altogether.

Those who attend regularly also learn a lot by paying attention and helping others in the group. This *secondhand* learning can shorten your search by weeks. When you hear the problems of others who are ahead of you in the search, you can avoid them completely. People in your group will come to know you and will point out subtleties you may not have noticed that interviewers will never tell you.

Will I Be with Others from My Field/Industry?

Probably not, but it's not that important. If you are a salesperson, for example, would you want to be with seven other salespeople? Probably not. You will learn a lot and have a much more creative search if you are in a group of people who are in your general salary range but not exactly like you. Our clients are from virtually every field and industry. The *process* is what will help you.

We've been doing this since 1978 and understand your needs. That's why the mix we provide is the best you can get.

Career Coaching Firms Charge $4,000-$6,000 Up Front. How Can You Charge Such a Small Fee?

1. We have no advertising costs, because 90 percent of those who attend have been referred by other members or an association you belong to. (Be sure to ask your alumni or trade association to contact us for a special rate for its members.).

A hefty up-front fee would bind you to us, but we have been more successful by treating people ethically and having them pretty much *pay as they go.*

We need a certain number of people to cover expenses. When lots of people get jobs quickly and leave us, we could go into the red. But as long as members refer others, we will continue to provide this service at a fair price.

2. We focus strictly on *job-search strategy,* and encourage our clients to attend free support groups if they need emotional support. We focus on getting *jobs that fit in with your career goals,* and that reduces the time clients spend with us and the amount they pay.

3. We attract the best coaches, and our clients make more progress per session than they would elsewhere, which also reduces their costs.

4. We have expert administrators and a sophisticated computer system that reduces our overhead and increases our ability to track your progress.

May I Change Coaches?

Yes. Great care is taken in assigning you to your initial coach. However, if you want to change once for any reason, you may do it. We don't encourage group hopping: It is better for you to stick with a group so that everyone gets to know you. On the other hand, we want you to feel comfortable. So if you tell us you prefer a different group, you will be transferred immediately.

What If I Have a Quick Question Outside of the Group Session?

Some people prefer to see their group coach privately. Others prefer to meet with a different coach to get another point of view. Whatever you decide, remember that the group fee does not cover coaching time outside the group session. Therefore, if you wanted to speak with a coach between sessions—even for *quick questions*—you would normally meet with the coach first for a private session so he or she can get to know you better. *Easy, quick questions* are usually more complicated than they appear. After your first private session, some coaches will allow you to pay in advance for one hour of coaching time, which you can then use for quick questions by phone (usually a 15-minute minimum is charged). Since each coach has an individual way of operating, find out how the coach arranges these things.

What If I Want to Start My Own Business?

The process of becoming a consultant is essentially the same as job hunting and lots of consultants attend Five O'Clock Club meetings. However, if you want to buy a franchise or existing business or start a growth business, you should see a private coach. Regardless of the kind of business you want to have, be sure to read our book: *Your Great Business Idea: The Truth About Making It Happen.*

How Can I Be Sure That The Five O'Clock Club Small-Group Sessions Will Be Right for Me?

Before you actually participate in any of the small-group sessions, you can get an idea of the quality of our service by listening to all 16 audio CDs that you purchased. If you are dissatisfied with the CDs for any reason, return the package within 30 days for a full refund.

Whatever you decide, just remember: <u>**Research shows that those who** regularly **attend the small-group strategy sessions get more satisfying jobs faster and at higher rates of pay than those who search on their own,** only **work privately with a career coach, or simply take a course**</u>. If you get a job just one or two weeks faster because of this program, it will have more than paid for itself. And you may transfer unused sessions to anyone you choose. However, the person you choose must be or become a member.

The Five O'Clock Club's Job-Search Buddy System

Do you wish you had someone to talk to—fairly often and informally—about the little things? "Here's what I'm planning to do today in my search? What are *you* planning to do? Let's talk tomorrow to make sure we've done it." You and your job-search buddy could keep each other positive and on track, and encourage each other to do what you told your small group you were going to do: Make that call, send out those letters, write that follow-up proposal, focus on the most important things that should be done—rather than (for example) spending endless hours responding to job postings on the Web.

With your buddy, practice your Two-Minute Pitch, get ready for interviews, bounce ideas off each other. Some job-search buddies talk every day. Some talk a few times a week. Most of the conversation is by phone and e-mail.

Sometimes, people match themselves up as buddies. Just pick someone you get along with in your small group. Sometimes, your coach can match you up. However you do it, stay away from negative people who talk about how bad it is out there. They will drag you down.

The small group changes over time: people get jobs; new people come in. If you lose one buddy who got a job, get another buddy.

Your buddy does not have to be in your field or industry. In fact, being in the same field or industry could keep you focused on the industry rather than on the process. But you do have to get along! The relationship may last only a month or two, or go on for years. Some buddies become friends.

Of course, you should see your Five O'Clock Club career coach privately for résumé review, target development, salary negotiation, and job interview follow-up. It's usually best to get professional coaching advice for these areas. And nothing beats the weekly small-group strategy sessions for making progress in the job search itself. Those who regularly attended the small group got jobs in half the time.

Using The Five O'Clock Club
From the Comfort of Your Home

A man who found the Five O'Clock Club books at his library near Denver calls to ask if there is a local branch. A woman in Seattle who bought the books on Amazon wants to know if she can attend our weekly seminars. A man in Phoenix who received *Targeting a Great Career* from his daughter also wants to attend. And an HR executive wants to know whether we can help her employees in an office closing in Miami.

In our early years, the reach of The Five O'Clock Club—because of the popular Club books—exceeded its presence, but systems have been in place for the past ten years to allow people anywhere to access the Club seminars and coaching by phone and computer.

The Launch of the Insider Groups

Teleconferencing has long come into its own, and for ten years we have offered weekly Club meetings on a nationwide basis. Our Insider Groups (via teleconference) were launched in February 2000, and the first teleconference group included executives from California, North Dakota and Maryland. Prior to the conference call, each person listens to the topic of the week on his or her audio CD or reads the topic in the books. They can listen to the "topic of the week" at their leisure and are then ready for the weekly teleconference.

Following the conference, participants can stay on the line and chat with each other—and most do. In addition, they can browse our LinkedIn Group and network with the almost 1,000 Five O'Clock Clubbers who participate. They can "reply all" to the emails sent to members of their small group and stay in touch with each other that way. And they can talk daily to their Job-Search Buddies, offering advice and encouragement that follow The Five O'Clock Club's methodology. What's more, they can talk to their private coach about a specific interview coming up, get advice on turning a job interview into an offer, or get help negotiating their compensation.

Website as a Public Service

Anyone can wander through the various areas of www.FiveOClockClub.com and tap into vast amounts of useful information—without being a member! For example, click on How To Get a Job to find a menu of 13 substantive articles that represent the heart of the Five O'Clock Club methodology. These articles cover job targeting, interviewing and salary negotiations—and how to start out on the right foot on your new job. There is also a free mini-course to help you assess the **quality** of your job search. Sure, you're working hard, but are you doing the right things?

Remember, The Five O'Clock Club is the ONLY organization devoted to conducting research on behalf of job hunters. We are the only organization with a research-based methodology for you to use rather than the vanilla job-search techniques that everyone else uses. We are the ONLY organization that has books and audios that document the methodology you should use in your job search.

In the Free Articles section you can access hundreds of articles that have appeared in our monthly magazine, *The Five O'Clock News*.

The Weekly Small-Group Strategy Sessions

You are assigned to a small group of your peers (same salary level). Each session is moderated by a certified Five O'Clock Club coach, lasts for an hour, and is guided by the same principles and techniques presented in our books and audios. These are not general discussions on job-search topics; each session moves you forward in your search by helping you to identify steps to take during the coming week. You leave the session with an assignment and proactive coaching on how to do it.

"Our group coach expects us to recap what we've done and we get an assignment. The momentum you get with The Five O'Clock Club makes the big difference," reports one Clubber.

One California Insider member said, "It's really been neat. I've been involved with other job-hunting groups, but they don't have the full breadth of job-search regimen that you have with The Five O'Clock Club. Reading the books and listening to the audios ahead of time helps keep us focused. Our coach expects us to recap what we've done and we get an assignment. The momentum you get with The Five O'Clock Club makes the big difference. I've stagnated with other groups." And he finds that there is a benefit in working with a group whose members are in California, Florida, Massachusetts and New Jersey. "It gives us a different perspective on issues. We have great rapport on the phone and we email and call each other after the session is over."

Reach Out and Touch Someone

You can get assigned to a Five O'Clock Club coach for private one-on-one coaching. Most of these match-ups result in telephone sessions—the coach may be in Maryland or Chicago, the client in California or Maine. Many clients want an hour or two of private coaching to help them determine goals and targets. You can find a sampling of coach bios and photos on our website.

Our coaches are trained in The Five O'Clock Club method and are committed to our ethical standards. At other such firms, a newly hired coach with experience is up and running that day. At The Five O'Clock Club, a coach with experience must go through our four-month certification program, un-learn what they thought they knew about job search, and master the methodology.

Seasoned career coaches are attracted to our certification program. Candidates for the Guild must study our 250-page training manual and pass exams to be admitted; they must do two "before" and "after" résumés so they don't give you a cookie-cutter résumé; they must observe 10 small-group coaching sessions and write an essay on what they have learned; and they must do an audition on some aspect of The Five O'Clock Club methodology so they can again prove that they have mastered it. With some 50 coaches in training, in addition to our certified coaches, we are in a position to meet the volume of coaching requests that may come our way in the future.

Be sure to tell your friends about us, and tell your employer that you want The Five O'Clock Club as your outplacement provider!

The Five O'Clock Club®

When Your Employer Pays

Does your employer care about you and others whom they ask to leave the organization? If so, ask them to consider The Five O'Clock Club for your outplacement help. The Five O'Clock Club puts you and your job search first, offering a career-coaching program of the highest quality at the lowest possible price to your employer.

Over 25 Years of Research

The Five O'Clock Club was started in 1978 as a research-based organization. Job hunters tried various techniques and reported their results back to the group. We developed a variety of guidelines so job hunters could choose the techniques best for them.

The methodology was tested and refined on professionals, managers, and executives (and those aspiring to be) from all occupations. Annual salaries ranged from $30,000 to $400,000; 50 percent were employed and 50 percent were unemployed.

Since its beginning, The Five O'Clock Club has tracked trends. Over time, our advice has changed as the job market has changed. What worked in the past is insufficient for today's job market. Today's Five O'Clock Club promotes all our relevant original strategies—and so much more.

As an employee-advocacy organization, The Five O'Clock Club focuses on providing the services and information that the job hunter needs most.

Get the Help You Need Most: 100 Percent Coaching

There's a myth in outplacement circles that a terminated employee just needs a desk, a phone, and minimal career coaching. The new trend is to provide job hunters with databases of fake job openings and other online help and call it "outplacement." The price is ridiculously low, but then an employer can claim that it is providing outplacement to all employees.

Our experience clearly shows that down-sized workers need qualified, reliable coaching more than anything else. Most traditional outplacement packages last only 3 months. The average executive gets office space and only 5 hours of career coaching during this time. Yet the service job hunters need most is the career coaching itself—not a desk and a phone.

Most professionals, managers, and executives are right in the thick of negotiations with prospective employers at the 3-month mark. Yet that is precisely when traditional outplacement ends, leaving job hunters stranded and sometimes ruining deals.

It is astonishing how often job hunters and employers alike are impressed by the databases of job postings claimed by outplacement firms. Yet only 10 percent of all jobs are filled through ads and another 10 percent are filled through search firms. Instead, direct contact and networking— done The Five O'Clock Club way—are more effective for most searches.

> **For the latest information on our outplacement services, go to our website, www.fiveoclockclub.com, and look in both the "For Employers" and "For Employees" sections.**

You Get a Safety Net

Imagine getting a package that protects you for a full year. Imagine knowing you can come back if your new job doesn't work out—even months later. Imagine trying consulting work if you like. If you later decide it's not for you, you can come back to The Five O'Clock Club.

We can offer you a safety net of one full year's career coaching because our method is so effective that few people actually need more than 10 weeks in our proven program. But you're protected for a year.

You'll Job Search with Those Who Are Employed—How Novel!

Let's face it. It can be depressing to spend your days at an outplacement firm where everyone is unemployed. At The Five O'Clock Club, half the attendees are working, and this makes the atmosphere cheerier and helps to move your search along.

What's more, you'll be in a small group of your peers, all of whom are using The Five O'Clock Club method. Our research proves that those who attend the small group regularly and use The Five O'Clock Club methods get jobs faster and at higher rates of pay than those who only work privately with a career coach throughout their searches.

So Many Poor Attempts

Nothing is sadder than meeting someone who has already been getting job-search help, but the wrong kind. They've learned the traditional tech-niques that are no longer effective. Most have poor résumés and inappropriate targets and don't know how to turn job interviews into offers.

You'll Get Quite a Package

You'll get up to 14 hours (or more, depending on the package) of private coaching—well in excess of what you would get at a traditional outplacement firm. You may even want to use a few hours after you start your new job.

And you get one full year of weekly small-group career coaching. In addition, you get books, audio CDs, and other helpful materials.

To Get Started

The day your human resources manager calls us authorizing Five O'Clock Club outplacement, we will immediately ship you the books, CDs, and other materials and assign you to a private coach and a small group.

Then we'll monitor your search. Frankly, we care about you more than we care about your employer. And since your employer cares about you, they're glad we feel this way—because they know we'll take care of you.

What They Say about Us

The Five O'Clock Club product is much better, far more useful than my outplacement package.

Senior executive and Five O'Clock Club member

The Club kept the juices flowing. You're told what to do, what not to do. There were fresh ideas. I went through an outplacement service that, frankly, did not help. If they had done as much as the Five O'Clock Club did, I would have landed sooner.

Another member

When Your *Employer* Pays for The Five O'Clock Club, *You* Get:

- **Up to 14 hours (or more, depending on the package) of guaranteed private career coaching** to determine a career direction, develop a résumé, plan salary negotiations, etc. In fact, if you need a second opinion during your search, we can arrange that too.
- **ONE YEAR of weekly small-group strategy sessions via teleconference** (average about 5 or 6 participants in a group) headed by a senior Five O'Clock Club career consultant. That way, if you lose your next job, you can come back. Or if you want to try consulting work and then decide you don't like it, **you can come back**.
- **LIFETIME membership** in The Five O'Clock Club: Beginners Kit and two-year subscription to The Five O'Clock News.
- **The complete set of our four books** for professionals, managers, and executives who are in job search.
- **A boxed set of 16 audio CDs** of Five O'Clock Club presentations.

COMPARISON OF EMPLOYER-PAID PACKAGES

Typical Package	Traditional Outplacement	The Five O'Clock Club
Who is the client?	The organization	Job hunters. We are employee advocates. We always do what is in the best interest of job hunters.
The clintele	All are unemployed	Half of our attendees are unemployed; half are employed. There is an upbeat atmosphere; networkng is enhanced.
Length/type of service	3 months, primarily office space	1 year, exclusively career coaching
Service ends	After 3 months—or before if the client lands a job or consulting assignment.	After 1 full year, no matter what. You can return if you lose your next job, if your assignment ends, or if you need advice after starting your new job.
Small group coaching	Sporatic for 3 months Coach varies	Every week for up to 1 year; same coach
Private coaching	5 hours on average	Up to 14 hours guaranteed (depending on level of service purchased)
Support materials	Generic manual; web-based info	• 4 textbooks based on over 25 yrs. of job-search research • 16 40-minute lectures on audio CDs • Beginners Kit of search information • LIFETIME subscription to the Five)'Clock Club magazine, devoted to career-management articles
Facilities	Cubicle, phone, computer access	None; use home phone and computer

The Way We Are

*The Five O'Clock Club means sobriety, refinement of
thought and speech, good breeding and good order. To
this, much of its success is due. The Five O'Clock Club
is easy-going and unconventional. A sense of propriety,
rather than rules of order, governs its meetings.*

J. HAMPTON MOORE, *History of The Five O'Clock Club*
(WRITTEN IN THE 1890s)

Just like the members of the original Five
O'Clock Club, today's members want an ongoing
relationship. George Vaillant, in his seminal work
on successful people, found that "what makes or
breaks our luck seems to be... our sustained relationships with other people." (George E.Vaillant,
Adaptation to Life, Harvard University Press, 1995)

Five O'Clock Club members know that much
of the program's benefit comes from simply showing up. Showing up will encourage you to do what
you need to do when you are not here. And over
the course of several weeks, certain things will
become evident that are not evident now.

Five O'Clock Club members learn from each
other: The group leader is not the only one with
answers. The leader brings factual information to
the meetings and keeps the discussion in line. But
the answers to some problems may lie within you
or with others in the group.

Five O'Clock Club members encourage each
other. They listen, see similarities with their own
situations, and learn from that. And they listen
to see how they may help others. You may come
across information or a contact that could help
someone else in the group. Passing on that information is what we're all about.

If you are a new member here, listen to others
to learn the process. And read the books and
listen to the presentations so you will know the
basics that others already know. When everyone
understands the basics, this keeps the meetings on
a high level, interesting, and helpful to everyone.

Five O'Clock Club members are in this
together, but they know that ultimately they are
each responsible for solving their own problems
with God's help. Take the time to learn the process, and you will become better at analyzing your
own situation, as well as the situations of others.
You will be learning a method that will serve you
the rest of your life, and in areas of your life apart
from your career.

Five O'Clock Club members are kind to each
other. They control their frustrations—because
venting helps no one. Because many may be
stressed, be kind and go the extra length to keep
this place calm and happy. It is your respite from
the world outside and a place for you to find
comfort and FUN. Relax and enjoy yourself, learn
what you can, and help where you can. And have
a ball doing it.

---

*There arises from the hearts of busy [people] a love of
variety, a yearning for relaxation of thought
as well as of body, and a craving for a
generous and spontaneous fraternity.*

J. HAMPTON MOORE, *History of The Five O'Clock Club*

Lexicon Used at The Five O'Clock Club

The LEXICON—to help you talk about your search

The Five O'Clock Club lexicon is a shorthand—a way to quickly analyze your search and to clearly speak about your search to other Five O'Clock Clubbers. We all speak the same language so we can help each other. Our counselors across the country also speak the same language.

Whether you are in a group or working privately with a Five O'Clock Club career counselor, you can learn our language and analyze your search. After you read the summary below, study our books "as if your were in graduate school." You will learn to better express where you are in your job search, and be better able to figure out what to do next.

The average person who attends The Five O'Clock Club regularly has a new job within just ten weekly sessions–even those who have been unemployed up to two years. Follow our method and you will increase your chances of getting a better job faster.

The following questions will help you to pinpoint what is wrong with your search.

I. Overview and Assessment

How many hours a week are you spending on your search?

Only two or three hours a week, you say? The good news is that you have not yet begun to search. That's why you're making so little prog-ress. To develop momentum in your search, spend 35 hours a week on a full-time search; if you are employed, spend 15 hours a week for a solid, part-time search.

What are your job targets?

If your job targets are wrong, everything is wrong. A target includes:
- industry or organization size,
- the position you want in that industry, and
- your targeted geographic area.

For example, let's say you want to target the health care industry. That's not a good target. It needs to be better defined. For example, perhaps you would consider hospitals. In the metropolitan New York area, for example, there are 80 hospitals. Let's say you're a marketing person, and you would consider doing marketing in a hospital in the NY area. That's one target: Hospitals is the industry, marketing is the position, and NY area is the geographic area. You could also target HMO's. Let's say there are 15 HMO's that you consider appropriate in the NY area. You could do marketing for them. That's a second target. You could also work for a consulting firm in the NY area that does health-care consulting. That's your third target.

But let's say you and your spouse have always loved Phoenix. You think you may like to investigate all three of those industries in the Phoenix area. That's three more targets. The reason you divide your search into targets is so you can have control over it, and tell what's working and what isn't. You make a list of all of the organizations in each of your targets—we call that your "Personal Marketing Plan." Then you find out the names of the people you need to contact in each of those targets—the hiring managers of the departments or divisions you are interested in.

That's the start of an organized search. At the very beginning of your search, you can assess how good your targets are and whether you stand a chance getting a job within a reasonable timeframe. Take a look at "Measuring Your Job Targets" in our books.

How does your resume position you?

The average resume is looked at for only ten seconds—regardless of length. When someone looks at your resume, will they pick up the most important information that you want them to know about you? The summary and body should make you look appropriate to your target. We recommend that the first line of your summary tell the reader exactly how they should see you, e.g., as an "Accounting Manager" or whatever. They will want to stereotype you anyway, so why not help them see you the way you want to be seen?

The second line should differentiate you from your competition: How are you different from all of those other Accounting Managers out there? Your second line could say, for example, "Expert in Cost Accounting."

That is followed by three or four bulleted accomplishments—the most important things you want them to know about you. That way, if they spend only 10 seconds on your resume, they will see what you want them to see. For the complete Five O'Clock Club approach, see our Resume book. It contains summaries related to over 100 industries and professions.

What are your back-up targets?

Decide at the beginning of the search before you start your first campaign. Then you won't get stuck later when things seem hopeless.

Have you done the Assessment?

If you have no specific targets, you cannot have a targeted search. Do the Assessment exercises in our books. You could see a counselor privately for two or three sessions to determine possible job targets. When a person joins the Club, we want them to do the exercises even if they are perfectly clear about what they want to do next. Doing the assessment helps a person to do better in interviews and helps them to have a better resume. Do not skip the assessment, especially the Seven Stories Exercise and the Forty-Year Vision.

II. Getting Interviews

How large is your target area (e.g., 30 companies)? How many of them have you contacted?

When you know your targets, you can research them and come up with a list of all of the companies in your target areas. Figure out how large your target market is. If you have contacted only a few companies in your target area, contact the rest. If you haven't contacted any, contact them all. That's a thorough—and fast—search.

How can you get (more) leads?

You will not get a job through search firms, ads, networking or direct contact. Those are techniques for getting interviews—job leads. Use the right terminology, especially when speaking to someone who has already landed a job. Do not say: how did you get the job, if you really want to know where did you get the lead for that job. In our books, you will find cover letters and approaches for each of these techniques. A good search does not rely on just one technique. We want our members to consider all four techniques for getting interviews in your target markets.

Do you have 6 to 10 things in the works?

When a job hunter is going after only one position—and hoping they will get an offer—that is a weak search. Our research shows that a good job hunter has 6 to 10 things in the works at all times. This is because five will fall away through no fault of your own: Maybe the company decides to hire a finance person instead of a marketing person, or maybe they decide to hire their cousin!

Do not put all of your eggs in one basket. When one offer falls through, you will have lost months in your search because you have to gear up all over again. To avoid losing momentum, make sure you have 6 to 10 things in the works at all times–through search firms, ads, networking or direct contact. It's not as hard as it sounds. Just follow our approach.

If you have 6 to 10 things going at once, you are more likely to turn the job you want into an offer because you will seem more valuable. Don't go after only one job.

How's your Two-Minute Pitch? (Who shall we pretend we are?)

A Two-Minute Pitch is the answer to the question, "So, tell me about yourself." Practice a tailored Two-Minute Pitch. Tell the group–or a friend–the job title and industry of the pretend hiring manager. You will be surprised how good the group is at critiquing pitches. Do it a few weeks in a row until you have a smooth presentation.

Practice it again after you have been in search a while, or after you change targets. Make sure your pitch separates you from your competition.

You seem to be in Stage One (or Stage Two or Stage Three) of your search.

Know where you are in the process. If you are in Stage One–making initial contacts you will recontact later–make lots of contacts so at least 6 to 10 will move to Stage Two: the right people at the right levels in the right companies. You will get the best job offers in Stage Three–talking to 6 to 10 people on an ongoing basis about real jobs or the possibility of creating a job.

Are you seen as insider or outsider?

Are people saying: "I wish I had an opening for someone like you." You are doing well in meetings. If your target is good, it's only a matter of time.

III. Turning Interviews into Offers

Want to go through the Brick Wall?

The brainiest part of the process is turning your job interview into an offer. First, make sure you want the job. If you do not want the job, perhaps you want an offer, if only for practice. If you are not willing to go for it, the group's suggestions will not work.

Who are your likely competitors and how can you kill them off?

"Outshine and outlast your competition" does not mean dirty tricks, but reminds you that you have competitors. You will not get a job simply because "they liked you". The issues are deeper. Ask: Where are you in the hiring process? What kind of person would be your ideal candidate?

What are your next steps?

The "next step" means: what are you planning to do if the hiring manager doesn't call by a certain date, or what are you planning to do to assure the hiring manager does call you.

Can you prove you can do the job?

Most job hunters take the "Trust Me" approach. Instead, prove to them that you can do the job, often by doing additional research or by writing a "proposal" of how you would handle the job.

Which job positions you best for the long run? Which job is the best fit?

Don't decide only on salary. Since the average person has been in his or her job only four years, … which … kes you a … ob that

… nality. If … well there. … ob is best

2019 SAT TEAM 2- REVISED: 5/30/2019 12:00 PM

THU. 05/30 10am-8pm	FRI 05/31 10am-6pm	SAT 06/01 10am-6pm	SUN 06/02 2pm-6pm
11:30-8	Off	9:30-6	9:30-6
9:30-6	9:30-6	9:30-6	
11:30--8	9:30-6		
11:30-8	9:30-6	9:30-6	
9:30-6	9:30-6		
11:30--8	9:30-6	9:30-6	
11:30--8	9:30-6		

… and a … you can … er… you … ted!"

… ub, you … ve … ed with … and job-search techniques, focusing on the experiences of real people.

- LIFETIME access to the *Members Only* section of our website containing, for example, all of our basic worksheets, our 111-page bibliography of research resources, and many other items.
- Access to reasonably priced weekly seminars featuring individualized attention to your specific needs in small groups supervised by our senior coaches.
- Access to one-on-one coaching to help you answer specific questions, solve current job problems, prepare your résumé, or take an in-depth look at your career path. You choose the coach and pay the coach directly.
- An attractive Beginners Kit containing information based on over 25 years of research on who gets jobs... and why... that will enable you to improve your job-search techniques—immediately!
- The opportunity to exchange ideas and experiences with other job searchers and career changers.

All that access, all that information, all that expertise for the one-time membership fee of only $49, plus seminar fees.

How to become a member— by mail or Email:

Send your name, address, phone number, how you heard about us, and your check for $49 (made payable to "The Five O'Clock Club") to our headquarters address: The Five O'Clock Club, 300 East 40th Street, New York, NY 10016, or sign up at www.fiveoclockclub.com. Or call us at 1-800-538-6645.

We will immediately mail you a Five O'Clock Club Membership Card, the Beginners Kit, and information on our seminars followed by our magazine. Then, call 1-800-538-6645 (or 212-286-4500 in New York) or email us (at info@fiveoclockclub.com) to:

- reserve a space for the first time you plan to attend, or
- be matched with a Five O'Clock Club coach.

Membership Application

The Five O'Clock Club

❏ **Yes! I want to become a member!**

I want access to the most effective methods for finding jobs, as well as for developing and managing my career.

I enclose my check for $49 for a LIFETIME membership, payable to The Five O'Clock Club. I will receive a Beginners Kit, a LIFETIME subscription to *The Five O'Clock News*, LIFETIME access to the Members Only area on our website, and a network of career coaches. Reasonably priced weekly small-group strategy sessions via teleconference are held every evening across the country.

Name:_____

Street Address:_____

City:_____ State:_____ Zip Code:_____

Work phone: (_____)_____

Home phone: (_____)_____

Email:_____

Date:_____

How I heard about the Club:_____

Packaging Yourself: The Targeted Résumé
The following *optional* information is for statistical purposes. Thanks for your help.

Salary range:

❏ under $30,000 ❏ $30,000-$49,999 ❏ $50,000-$74,999

❏ $75,000-$99,999 ❏ $100,000-$125,000 ❏ over $125,000

Age: ❏ 20-29 ❏ 30-39 ❏ 40-49 ❏ 50+

Gender: ❏ Male ❏ Female

Current or most recent position/title: _____

Please send to:
Membership Director,
The Five O'Clock Club Headquarters
300 East 40th St.,
New York, NY 10016

The original Five O'Clock Club® was formed in Philadelphia in 1893. It was made up of the leaders of the day who shared their experiences "in a setting of fellowship and good humor."

Index

About the Author

Kate Wendleton is a nationally recognized authority on career development. She founded The Five O'Clock Club in 1978 and developed its methodology to help job hunters, career changers and employees of all levels, making The Five O'Clock Club the only organization to conduct ongoing research on behalf of employees and job hunters.

Kate was a nationally syndicated columnist for eight years and a speaker on career development, having appeared on the *Today Show*, CNN, CNBC, Larry King, National Public Radio and CBS, and in *The Economist, The New York Times, The Chicago Tribune, The Wall Street Journal, Fortune* magazine, *Business Week* and other national media.

For the past two years, Kate has spent every Saturday with young adults who have aged out of foster care, trying to give them the opportunity to make the most of their lives. This organization, Remington Achievers, is a not-for-profit arm of The Five O'Clock Club.

Kate also founded Workforce America, a not-for-profit Affiliate of The Five O'Clock Club, that served adults in Harlem who were not yet in the professional or managerial ranks. For ten years, Workforce America helped each person move into better-paying, higher-level positions as each im-proved in educational level and work experience.

Kate founded, and directed for seven years, The Career Center at The New School for Social Research in New York. She also advises major corporations about employee career-development programs.

A former CFO of two small companies, she has twenty years of business-management experience in both manufacturing and service businesses.

Kate attended Chestnut Hill College in Philadelphia and received her MBA from Drexel University. She is a popular speaker with groups that include associations, corporations, and colleges.

While living in Philadelphia, Kate did long-term volunteer work for the Philadelphia Museum of Art, the Walnut Street Theatre Art Gallery, United Way, and the YMCA. Kate currently lives in Manhattan with her husband, and she has a number of children, including young men who have aged out of foster care.

Kate is the author of The Five O'Clock Club's five-part career-development and job-hunting series for professionals, managers and executives as well as *Your Great Business Idea: The Truth About Making It Happen*, *WorkSmarts (co-editor)* and The Five O'Clock Club's boxed set of sixteen lectures on audio CDs as well as via downloads.

About The Five O'Clock Club and the "Fruytagie" Canvas

Five O'Clock Club members are special. We attract upbeat, ambitious, dynamic, intelligent people—and that makes it fun for all of us. Most of our members are professionals, managers, executives, consultants, and freelancers. We also include recent college graduates and those aiming to get into the professional ranks, as well as people in their 40s, 50s, and even 60s. Most members' salaries range from $30,000 to $400,000 (one-half of our members earn in excess of $100,000 a year). In addition to attending the weekly small-group strategy sessions at the Club, The Five O'Clock Club Book Series contains all of our methodologies—and our spirit.

The Philosophy of The Five O'Clock Club

The "Fruytagie" Canvas by Patricia Kelly, depicted here, symbolizes our philosophy. The original is actually 52.5 by 69 inches. It is reminiscent of popular 16th century Dutch "fruytagie," or fruit tapestries, which depicted abundance and prosperity.

I was attracted to this piece because it seemed to fit the spirit of our people at The Five O'Clock Club. This was confirmed when the artist, who was not aware of what I did for a living, added these words to the canvas: "The garden is abundant, prosperous and magical." Later, it took me only 10 minutes to write the blank verse "The Garden of Life," because it came from my heart. The verse reflects our philosophy and describes the kind of people who are members of the Club.

I'm always inspired by Five O'Clock Clubbers. They show others the way through their quiet behavior... their kindness... their generosity... their hard work... under God's care.

We share what we have with others. We are in this lush, exciting place together—with our brothers and sisters—and reach out for harmony. The garden is abundant. The job market is exciting. And Five O'Clock Clubbers believe that there is enough for everyone.

About the Artist's Method

To create her tapestry-like art, Kelly developed a unique style of stenciling. She hand-draws and hand-cuts each stencil, both in the negative and positive for each image. Her elaborate technique also includes a lengthy multi-layering process incorporating Dutch metal leaves and gilding, numerous transparent glazes, paints, and wax pencils.

Kelly also paints the back side of the canvas using multiple washes of reds, violets, and golds. She uses this technique to create a heavy vibration of color, which in turn reflects the color onto the surface of the wall against which the canvas hangs.

The canvas is suspended by a heavy braided silk cord threaded into large brass grommets inserted along the top. Like a tapestry, the hemmed canvas is attached to a gold-gilded dowel with finials. The entire work is hung from a sculpted wall ornament.

Our staff is inspired every day by the members of The Five O'Clock Club, and our mantra, which is to "always do what is in the best interests of the job hunter." We all work hard—and have FUN! The garden is abundant—with enough for everyone.

We wish you lots of success in your career. We—and your fellow members of The Five O'Clock Club—will work with you on it.

—Kate Wendleton, President

The original Five O'Clock Club was formed in Philadelphia in 1883. It was made up of the leaders of the day, who shared their experiences "in a spirit of fellowship and good humor."

THE GARDEN OF LIFE IS abundant, prosperous and magical. ❦ In this garden, there is enough for everyone. ❦ Share the fruit and the knowledge ❦ Our brothers and we are in this lush, exciting place together. ❦ Let's show others the way. ❦ Kindness. Generosity. ❦ Hard work. ❦ God's care.

The Five O'Clock Club Job-Search Series
for Professionals, Managers and Executives

We'll take you through your entire career:

1. First, understand yourself and what you want: **Targeting a Great Career** (1-285-75342-9).

2. **Package Yourself with a Targeted Résumé** (1-285-75358-5) done The Five O'Clock Club Way.

3. **Shortcut Your Job Search** (1-285-75346-1) by following our techniques for Getting Meetings.

4. Turn interviews into offers with **Mastering the Job Interview and Winning the Money Game**. (1-285-75349-6) **5.** Learn from successful job hunters and their coaches: **Report from the Front Lines**. (1-4180-3784-2)

- Figure out what to do with your life and your career
- Develop a résumé that separates you from your competitors
- Shortcut your search by using the Internet and other techniques *properly*
- Learn how to turn those job interviews into job offers
- Use our Four-Step Salary Negotiation Method to get what you deserve
- Learn from others: Be inspired and save time in your search.

The Five O'Clock Club has enabled thousands of professionals, managers, and executives to correct their job-search mistakes. Most who attend regularly and read our books—even those unemployed up to two years—have a new job within only ten weekly sessions.

Most people conduct a passive job search. Their approach is ordinary, non-directed, fragmented, and ineffective. The Five O'Clock Club methodology was tested and refined on professionals, managers, and executives (and those aspiring to be) —from all occupations and economic levels.

The members who do best read and re-read the books, mark them up and take notes. Do the same and you will do better in your search.

Advanced Concepts:

For Executives Only
Applying Business Techniques to Your Job Search
978-0-944054-12-3; $12.95
Five O'Clock Books

Your Great Business Idea
The Truth about Making It Happen
978-0-944054-13-0; $14.95
Five O'Clock Books

Achieving the Good Life After 50
Tools and Resources for Making It Happen
978-0-944054-14-7; $12.95
Five O'Clock Books

Doing Well in Your Present Job:

Work Smarts
Be a Winner on the Job
How to build relationships at work and achieve result.
978-0-944054-15-4; $14.95
Five O'Clock Books

Navigating Your Career
Develop Your Plan. Manage Your Boss. Get Another Job Inside
1-4180-1501-6; $12.95
Thomson Delmar Learning

Becoming a Better Person:

The Good Person Guidebook
Transforming Your Personal Life
978-0-944054-16-1; $14.95
Five O'Clock Books

For Students / Recent Grads:

Launching the Right Career
Students, recent grads, and those who want a career instead of a job.
1-4180-1505-9; $12.95
Thomson Delmar Learning

Additional Search Help:

Job Search Workbook
8.5 x 11 format
1-4180-4050-9; $12.95
Thomson Delmar Learning

A Boxed Set of 16 Audio CDs

40-minute presentations covering every aspect of The Five O'Clock Club Job-Search Methodology (also available via download)

At major bookstores or through www.fiveoclockclub.com or Amazon.com.
For bulk orders, call The Five O'Clock Club at 1-800-538-6645